To Advance Their Opportunities

To Advance Their Opportunities

Federal Policies Toward African American
Workers from World War I to the
Civil Rights Act of 1964

Judson MacLaury

Foreword by Ray Marshall

Newfound Press
THE UNIVERSITY OF TENNESSEE LIBRARIES, KNOXVILLE

To Advance Their Opportunities: Federal Policies Toward African American Workers from World War I to the Civil Rights Act of 1964
©2008, reprinted 2014 by Judson MacLaury

Digital version at www.newfoundpress.utk.edu/pubs/maclaury2

Newfound Press is a digital imprint of the University of Tennessee Libraries. Its publications are available for noncommercial and educational uses, such as research, teaching and private study. The author has licensed the work under the Creative Commons Attribution-Noncommercial 3.0 United States License. To view a copy of this license, visit <http://creativecommons.org/licenses/by-nc/3.0/us/>.

For all other uses, contact:

Newfound Press
University of Tennessee Libraries
1015 Volunteer Boulevard
Knoxville, TN 37996-1000
www.newfoundpress.utk.edu

ISBN-13: 978-0-9846445-7-5
ISBN-10: 0-9846445-7-1

MacLaury, Judson.
To advance their opportunities : federal policies toward African American workers from World War I to the Civil Rights Act of 1964 / Judson MacLaury ; foreword by Ray Marshall.
Knoxville, Tenn. : Newfound Press, University of Tennessee Libraries, 2014, ©2008.
1 online resource (xx, 298 p.)
Slightly edited reprint. Originally published in 2008.
Includes bibliographical references (p. [281]-298).
1. African Americans – Employment -- Government policy – History -- 20th century. 2. African Americans -- Employment -- Law and legislation – History -- 20th century. 3. Discrimination in employment -- Government policy -- United States – History -- 20th century. I. Title.
HD8081.A65 M33 2014

Book design by Jayne Smith
Cover design by Hannah Barker

Contents

Foreword   vii

Preface 2014   xv

Preface 2008   xvii

PART I. Crisis-Driven Federal Action from World War I through the Great Depression, 1914-1940

Chapter 1. World War I and After   3

Chapter 2. Depression and New Deal   43

PART II. Institutionalization of Executive Action, 1940-1960

Chapter 3. World War II and the FEPC   85

Chapter 4. Truman Administration, 1945-1952   105

Chapter 5. Eisenhower Administration, 1953-1960   129

PART III. Culmination of Executive Action, 1960-1964

Chapter 6. Birth of the President's Committee on Equal Employment Opportunity   157

Chapter 7. The Committee Gets Underway   181

Chapter 8. *The Kheel Report* and Beyond   199

Chapter 9. The Department of Labor in the Kennedy-Johnson Era   217

Epilogue   237

Notes   241

Bibliography   281

Foreword

In *To Advance Their Opportunities*, Judson MacLaury, retired Department of Labor (DOL) historian, traces the evolution of federal policies toward African American workers from World War I to the passage of the Civil Rights Act of 1964. This is a valuable contribution to our understanding of this topic, not only because of Judson MacLaury's knowledge of his subject, but also because this book is based on a thorough review of the relevant literature and unpublished materials at the DOL and the National Archives.

MacLaury's focus is on the federal executive, which was much more responsive to pressures from African Americans than the Congress, where a small number of segregationists could use Senate rules, especially the filibuster, to block civil rights legislation. Southern segregationists were able to acquire seniority and inordinate influence in the Democratic Party because most African Americans in their regions were disenfranchised and, before FDR's second term, most black voters and community leaders supported Republicans.

African Americans' ability to influence the federal government began to change when migration out of the rural South greatly enhanced their political power. These migrations accelerated significantly during World War I, when the cessation of mass immigration from Europe opened urban job opportunities to African Americans.

Black political power was enhanced both by their movement to urban areas (North and South), where racial oppression was more visible, and their movement from the one-party South, where they were disenfranchised, to two-party areas outside the South where black voters could significantly influence close elections. The urbanization of African Americans also strengthened civil rights organizations like the National Association for the Advancement of Colored People (NAACP) and the National Urban League (NUL), as well as unions like the influential Brotherhood of Sleeping Car Porters (BSCP), led by A. Philip Randolph.

The dramatic expansion of direct and indirect federal employment during the New Deal period enabled the Roosevelt administration to expand African American employment. In addition, millions of black workers participated in New Deal programs like the National Youth Administration (NYA), the Civilian Conservation Corps (CCC), and public employment programs. That said, African American participation in these recovery programs was generally below their relative unemployment rate, which approached 50 percent, about double the overall rate. And while progress was made in reducing discrimination against black participants, unequal treatment characterized even the best of these programs.

There was, moreover, a continuing tug-of-war between a few influential pro–civil rights New Dealers—like Interior Secretary Harold Ickes, Labor Secretary Frances Perkins, presidential adviser Harry Hopkins, and FDR's wife Eleanor—and those who were influenced by militant segregationist politicians. The progressives were, however, supported by black community protests against discrimination in New Deal programs and in federal employment. FDR, who had never shown much interest in race matters, had to balance appeals from the progressives and opposition from segregationists in his own party.

Because FDR thought sustainable, broadly shared prosperity was not possible unless all major groups were included, his administration did much to help African Americans. And, despite their continuing protests against discrimination in federal employment and by government contractors, most black leaders and voters, who had previously strongly supported Herbert Hoover, made a dramatic switch to the Democratic Party and voted overwhelmingly for FDR in his reelection campaign.

The depression—and most New Deal recovery programs—ended with World War II, which opened a new chapter in the march toward racial equality. Although discrimination continued, and was even sometimes acquiesced to by staunch civil rights champions like Harry Hopkins and Frances Perkins, African Americans doubled their proportion of federal jobs from 5 percent to 10 percent. Although most of these jobs were in lower pay grades, the administration also increased the number of black professionals and administrators.

The tight World War II labor markets boosted the expansion of black employment, especially among defense contractors. Under intense pressure from the black community, including a threatened march on Washington, FDR issued an executive order creating the Fair Employment Practice Committee (FEPC) to outlaw discrimination by federal contractors.

The proposed march on Washington, led by A. Philip Randolph, was particularly embarrassing to FDR because discrimination exposed a serious weakness in America's fight to "make the world safe for democracy." Indeed, the tension between tolerating discrimination while fighting totalitarian regimes made American leaders more likely to act on antidiscrimination pressures. As President Johnson remarked, "Race relations don't look the same from the banks of the Potomac as they do from the banks of the Pedernales" (where his ranch was located).

The experiences of the Kennedy and Johnson administrations revealed the strengths and weaknesses of executive orders and voluntary fair employment programs. The use of executive powers enabled administrations to combat discrimination despite Congressional opposition. The executive orders were enforced mainly by moral suasion and the threat of contract cancellation or debarment. Presidents likewise could use their "bully pulpit" to persuade the public that discrimination was not only bad for the economy, society, and polity, but also weakened America's contest against totalitarian regimes.

Voluntary antidiscrimination programs had some advantages in changing private employment practices. These programs were introduced not only because of inadequate support for civil rights legislation, but also because legal processes were more effective against specific overt discriminatory acts than against the more pervasive and entrenched institutional forms that permit discrimination to persist even after it has become illegal. One of the clearest effects of executive-order-based programs was to give those employers and unions who were inclined to adopt fair practices some protection from adverse reactions by racist customers or members.

Despite these advantages, executive orders and voluntary approaches had many shortcomings: they lacked the credibility afforded by Congressional action; they were relatively ineffective against determined defenders of the status quo; government contracting sanctions had limited impact on unions, which were not parties to the contracts; government agencies were reluctant to cancel contracts because they were more interested in the goods and services provided than combating discrimination;[1] and administrations likewise were deterred from vigorous enforcement by pow-

---

[1] This defect was overcome somewhat by the Carter administration, which not only demonstrated its willingness to cancel contracts, but also consolidated enforcement in the Department of Labor.

erful members of Congress, who controlled their budgets. These weaknesses, and subsequent experience, demonstrated that voluntary programs are more effective when backed by the threat of vigorous enforcement.

The limitations of executive orders and voluntary programs established the political bases for the civil rights acts of 1964 and 1965, which were passed with strong political leadership from President Lyndon Johnson and vigorous opposition from many Republicans and Southern Democrats. It would, however, be a mistake to assume that the civil rights acts ended discrimination. Affirmative action programs were required to address institutional discrimination that was beyond the reach of statutory law.

An example of the kind of targeted affirmative action programs that produced significant change was the apprenticeship outreach programs that greatly increased the number of minority apprentices. Joint employer-union apprenticeship programs had a long history of discrimination against minorities and women, which meant that few counselors recommended that black students prepare for apprenticeable occupations. As a result, when the Civil Rights Act of 1964 outlawed discrimination by unions and apprenticeship sponsors, there were very few qualified minority applicants to take advantage of these opportunities. Institutional discrimination causes people to avoid programs they believe will not accept them. Pragmatic civil rights leaders like A. Philip Randolph responded to this impasse by creating specific outreach programs to recruit, prepare, and place qualified minority apprentices. Secretary of Labor Willard Wirtz commissioned an evaluation of these programs, which documented their success.[2] The Department of Labor then funded these programs

---

[2] Ray Marshall and Vernon Briggs, *The Negro and Apprenticeship* (Baltimore: Johns Hopkins Press, 1967).

on a larger scale, causing minorities in apprenticeship programs to approximate their proportion of the work force by the end of the 1970s.

The outreach concept was applied successfully to the Minority Women's Employment Project, directed by Alexis Herman, later secretary of labor in the Clinton administration. Federal employment programs provided opportunities for millions of African American workers while the administration of these programs trained many black leaders.

Judson MacLaury's research leads him to three central conclusions: "First, there were significant, measurable advances for African American workers; second, the concept of affirmative action was born and underwent considerable development during this period; and third, most major actions by the executive were only taken in response to pressure, direct or indirect, from the African American community."

The evidence fully supports these conclusions. Despite a counterattack on affirmative action during the 1980s and 90s, it seems fairly clear that reducing institutionalized discrimination requires positive action to include those who have been excluded, in tandem with legal measures to combat specific, overt acts of discrimination.

The evidence likewise demonstrates the critical importance of continuous pressure from the victims of discrimination; even well-meaning political champions of equal opportunity seldom assign as high a priority to effective remedies as the victims themselves. Political champions are often satisfied with token breakthroughs, while the victims rarely, if ever, are. This reality is well understood by civil rights leaders and sympathetic politicians alike. A. Philip Randolph, for example, demonstrated the moral power of open and massive protests against a sympathetic, but cautious, president who tolerated discrimination, despite his dedication to democracy and broadly shared prosperity. Randolph often told his followers: "Your friends can help you but they can't save you; you have to save yourselves." Similarly, in his 1963 letter from a Birmingham jail, Martin Luther King Jr. wrote: "Freedom is never voluntarily given by the oppressor; it must be demanded by the oppressed." President Johnson, the consummate politician, understood this principle very well. He told a group of labor and civil rights leaders who called on him to support the Civil Rights Act of 1964 that this legislation was good for them and the country and he was all for it, adding: "Now go make me do it."

The lessons from *To Advance Their Opportunities* are as valuable for other victims of discrimination—especially women—as they are for African Americans. Indeed, MacLaury writes that women, for example, were excluded from the CCC and other important New Deal programs. It is also noteworthy that President Truman, a civil rights champion who defied members of his party and, among other things, desegregated the armed forces, nevertheless acquiesced to pressure from male members of his cabinet not to reappoint Frances Perkins, the most effective and influential secretary of labor in history.

The elimination of discrimination against people for reasons unrelated to merit therefore will require a combination of strong leadership from public and private officials, but especially from the victims of discrimination.

The evolution of the slow march to equal opportunity reveals the interaction between attitudes and behavior. In employment situations, discrimination is only partially responsive to attitudes. Changed behavior is required to overcome specific overt racial discrimination. Affirmative action and African American performance in all sectors of American life changed racial attitudes. Barriers to further change were created by racial politics, which appealed to whites through thinly veiled racist code words. The fact that racial appeals have to be veiled is a sign of progress; the fact that they are made at all shows how far we still have to go.

It could be that a number of developments will cause even thinly disguised racial appeals to be less effective in the 21st century. After the initial breakthroughs—the positive effects of tokenism—African Americans' accomplishments in all sectors of national life challenged the enduring myth of inherent racial differences. A second important force for change was the rise of both black political and black economic power after the Voting Rights Act of 1965, which enabled two pro-civil rights Southerners, Jimmy Carter and Bill Clinton, to get elected president despite losing the Southern white vote. Racist appeals were further weakened by welfare reform and the decline in urban violence, which made many code words much less effective, and by growing embarrassment about the treatment of African Americans throughout most of our history. This is not to argue that racism is dead—only that it has become much less acceptable and there are fewer ways to camouflage racist signals.

Judson MacLaury's detailed study of efforts to reduce discrimination against African Americans is important because it teaches the kinds of actions and leadership required to combat the deadly effects of discrimination against people for reasons unrelated to their personal merit.

Ray Marshall
June 2008

Mr. Marshall was secretary of labor during the Carter administration, 1977-1981.

Preface 2014

In June 2013 I had the opportunity to meet with Holly Mercer, the current director of Newfound Press, and her team. We discussed the original 2008 printing of this book and unanimously agreed that after a little touching up and redesign, the book should be reintroduced to the public as a reprint. Holly thereupon assigned Jayne Smith of her staff to prepare a thorough copyedit. While I did not change the factual substance of the original publication, I did work with Jayne on the editing, and along the way I reshaped some of the language.

I can only hope that my own efforts have made this a better book. I am convinced, however, that Jayne's dedication and sharp editorial skills have made it a more solid and professional publication. Applying her thorough knowledge of the *Chicago Manual of Style*, she has introduced a sound and consistent style throughout the book. She also created the new design, and I recently learned that she had played a key role in completing the layout and design of the 2008 printing as well. I thank her for all her superb work.

Like the original publication, this reprint, both hard copy and online, does not come with an index (always a sore point with book reviewers). But none is really necessary. Hard-copy users need only to visit the book's website at the University of Tennessee (http://newfoundpress.utk.edu/pubs/maclaury2), where they can create their own virtual index.

PREFACE 2014

The year 2014 is a highly auspicious and appropriate one for a new printing of a book dealing with fair employment of black workers. For one thing, 2014 marks the fiftieth anniversary of the Civil Rights Act of 1964 and its Title VII, which banned racial and other discrimination in virtually all private employment. It also marks the one-hundredth anniversary of the beginning of World War I, an event I write about that indirectly triggered the Great Migration, which in turn set in motion both vast social change in the United States and also the birth of engagement by the federal government with the African American workforce.

Furthermore, in this year the presidential administration of Barack Obama, the first African American and indeed nonwhite US president, is a ripe old five years of age. Without the Civil Rights Act and the Great Migration, it is doubtful that Obama would ever have been in a position to be elected in 2008 or reelected in 2012. At the conclusion of my Epilogue to the 2008 printing, I raise the issue of when our country will truly be able to say that it is at last color-blind. To paraphrase Ronald Reagan in 1980, are we better off (more equalitarian) five years later? I believe that with Obama's election, with greater recent acceptance of gay men and women as legally married couples and full participants in the American mainstream, and with greater tolerance of diversity of all kinds, we have taken a few giant steps in that direction. Now we need to secure that hard-won progress and *demand* that it continue.

Judson MacLaury
January 2014

Preface 2008

After the abolition of slavery, African Americans were soon oppressed at the local level by discriminatory Jim Crow laws and practices that made the vast majority of them second-class citizens. Because of that, disproportionate numbers of them were relegated to low-paying, low-prestige employment. It was not until the Civil Rights Act of 1964, Title VII, that it was made a violation of federal statute law to discriminate against African Americans in the workplace.

Long before the Civil Rights Act, however, the federal government had begun to recognize the importance of African American workers to the economy and the legitimacy of their desire for, and right to, an equal chance to share in its opportunities. This book is the story of the origins and growth of the federal executive branch's role in addressing the emergence of black labor in the national economy and in improving their opportunities for good jobs. It will show that, beginning with the Great Migration of black workers out of the rural South to the industrial North and Midwest during World War I, the federal government slowly initiated a series of steps to deal, at least partially, with the economic issues and social problems that arose. A key finding of the book is that virtually every major step the government took was the result of strong pressure from the growing civil rights movement.

The story of executive branch action is divided into three eras. "Part I: Crisis-Driven Federal Action from World War I through the Great Depression, 1914-1940" shows how the government operated initially in an ad hoc way, responding to circumstances resulting from the two world wars that bookended the Roaring 20s and the Great Depression. "Part II: Institutionalization of Executive Action, 1940-1960" and "Part III: Culmination of Executive Action, 1960-1964" describe the development of policy, implemented through presidential executive orders and other measures, into a more continuous and systematic effort.

As the book shows, in the period from 1914 to 1964, the federal government operated primarily in the spheres where it had the greatest control: federal employment, whether within the bureaucracy or on government projects; and employment by contractors providing goods or services to the federal government. Control was implemented either through direct administration, in the case of federal employment, or through executive order and moral suasion, in the case of private employers. Relevant legislation and court cases are discussed, but the focus is on the executive branch, the main actor during the "pre-history" of government action on civil rights before Title VII.

The federal government adopted a largely cooperative, voluntaristic approach to seeking compliance with goals of fairness in the workplace. Even after it developed regulations that allowed various sanctions, it was generally reluctant to enforce them against violators. The political and social realities of the period before the Civil Rights Act were not conducive to mandatory enforcement of equal opportunity rules. The government did, however, seek to persuade private employers to take extra steps, which became known as Affirmative Action, to hire and promote African Americans. Governmental bodies probably carried voluntarism as far as it could effectively go, until the Civil Rights Act introduced a paradigm shift that ushered in a new era of mandatory compliance with federal antidiscrimination goals.

The literature on which I base this book is rich and extensive. However, that literature is a bit of a patchwork. There are excellent individual studies of civil rights under various presidents, but they do not focus on employment. There are a few studies that do focus on the topic, but none covers the entire period from 1914 to 1964. One goal of the book is to synthesize this collective historical effort.

Another goal is to show, in detail, how various programs and executive orders came about and how they were implemented. While the literature is very rich in coverage of the macro political and social background, there is relatively little coverage of the micro aspects. In order to adequately address this area, I delved into the wealth of government records in the National Archives and the rich collections of the Wirtz Labor Library of the US Department of Labor. Hopefully, the book will provide the public with a clearer picture of how their federal government went about promoting equal employment opportunities for African American workers.

In the interest of full disclosure, I should note that I served as the Department of Labor historian from 1972 until my retirement in 2006. As the book has been completed since I left the federal government, hopefully removal has provided additional perspective and objectivity. I would like to acknowledge those at the department who made my research possible. First, I wish to express my deep gratitude to Dr. Jonathan Grossman, my predecessor as departmental historian. He not only hired me, he encouraged me to write the book that he always said I had in me. I also want to thank Gary Reed, a later supervisor, who encouraged me to start work on this book and to concentrate my time and efforts on a project that he knew would bear fruit only years later. His only requirement was to "just write a good book." I hope I have met his expectations. To Linda Stinson, my successor as departmental historian—words cannot express my thanks for the superb developmental editing job she did. She helped me turn an unwieldy early draft into a much more readable book. Finally, I should credit the Department of Labor itself for giving me the idea for the title, which I shamelessly stole from the law that created the department in 1913. The title is part of the mission statement requiring the new department "*to . . . advance their opportunities* for profitable employment" [emphasis added]. There was no congressional intent to make sure those opportunities were equally available to all, but fortunately time and change made that a preeminent national mission.

Professor Robert Zieger, a labor historian at the University of Florida, kindly served as my unofficial adviser throughout the project. He reviewed my early outlines of the book and plans for research and writing, and he provided encouragement and support as I grappled with the daunting and, to me, unfamiliar challenges of writing a book.

Lastly, I want to thank the wonderful and talented people at Newfound Press and the University of Tennessee Library. Linda Phillips, chair of the press's editorial board, shepherded my manuscript through the review process and was a joy to work with. Casie Fedukovich did a superb job of copy and substantive editing. My book is a better one for her efforts. The book design by Jayne Rogers and cover design by Hannah Barker perfectly express the theme and period of the book. To all, my profound thanks.

I dedicate this book to the memory of my parents, James and Ruth. To my wife, Judy, I can only say thank you for steadfast moral support during the book's ten-year, and seemingly endless, gestation period.

Judson MacLaury
Seattle, Washington
June 2008

Part I
Crisis-Driven Federal Action from World War I through the Great Depression, 1914–1940

The period from World War I through the Great Depression and the New Deal marked the first large-scale influx of African American workers into the nation's industrial workforce. It also saw the initiation of significant federal involvement with and assistance to African American workers. It was a period of mostly ad hoc government responses driven first by the emergency of World War I and then by the Depression. The intervening period of peace and prosperity during the 1920s produced relatively little federal action in this area.

Chapter 1, "World War I and After," focuses on several factors that came together in this period to affect black workers. First was the widespread institution of discriminatory Jim Crow practices in the administration of President Woodrow Wilson, prompting a strong backlash from the black community. At the same time that black workers began migrating from the rural South to fill industrial jobs in the North, the supply of white immigrant labor from Europe was drying up because of the war. The migration and America's entry into the war in Europe, combined with pressure from black leaders, led to federal efforts to assist black workers and fully integrate them economically into the war effort. The principal federal vehicle for these efforts was the Department of Labor's Division of Negro Economics, a temporary wartime agency headed by black sociologist George Haynes.

PART 1

Chapter 2, "Depression and New Deal," covers a period of remarkable efforts by the government to assure full and equal participation by African Americans in the work and relief programs of the New Deal. The leadership of the administration of President Franklin D. Roosevelt included racial progressives like Harold Ickes, Harry Hopkins, and the First Lady, Eleanor Roosevelt. They were joined by an unprecedented number of senior black appointees who organized themselves into an unofficial "Black Cabinet" that guided and promoted equal treatment efforts.

Depression-era equal opportunity efforts largely expired with the demise of their host agencies. However, new laws like the Wagner Act, the Fair Labor Standards Act, and the Social Security Act—which instituted unemployment insurance—left a long-term legacy of benefits to the African American workforce.

CHAPTER 1

World War I and After

On July 28, 1914, Austria-Hungary invaded Serbia and World War I began. This conflict set in motion a chain of events that would have profound consequences for the African American workforce and for federal government policies toward them. For several decades before the war, the flow of European immigrants was the main source of labor fueling America's burgeoning industrial economy. According to the federal Dillingham Immigration Commission's reports of 1907-1910, workers from Eastern Europe virtually monopolized employment in many sectors of industry. By 1915 the flow was reduced from a torrent to a trickle. In 1914 more than 1.2 million Europeans came to the United States; in 1915 only 327,000 entered the country.[1] European armies soaked up conscription-age workers, and many immigrants returned to their homelands from the United States.

The Great Migration

While the influx of new laborers dwindled, the demand for US agricultural and industrial products soared. In response, the country turned to its main underused domestic source of labor: the black population. Concentrated largely in the rural South, African Americans at that time were subjected to Jim Crow laws in that region. Discriminatory practices, instituted in the decades after the end of Reconstruction in 1877, segregated them socially and severely limited their economic opportunities. Consequently, the allure of jobs and better lives outside of the South prompted massive numbers to move north.

The groundwork for this large-scale relocation had already been laid by decades of the temporary movement of southern black laborers as they took seasonal jobs in the North and then returned home.[2] But the growing threat of racial violence—including lynching, along with heavy flooding and boll weevil infestations that routinely combined to ruin the cotton crops of black sharecroppers and tenant-farmers—provided African Americans with a strong motivation to relocate permanently. During the 1910s, more than half a million of them left the South for good, beginning the Great Migration of African Americans that endured for the next half century and more.

These migrants settled mainly in the large cities of the Northeast and Midwest. They found employment in industries that had formerly relied on European immigrants, such as railroads, packing houses, steel mills, and heavy manufacturing. Significant numbers also moved to nonurban areas, such as the coalfields of the southern Appalachians.[3]

The search by large numbers of African Americans for better economic and social opportunities in the cities of the North and Midwest brought them into contact with white workers and white society in a much-freer environment than existed in the Jim Crow South. The result was often racial friction and, occasionally, explosive violence. In their new homes, free of restrictions on their voting rights, African Americans increasingly exercised their franchise in a more balanced two-party system, and thus began to affect elections. The result of these social and political pressures was that the federal government was forced to pay serious attention to the issues raised by the presence of large numbers of blacks in the urban industrial workforce. Thus began fifty years of federal efforts, principally through the executive branch, to assimilate African Americans into the industrial workforce and to attempt to satisfy, however gradually, their growing desire for fair treatment.

Woodrow Wilson Administration and Blacks

Ironically, federal engagement in the issues of working African Americans developed under an administration that was generally unsympathetic, and often openly hostile, to their plight. The White House was occupied by Woodrow Wilson, a Virginia Democrat who took office on March 4, 1913.[4] During the 1912 presidential elections, the Wilson campaign made a strong bid for the support of the growing block of black voters. Black groups worked vigorously for Wilson's election, and late in the campaign, he was endorsed by the National Association for the Advancement of Colored People (NAACP). While it turned out that their support was not crucial to Wilson, many blacks felt it gave them influence in the administration, and they looked forward to turning campaign promises into action for black rights. However, the executive branch was still dominated by segregationist Southern Democrats. As a result, Washington remained resistant to meeting either the political or economic expectations of the black community.[5]

Despite his campaign promises for racial fairness, Wilson actually favored segregation. He shared the belief, widespread among white Americans, that African Americans were racially distinct from and inferior to white people. Wilson also needed the support of Southern Democrats, who were uninterested in a goal of racial justice, in order to win their support for his main priority: an ambitious program of economic reform.[6]

While the southern states began instituting segregation and discrimination in the 1880s, the federal government moved in the opposite direction, at least regarding its own employees. Blacks began to be appointed to diplomatic posts and political positions, and the government even held recruitment campaigns. Thirty years later, Wilson reversed that policy. He appointed only two blacks in his first two years in office, while allowing a total of twelve traditionally black positions to lapse into white hands.[7] In perhaps the unkindest cut of all, Wilson's Secretary of State William Jennings Bryan broke with the tradition of appointing black ambassadors to Haiti, a tradition that had been initiated with the selection of black abolitionist Frederick Douglass. Bryan's naming of a white to that position aggrieved both American blacks and Haitians. Leaders from the National Colored Democratic League and the National Black Democratic League called on Wilson to resume the tradition of patronage appointments for members of their race.[8]

Before the Wilson administration, black participation in career federal government employment had been even higher than in the political appointment realm. Under the Pendleton Civil Service Act of 1883, most federal jobs were gradually removed from patronage and brought under a competitive civil service. By law, hiring was now to be based solely on merit. The Civil Service Commission (CSC), that administered the Pendleton Act, saw to it that qualified blacks had a fair opportunity to be hired. While many obtained only menial positions, a significant number held managerial and professional posts. The CSC also promoted fair treatment after hiring. Segregation in federal offices was virtually nonexistent. As a result, the number of blacks in civil service positions grew steadily from about six hundred in 1883 to twelve thousand by 1913.[9]

When the Wilson administration took office in 1913, the National Democratic Fair Play Association objected to a federal landscape where white women were working alongside, or even reporting to, black men and women. Southern members of the cabinet were very sympathetic to these concerns. At an early cabinet meeting, several of them complained about alleged friction between black and white federal employees. As a proposed solution, they called for the introduction of segregation. Wilson went along with the idea, rationalizing it as being not only good for the government, but also in the best interest of blacks.

Secretary of the Treasury William Gibbs McAdoo (Wilson's son-in-law) and Postmaster General Albert S. Burleson were particularly strong proponents of segregation. Burleson claimed to have the support of moderate black leaders, including Bishop Alexander Walters, president of the National Colored Democratic League. Wilson's cabinet, while not formally endorsing segregation, did not oppose as a body the racist efforts of Burleson, McAdoo and others.[10]

Consequently, Jim Crow practices were soon widely adopted. Such institutionalized racism affected black federal workers adversely in three main ways: physical segregation in the workplace, numerous downgrades to lower-paying jobs, and outright termination. Officially, there was no change in the CSC's merit-based hiring policies. But in May 1914 it began requiring that photographs be attached to all job applications, making it easier to discriminate against black candidates.[11]

Some departments adopted Jim Crow practices more enthusiastically than others. Not surprisingly, Secretary McAdoo's Treasury Department instituted it widely. The impact of this endorsement was magnified by Treasury auditors' offices being in almost every department of the government. Because of this presence, segregation and other Jim Crow practices often existed in buildings occupied by departments that did not support these policies. The Treasury Department even took the extreme step of setting up partitions in some offices so that white and black employees would not be able to see each other. While other federal agencies instituted Jim Crow informally and through verbal orders, the Treasury Department was alone in issuing written orders.

Albert Burleson's Jim Crow Post Office Department was the largest federal employer of African Americans, and it had a wide national reach with post offices in virtually every county. Black employees in post offices and railway mail cars in the South suffered acutely from workplace discrimination. Elsewhere, restrooms were segregated in such agencies as the Government Printing Office, the Marine Hospital building, and the Navy Department. In some cases, the black restrooms had to be used by both sexes. Even more incredibly, at times, bathrooms doubled as eating areas for blacks excluded from the regular dining rooms.[12]

Segregation was not universally adopted in the federal government, however. Secretary of Agriculture David F. Houston, a Southerner, did not impose it on the US Department of Agriculture (USDA), though racial practices were far from uniformly fair from one office to another within the USDA. Relatively few blacks were appointed as county agricultural agents, but these small numbers were due in part to the power of local offices to reject applicants on racial or other grounds. On the other hand, at the Office of Public Roads and the Bureau of Plant Husbandry, blacks and whites were allowed to work side by side. The Labor Department also remained relatively free of discrimination. Perhaps because adoption was not universal, the impact of Jim Crow on the federal workforce during the Wilson administration was somewhat mitigated. While the proportion of black civil servants declined from 6 to 5 percent of the government-wide total, their absolute numbers actually increased.[13]

Responses to Federal Segregation

The nascent black civil rights community did not take the wave of federal segregation lying down. In May 1913 Ralph Tyler, a black

Treasury Department auditor and career employee working in the Department of the Navy, called on President Wilson to speak out against discrimination in the Bureau of Printing and Engraving and in the auditor's office of the post office. More influential voices soon joined Tyler's. Concerned about Jim Crow in the Wilson administration, the NAACP concurrently authorized *New York Post* editor Oswald Garrison Villard, the chair of the body, to develop a plan for a "National Race Commission" and present it to the president. Villard was the leading white advocate of equal treatment for blacks and also a personal friend of President Wilson. In May 1913 Villard had an opportunity to present his plan to the president. At first, Wilson approved of the idea, but months passed and nothing happened. Villard repeatedly urged Wilson to appoint the commission, but finally Wilson informed him that he had decided against it because of opposition within the Senate.[14]

In the meantime, the NAACP collected substantial inside information on Jim Crow in Washington, based on reports from a special investigator and other sources. By August 15, 1913, when it seemed unlikely that there would ever be a National Race Commission, the NAACP sent Wilson a strong letter objecting to the growing Jim Crow practices in the government. They followed up with a comprehensive publicity campaign among sympathizers, newspapers, members of Congress, and others, encouraging them to join the NAACP in opposition.[15]

On November 6, 1913, Wilson unenthusiastically received a delegation from the National Independent Political League (NIPL), headed by the *Boston Guardian*'s crusading editor William Monroe Trotter. On behalf of the NIPL, a black advocacy group operating independently of the NAACP, Trotter presented the "National Petition Against Jim Crow and Color Segregation in the Federal Government," signed by twenty thousand supporters. At first, Wilson denied there was a formal Jim Crow effort. But when confronted with the documentation of segregation in his administration, the president reluctantly acknowledged its existence and vaguely promised that the situation would be "worked out."[16]

The anti–Jim Crow campaigns continued and, on November 16, 1914, a year after the 1913 meeting, Trotter led an almost identical delegation to Washington, this time under the auspices of the National Independent Equal Rights League. Meeting with Wilson, the group presented resolutions from the Massachusetts legislature protesting segregation in the federal government. Members took turns addressing the president and urging an end to Jim Crow. Trotter spoke last and made an impassioned plea for racial justice. He eschewed the deference normally expected in addressing the President of the United States, boldly rebuking Wilson for allowing rampantly unfair treatment of black employees in the federal government. Wilson responded that these employees were not being ill-treated in their separate work arrangements and claimed that segregation actually helped assure racial harmony. Trotter rejected the argument and asserted that because of these policies, African Americans might be less likely to support the Democratic Party in the future. Wilson took offense at this political threat, and the conversation degenerated into a heated argument. Although the meeting ended on a calmer note, this fiery confrontation between a black leader and the president generated intense news coverage and enormous publicity for the movement against Jim Crow in the government.

Presidential aide Joseph Tumulty was impressed with Trotter's eloquence and continued to urge Wilson to reconsider the issue of segregation. While discrimination and segregation remained in existence for some time, after 1914 there was little, if any, further growth of Jim Crow in the federal establishment.[17]

African Americans and World War I

With the US declaration of war against Germany on April 6, 1917, black support and black labor were now crucial to both war munitions production and the military buildup. Administration officials worried, perhaps out of a guilty conscience, that German propagandists would find blacks responsive to their message promoting nonintervention by the United States and less willing to contribute to the war effort. Rumors abounded of German agents stirring up black field hands. Unsubstantiated incidents were blown out of proportion and widely disseminated. A black man was reported to have said, "The Germans ain't done nothin' to me, and if they have, I forgive 'em."[18] To help counteract this perceived threat, Wilson and his cabinet sought to rebuild ties with the black community that had been damaged by the onset of Jim Crow under Wilson's administration.

As it turned out, doubts about the loyalty of African Americans and plots to undermine their support of the war effort were misplaced. After hundreds of federal investigations of alleged German subversion, there was no proof of a single bona fide plot to turn black people against the US government during the war.[19] On the contrary, a national meeting of the NAACP and allied groups in May 1917 resolved that blacks should enthusiastically support the United States and work for a victory that the delegates believed could lead to freedom for the "darker races" throughout the world. Further, while pledging absolute loyalty to the military's aims, the delegates also vowed to continue seeking equal rights for blacks. These rights included the right to serve at all levels of the military, to fully exercise the voting franchise, to be free from Jim Crow practices, and to be safe from lynch mobs—an escalating problem of the early twentieth century. This resolution characterized the wartime positions of most black leaders who advocated loyalty to the government, but who also demanded fairness.

Meanwhile, the most pressing need after the declaration of war was a rapid mobilization to expand the United States Armed Forces. Hundreds of thousands of civilian blacks freely and enthusiastically joined patriotic rallies and volunteered to serve on the home front and in the military.[20] Consequently, it was in the military that the first serious wartime issue involving blacks arose. The Selective Service Act of 1917 allowed the induction of black conscripts by local draft boards. Large numbers were drafted, but the US Army sought to hold to long-established traditions of discrimination. In an attempt to break this mold, the NAACP campaigned to convince Secretary of War Newton D. Baker, one of the nonsouthern members of the cabinet, to try to improve conditions for black soldiers. Adding pressure on the government, in August 1917 race riots broke out in Houston, Texas, stemming from police brutality toward black soldiers.[21]

In response to the military's discrimination and the violence in Houston, Secretary Baker ordered the training of black officers and created an all-black combat division—the legendary Ninety-Second. This new division and several black regiments in existing divisions broke the barriers to military service by blacks in combat duty and acquitted themselves well in battle on the Western Front.[22] Despite these opportunities, the NAACP was critical of the lack of further progress in the army. It objected to the facts that segregated units remained the norm, white officers publicly belittled the combat abilities of black soldiers, and blacks were discriminated against in matters of leave and recreation.[23]

In October 1917 Secretary Baker sought to respond to the NAACP and help defuse racial tensions. He met first with President Wilson and black educator Robert Moton; later he met separately with W. E. B. DuBois, one of the founders of the NAACP. After these dialogues, Baker created the post of confidential adviser in the

War Department to address black concerns within the military. He named Emmett Scott, an African American and long-time associate of Booker T. Washington, to fill the post. At that time there was only one other federal office dedicated to black affairs—an obscure Division of Racial Groups in the Bureau of Education. Scott's duties included inspecting training camps and investigating discrimination claims against the military and southern draft boards. He also strove tirelessly to require the US Public Health Service to hire black doctors and nurses.[24]

Like the military, federal civilian agencies had a mixed wartime record of promoting equal opportunity and fair treatment of black workers. The National War Labor Board, established to eliminate disruptions in war production due to labor disputes, intervened in a number of cases affecting black workers and generally supported their rights. In a case involving white and black laundry workers in Little Rock, Arkansas, for example, the board ordered equal pay for equal work regardless of race. The US Railroad Administration (USRA), which operated the railroads after the federal government nationalized them in late 1917, also sought with some success to equalize opportunities. On a number of occasions, the USRA defended the rights of black workers and their unions in the historically white-dominated realm of train operations. In one notable instance, sleeping-car porters were granted a pay increase after appealing to the USRA. On several occasions, the agency cancelled union contracts that discriminated against blacks. The USRA's impact was limited, however, because Treasury Secretary McAdoo, a leading proponent of Jim Crow, was its director. Like McAdoo, many USRA investigators were far from racially progressive and usually sided against the rights of black railroad workers. Likewise, the USDA generally sided with southern farmers who feared losing their cheap black labor to new jobs in defense plants. The USDA helped farmers by promoting local "work or fight" orders that forced black farm workers to remain in their jobs or else face conscription into the army.[25]

Secretary of Labor William B. Wilson and the War Labor Administration (WLA), that he directed, had the massive and difficult job of facilitating the mobilization of the labor force for defense production.[26] Though hampered by lack of preparedness planning by the White House and inefficient defense procurement procedures, the WLA and the Department of Labor placed millions of workers in defense jobs. In the process, Secretary Wilson and the agencies he headed were faced with the situation of hundreds of thousands of black workers who had migrated in search of defense work. Unlike the many government officials who favored Jim Crow, William Wilson, a former labor leader, was sympathetic to the plight of African Americans. The campaign against segregation in the government had reached the Labor Department in late 1913 when Secretary Wilson received letters, from groups as diverse as the NAACP and the New York City Republican Club, calling for equal treatment of black federal employees. These missives found a receptive ear at the Labor Department that staunchly resisted the Jim Crow tide. Wilson's biographer, Clark Wilhelm, wrote that Wilson "was willing to use his labor administration to help Negroes, showing himself a courageous innovator." Wilson's second-in-command, Assistant Secretary Louis Post (also a white), had a strong record of supporting black causes. He worked for the Freedmen's Bureau after the Civil War, participated in the founding of the NAACP in 1909, and maintained strong relations with the black leadership.[27]

The Department of Labor and the Great Migration

Even before the war, the Department of Labor became involved with black workers and the Great Migration through the work of an agency known as the US Employment Service (USES)—not to be confused with the agency of the same name created by law in 1933. The first USES was created in 1915 as part of a plan to find jobs for those left without employment during a recession.[28] However, the new agency built upon a preexisting Division of Information, established in 1907 within the Bureau of Immigration that operated labor distribution (i.e., placement) offices at major ports to help guide arriving immigrants to jobs.[29]

The recession of 1915 proved to be short-lived, but the USES continued and played a surprising role in the Great Migration. A secretary of labor's circular in January 1915 ordered the USES to expand the labor distribution network. The scope of the system was also greatly extended through a strategy involving the Post Office Department and using the Bureau of Immigration field staff to oversee operations. Every post office in the country was directed to prominently display a notice advising employers and workers of a new employment program. Interested parties were to fill out application forms and turn them in to the postmaster to be sent to USES distribution branches where job seekers would be matched with job offers on a nationwide basis.[30]

Although the job matching system was never fully implemented, post offices did display notices from the Labor Department announcing employment opportunities. The USES also facilitated transportation arrangements for relocating employment candidates, many of them southern blacks who could not afford the rail ticket north to a new job, by asking employers to advance one-way railroad tickets when needed. The trunks of new hires were checked straight through and consigned to the employer as security to assure reimbursement for the tickets.[31]

In this way, the Department of Labor provided an assist to the Great Migration just when demand for labor in the industrial North was swelling. In its annual report for 1917, the department acknowledged that "some of the black migration northward had been through agencies of the US Employment Service." Charles Johnson, a leading black sociologist, asserted in 1930: "Quite unwittingly the [department], through its practice of assisting in the movement of labor to acute points of demand, was giving the first impetus to the Negro migration."[32]

By June 1916 southern planters were becoming intensely concerned about the impact on production of the actual and anticipated shortages of cheap black labor due to migration. Rising wartime agricultural prices provided a strong incentive for them to maintain production.[33] In response, they supported "work or fight" laws and orders to force black workers to stay in the fields. They also complained to their elected representatives in Washington that the USES was encouraging migration. Several southern congresspersons importuned the Department of Labor to put the brakes on. In a rare about-face on racial policies, the Labor Department, while continuing to assist individual black workers, yielded to pressure and "withdrew its facilities from group migration."[34]

In further response to mounting criticism generated principally by southerners, the Department of Labor ordered studies of the migration's economic and social impact. In the summer of 1916, the department sent Charles Hall and William Jennifer, black investigators on detail from the Commerce Department, on a fact-finding mission to determine the impact of the migration.[35] Based on numerous interviews with individuals of both races, the researchers concluded—contrary to assertions by the planters—that the migration was neither flooding the labor market in the North nor shrinking the labor force in the South.[36]

Hall and Jennifer called for further study of the complex and changing nature of the migration. By 1917 they wrote, it had "excited widespread concern for its possible effect upon the prosecution of the war." The perceived black migration problem was now a war problem. To look into these and other issues, Secretary Wilson commissioned a more thorough investigation in 1917. To supervise the study, he appointed Dr. James H. Dillard, a distinguished white academician and president of the Jeanes-Slater Funds for Negro Education. Wilson considered Dillard a credible investigator who had the confidence of blacks and whites alike.[37]

Dillard engaged a team of investigators from both races to conduct field work in several southern states. He compiled their findings in a detailed report submitted to Secretary Wilson at the end of 1917. The report, however, was not published until 1919, but its purpose was to uncover both the causes of the migration and also its effects on the economy of the South. While Dillard worried about the impact of the migration on the South, he found that the effects were fundamentally positive. The study asserted that the movement of blacks to the North was a "commendable effort" that reflected the natural desire of human beings to improve their circumstances. In Dillard's view, national progress depended upon broadly shared improvement that was not confined to one class or race.[38] In regard to labor shortages in the South, he concurred with Hall and Jennifer and wrote that "the danger seems not to have been so extensive or so acute as was feared."[39]

Despite Dillard's findings, Secretary Wilson continued to receive complaints about alleged labor shortages. G. S. Cullinan, president of the Houston, Texas, Chamber of Commerce, charged that a Pennsylvania Railroad agent sought to hire five hundred blacks away from Houston by spreading a rumor that the federal government planned to force remaining blacks into farm work. Congressman John T. Watkins (Democrat–Louisiana) charged that hundreds of black farm laborers were heading to the north from his district. But it was not only the southerners who complained. The governor of

Minnesota called on Wilson to halt the entry of blacks into his state. A group of labor leaders from Illinois blamed a series of racial assaults in East St. Louis on the large number of black migrants in that area. Further, many labor unions were unhappy about the widespread use of black migrants as strikebreakers in the North and Midwest.[40]

Secretary Wilson was conciliatory toward Congressman Watkins. He responded that the department had no authority to interfere with the movement of workers and admitted it was "an embarrassing situation." Wilson expressed the hope that in the North, employers would cease using black strikebreakers, and in the South, they would be "as solicitous as others for the welfare of the workers of their region." The Labor Department's policy, he wrote, was to balance the individual interests against the "industrial interests of the country as a whole."[41] To further address southern concerns about labor shortages, Wilson instituted a program to temporarily admit Mexican workers, including agricultural labor.[42]

Wilson was only compromising with political realities and wartime needs, but USES Director John Densmore went beyond practical needs in responding to southern employers. When the operator of a sawmill charged that blacks were being lured away from his firm to higher paying federal munitions work in Muscle Shoals, Alabama, Densmore assured him that the government would not give black workers any information "showing what they do at Muscle Shoals to get [them] to move away from there. We will let [them] alone."[43]

Birth of the Division of Negro Economics

In response to the Great Migration and continuing into the war period, African American leaders increasingly called for federal action to assist black workers. Initially spearheading the drive was Giles Jackson, an ambitious Virginian who was president of the National Civic Improvement Association. Jackson advocated a self-help program for blacks that would focus on agricultural work. Beginning in 1916, he lobbied Washington for the creation of a "Bureau of Industrial Aid and Economics" that his association would operate under the umbrella of the Department of Labor with a substantial federal funding level of $700,000. The main purpose of the bureau was to encourage blacks to farm in the South instead of migrating, thereby helping to maintain food supplies and holding farming costs down. In a region where growers were increasingly worried about losing low-wage black labor, this approach gained political support. The Richmond Chamber of Commerce and Senator Thomas Martin of Virginia endorsed Jackson's approach.[44]

Jackson's strategy, with its unorthodox mixture of private and public resources, gained enough support to have the matter taken up in the White House in May 1917. President Wilson's personal secretary, Joseph Tumulty, referred the plan to the wartime Council of National Defense, which informed Jackson that Congressional approval of funding would be needed. Jackson petitioned members of Congress to approve the necessary legislation. In order to gain more support in the administration, Jackson joined Congressman W. Schley Howard (Democrat-Virginia) and members of the Richmond Chamber of Commerce to discuss the plan with Secretary Wilson. Jackson also met with Samuel Gompers, president of the American Federation of Labor (AFL), around the same time. Gompers, concerned about the use of black migrants as strikebreakers in the North, endorsed Jackson's plan and urged Secretary Wilson to join him. Additional support came from John A. Ross, president of the Associated Colored Employees of America, headquartered in New York City.[45]

Jackson's proposal was never adopted, but it did establish the idea of a permanent federal office dealing with black labor issues. At the end of January 1918 the National Urban League (NUL)—long involved in the issue of the black migration and concerned that the exodus was about to intensify—held a conference in New York City with representatives of business, social service agencies, other black organizations, and organized labor in attendance. The NUL's primary focus was on winning the support of the AFL for greater union membership for black workers who were now entering the industrial workforce in droves and were, at the same time, subjected to significant discrimination by organized labor. To supplement this effort, the conference included in its resolutions a call for "one or two competent blacks" to be appointed in the Department of Labor to assist in the distribution of black labor.[46]

On Lincoln's birthday, February 12, 1918, a group of black leaders from the NUL, the NAACP, and other bodies acted on this resolution. A preliminary meeting with Louis Post paved the way, and the group presented Secretary Wilson with a more detailed version of their January conference recommendation. The memo cited the war emergency as creating "the most critical labor problem in its history." It noted that the Department of Labor had already set up mechanisms to provide an adequate labor supply, deal with war-production labor disputes, and assure decent working and living conditions for war industry workers. The petitioners made it clear that they believed it was now time to pay attention to the black labor force whose migration posed a social challenge to the nation. Unlike Giles Jackson, who sought to keep blacks in the rural South, this group accepted migration as a continuing reality that required understanding and action to prevent further social problems in the North. Specifically, they asked for the appointment of "a black expert on labor problems" to advise the secretary of labor. They cited the service of Emmett Scott in the War Department as a precedent. To supplement the proposed "black expert," they called for the appointment of black assistants in the various offices of the war labor program as recommended in the January resolution. They also offered to suggest names for black appointees.[47]

Post forwarded their request to Secretary Wilson, along with his personal endorsement. Although Post felt that simply adding a black to the Department of Labor's Advisory Council would be "mere race recognition" or *tokenism*, he and Wilson agreed that the department should pursue the matter. Post noted that "there is an absolute necessity that the Department of Labor come into comprehensive and comprehending relations with ... the black race." He recommended to Wilson that the department hold an "authoritative conference" to decide how best to act on the petition. With his scribbled "Approved Feb. 16-18, WBW" on Post's decision memo, Wilson endorsed the first step toward applying to black workers the broad federal mandate stated in the Department of Labor's 1913 Organic Act: to "foster, promote and develop the welfare of the wage earners of the United States, improve their working conditions, and advance their opportunities for profitable employment." With this action, the federal government also began laying the groundwork for outreach efforts that evolved over the next half century into affirmative action.[48]

The recommended "authoritative conference" took place later in February 1918 at a meeting between several signers of the Lincoln's Birthday proposal and the Department of Labor's Advisory Council. L. C. Marshall, of the council, reported to Wilson that what the black group really wanted was to have a black adviser serving within the department. The council agreed with this idea. However, it rejected the call to have the black adviser serve on the Advisory Council itself because of the temporary nature of the council's existence. They recommended that Wilson appoint a black expert who could provide advice and also help administer any programs that were developed. They left open the question of where the adviser would be located and what kind of organization (if any) would be needed.[49]

Wilson followed the Advisory Council's recommendation and created the position of Director of the Division of Negro Economics (DNE), the purpose of which was to advise him "in all matters affecting Negroes." The director would report to Wilson. To fill this historic post, he appointed George Haynes, professor of sociology and economics at Fisk University. James Dillard, the Urban League, the NAACP, and others supported Haynes for the position. The appointment was effective May 1, 1918.[50]

Haynes, by then, was already a groundbreaking black pioneer. Born in 1880 to a domestic servant in Pine Bluff, Arkansas, Haynes graduated from Fisk University in 1903. After several years divided between pursuing graduate studies in sociology and working to support his mother and sister, he enrolled at Columbia University and, in 1912, became the first black to receive a doctorate there.

During the course of his graduate studies, Haynes focused on the causes and effects of the Great Migration. He became convinced that it was not, contrary to the hopes of many both within and outside of the South, about to be reversed. He believed that blacks and whites should apply social work techniques to ease racial friction and promote black adjustment to urban life. To that end, he helped found the NUL in New York City while teaching at Fisk. While working with the fledgling organization, he endeavored to develop cooperation between white and black groups. After his service at the Department of Labor, he returned to the field of social work, spending the balance of his career with the Federal Council of Churches as head of the department of race relations.[51]

As DNE director, Haynes had beaten out a powerful rival—Giles Jackson. Although Jackson's original proposal for a black workers' program had been rejected, he received endorsements for director of the DNE from the AFL, both senators from Virginia, and the White House. Louis Post, however, derailed the nomination because of his doubts about Jackson, both personally and professionally. These doubts were reinforced by the NAACP and other black organizations that considered Jackson persona non grata. W. E. B. DuBois termed Jackson *disreputable*, while the *Washington Bee*, a black newspaper, charged that he was "not fit to be a dog catcher."[52]

Though he failed to land the big prize, Jackson was able to secure an appointment within the USES as chief of its new Negro Division. He took office on May 1, 1918, the same day Haynes became director of the DNE. Jackson's Negro Division was mandated to develop a program "for the mobilization, employment, and housing of black labor," a mission very similar to that of the DNE.[53]

Such a duplication of functions had the potential for generating a disruptive rivalry in leadership between Haynes and Jackson. The rivalry never materialized. The Negro Division and Giles Jackson were briefly cited in the 1918 Annual Report of the USES but were not mentioned in any subsequent annual reports. The fact was that, while Secretary Wilson had appointed Jackson to please Jackson's politically powerful supporters, he never intended to allow him to play a significant role. Starved of staff and budget, Jackson was virtually ignored. Haynes and the DNE held sole responsibility for the department's efforts to mobilize black labor.[54]

Wilson met with George Haynes on May 1, 1918, Haynes's first day in office, and laid out some initial goals for the DNE. As the Advisory Council had suggested, Haynes was to advise the secretary and other top Department of Labor officials "on matters relating to black wage earners" and to direct programs promoting cooperation between blacks and whites in both agricultural and industrial workplaces. Wilson asked Haynes to develop specific plans for such programs, based on this broad mandate. Wilson also stressed his own belief that such public programs were important because blacks were such a significant portion of the populace, constituting one-tenth of the US population and one-seventh of the workforce.[55]

In April 1918 just before Haynes (and Jackson) took office, the USES prepared a memo of suggested policies for the DNE. The main recommendation was to create within the DNE a "Farm Service Reserve," a cohort of black workers for "the farms in sections of the country where farmers are dependent on colored laborers." The Farm Service Reserve (FSR) bore the fingerprints of Giles Jackson and was never adopted. Nevertheless, the USES memo played an important part in the development of the DNE. Clearly aimed at the South, the FSR also reflected the thinking of USES Director John Densmore, who was sympathetic to southern growers. The leadership of the proposed FSR would be chosen from the black community, with special consideration given to leaders of secret societies who, it was believed, would be better able to gain the cooperation of black workers. These leaders would also counteract racially inflammatory wartime propaganda supposedly spread by German agents through Gypsy fortune-tellers and others. There was to be a campaign to enlist white cooperation with the FSR, with strong reliance on publicity in the press and on support from state government and local leadership.[56]

The USES memo and FSR proposal soon circulated to Wilson, who referred it to Haynes. Haynes prepared a detailed response in which he expanded on its ideas and broadened its scope. Haynes's memo became the basis for the DNE program.[57] While not fully endorsing the FSR, Haynes did approve of many of its features. He favored utilizing black staff, tapping into black organizations, presenting workers with a certificate and badge, and obtaining publicity from black leaders and newspapers. Haynes pointed out, however, that with the planting season nearly over, there was less need for emergency farmworkers. Yet, in his view, there remained a need for long-range planning for both agricultural and industrial labor. Haynes also stressed that the needs of the whole country, and not just the South, should be considered. Furthermore, the black labor program would have to be coordinated with the broader mandate of the Department of Labor to improve conditions for all workers. Finally, Haynes pointed out that, given efforts in the South to forcibly prevent blacks from leaving, workers would probably be suspicious of any program that sought to send them back to the farm.[58]

Based on these considerations and building on the USES proposal, Haynes formulated a four-point approach to helping blacks find jobs, while maintaining peace between the races. First, he proposed that a farm reserve–type program should be part of a wider effort to deal with black employment in all sectors and regions. Second, he suggested that the plan provide a mechanism for bringing black and white representatives of various local bodies together to promote mutual understanding and to establish permanent committees comprised of both blacks and whites.[59] Third, Haynes wanted to mount a careful campaign to publicize the effort among both whites and blacks, again using local leaders and organizations. Fourth, he wished to appoint black staff members (e.g., assistant directors and examiners) to work in the field to help administer the program. Though his plan was comprehensive, Haynes stressed that the most delicate and difficult problems will be

> 1. to have the colored people understand the large purpose and liberal spirit of the department;
>
> 2. to find and secure the right type of black workers; and
>
> 3. to determine the approach to the local white people, especially in the South.

The first two are the keys to the third.[60]

Post forwarded Haynes's proposal to Wilson. To implement Haynes's four-point approach, Wilson, Post, and Haynes formulated the guiding strategy of the DNE as follows: (1) organization of local interracial committees, (2) publicity campaigns to promote racial harmony and cooperation with the department's war effort, and (3) development of a staff of blacks in the DNE to assist in those efforts and to work with other war agencies of the Labor Department. In addition, Haynes and the USES were to work jointly to keep Wilson informed about "industrial" (i.e., race) relations between blacks and whites.[61]

A Federal-State Partnership

The Division of Negro Economics implemented its dual mission of mobilizing black labor for the war effort and promoting fairness and racial harmony through a federal-state partnership, with an emphasis on the states. This effort concentrated on the regions most affected by the migration: the South, the root homeland of most of the nation's blacks and the base for their exodus; and the Northeast and Middle West, the primary destinations of that migration. Assisted by a corps of newly appointed state supervisors of Negro economics, Haynes set the stage for grassroots action within the states. Grassroots action was implemented primarily by means of multiracial Negro Workers' Advisory Committees (NWACs). Together the DNE and the state Supervisors of Negro Economics complemented the mobilization and antidiscrimination efforts of the Negro Workers' Advisory Committees. These corresponding efforts were then, in turn, supplemented by other federal agencies.

Haynes's first step in the national black labor program was to organize and set the course for the DNE. Given the triple mandate approved by Secretary Wilson, Haynes had to take into account several factors when planning new programs and establishing his national organization. Primary among these was the impact of the black migration upon the balance of labor in both the North and the South. In the North, migration put the races into close contact and resulted in deplorable living conditions for blacks. Haynes recognized that confrontations between the races in shops and factories gave rise to "misunderstandings, prejudices, antagonisms, fears, and suspicions." He considered these problems to be local issues that should be understood and remedied in their local context. He also recognized the need to forestall both black and white suspicions about the goals and intentions of his agency. "From the start," he later wrote, "we have wanted both races to understand and firmly believe that the Department wishes to promote cooperation and to help solve local labor problems."[62]

With these factors in mind, Haynes began developing a multifaceted program to utilize existing governmental and nongovernmental bodies. The strategy was for the DNE to work with the USES, which was the prime placement agency for war-related jobs, and with other war-related agencies throughout the federal government to deal specifically with African American issues. The DNE would also coordinate with private welfare organizations around the country. Finally, to improve black morale, enthusiasm for the war effort, and race relations, Haynes planned a nationwide publicity program.[63]

While he planned these massive coordinations, Haynes also had to deal with bureaucratic issues, such as planning the organization and finding qualified candidates to serve as staff. Wilson, mindful of suspicions about the program around the country and particularly in the South, made it clear that the DNE was largely advisory and had no enforcement powers. He also stressed that it was not a separate "Negro Bureau" but rather an integral part of the office of the secretary that reported directly to him. The staff in the national office was kept small to reduce the visibility of the program, but this concession was not as crippling a limitation as it might seem. The key component of the organization was not the national but the state segment.[64] Appointing African Americans as DNE staff, state supervisors, and racial specialists in the USES was a priority for Haynes. Mindful that there was "serious doubt about the expert efficiency of blacks in official positions," he ensured that staff members were well-trained and fully experienced in their specialties. The job of mediating between whites and blacks in the workplace and promoting black morale required staff with exceptional human relations skills and sensitivities. Haynes was convinced that his personnel measured up to these standards. Appointed supervisors in key states were two experts from the Bureau of the Census: Charles E. Hall and William Jennifer who coauthored the department's 1916 study on migration and who served in Ohio and Michigan, respectively. Haynes also hired black clerks for his office and reviewed black appointees in the USES with whom he worked out a joint supervisory arrangement. DNE Assistant Director Karl Phillips supervised the Washington office and worked closely with the director. Haynes later praised the entire staff for their performance under difficult circumstances. Looking at the broader context of black people functioning in a largely white world, he wrote: "Their services as a part of this experiment in the Federal Government's relation to black wage earners has been a contribution to the experience with blacks in important administrative positions."[65]

While still developing the DNE staff and program, Haynes began to establish contact with local leaders and groups in the states. He embarked on a ten-day tour in early June 1918 to meet with white and black representatives in the eight southern states where the problems of black workers were particularly urgent. Setting the stage for the tour was a Department of Labor press release dated May 31, 1918. Citing problems in both the South and the North resulting from black migration, the department called on patriotic whites and blacks to form local alliances. In the case of the South, it asked the alliances "to make those [blacks] who have not yet left the South satisfied." On his tour, Haynes developed what he called *sympathetic contacts* and laid groundwork for local efforts. He won promises of assistance from white and black educators, chambers of commerce, state Councils of Defense, and local offices of the USES. In many areas, his visits sparked the spontaneous formation of local cooperative groups that proved useful in the national effort.[66]

Haynes chose North Carolina as the place to initiate the federal-state phase of the DNE program. Two weeks after Haynes paid a visit to Raleigh, Governor T. W. Bickett called a conference of white and black leaders. Haynes met with the group to explain the federal program and offer his assistance. After the conference, Bickett appointed a working group to set up a North Carolina NWAC, with provision for county and city NWACs as well. Haynes was particularly pleased to see the governor accept the post of Honorary Chairman of the State Committee. The committee organized a wide-ranging coalition of educators, government officials, and representatives of the major towns and cities. While the participants were predominantly black, many white citizens were also involved. A number of cities and counties developed local NWACs to work with the state body. Haynes appointed Dr. A. M. Moore as North Carolina's Supervisor of Negro Economics. Moore reported jointly to Haynes and the USES and worked closely with the North Carolina NWAC system. Haynes also helped get the USES involved in the program. The state Council of Defense and the governor also played major roles.[67] Thanks to their efforts, North Carolina was able to report that several progressive employers asked the NWAC for advice as they voluntarily set up programs for the welfare of their black employees.

The North Carolina system became a model for other southern states, with numerous variations in types of participant, organizational structure, and mission—differences which were to be expected in such a decentralized program. Mississippi, Florida, and Virginia soon held conferences and organized their own NWACs, followed by other southern states. The Council of National Defense played a key role in the development of such programs in the South, both through endorsements and through efforts by the state councils to bring white members to the NWACs.

Attention then turned to the North. Haynes selected Ohio, a major employer of black migrants, to lead the way in that region. Jointly with the USES and Governor James M. Cox (later the unsuccessful Democratic nominee for president in 1920), Haynes convened a state conference. Cox, who had visited Tuskegee Institute that year, assured an enthusiastic audience that "we . . . need [black] people and need them badly in the war . . . [and] in the industrial life of this country."[68] Ohio soon set up a program similar to that in North Carolina and served as a regional leader and example.

To deal with large new concentrations of blacks in Ohio's cities, Charles Hall worked with the USES and also directly with the black workforce. He sought to assure that blacks would be able to find available work, the pay and hours of these jobs, and details on the attitudes of surrounding white communities.[69] A local Ohio committee reported to the state conference that blacks were being denied skilled jobs in defense work. It called on the federal government to prohibit discrimination in contract work (see chapter 3 on the Fair Employment Practice Committee). An Ohio committee on black women in industry also called for greater attention to the needs of this group of workers.[70]

The Florida NWAC defused a tense situation caused by rumors that black women, receiving military allotments from family members in the armed forces, were refusing to work. The committee investigated and announced the finding that many of these women were actually employed.

In Illinois, a special committee reported to the state conference on the general conditions of black war workers. It found that union organizing in the Chicago stockyards had actually improved race relations, and that in other parts of the state blacks were well accepted. Although race riots erupted in Chicago, through the efforts of local NWACs and other groups in Illinois, "much friction . . . was removed by this cordial effort." In several Illinois cities, these groups defused tense racial situations and calm prevailed.[71]

The work of the states was varied and wide-ranging, including investigating conditions of black workers, educating blacks and whites on race relations improvement, helping with job placements, alleviating discrimination and race friction, and developing recommendations for federal action. The DNE report *The Negro at Work during the World War and during Reconstruction*, published in 1921, provides many illuminating examples of this work. Before the end of the war, most large states east of the Mississippi River had developed a black labor program. A total of 11 states had formal NWACs, buttressed with 225 local committees with a membership of over 1,000. This aggregation of local white and black leadership generally worked well together, and both races gave freely of their time for little or no pay. Haynes noted that there was only one known case of friction among committee members serious enough to cause a resignation.[72]

In addition to these efforts in their own backyards, the states also kept the Department of Labor and the DNE informed of conditions and morale in their workforces and assisted the department and the Supervisors of Negro Economics in their work.[73] The state supervisors worked closely with the local USES offices. When the USES was given the responsibility for recruiting labor for defense work, many members of NWACs and state Supervisors of Negro Economics volunteered to assist. While not technically supervised by Haynes, they kept him informed of their activities and of conditions in their states. The supervisors assisted the NWACs and associated groups and also worked directly with employers and others to reduce discrimination, place blacks in defense jobs, and improve black morale and productivity. Since the NWAC system handled the bulk of this work in the southern states, the supervisors were most active in the northern states.[74]

Like the NWACs, the supervisors engaged in a wide range of activities, but they had to be very selective since they were operating with little or no staff. One of the most notable supervisors was Charles Hall in Ohio. He took particular interest in housing and promoted the organization of black building and loan associations. Based on Ohio law, he developed a model constitution for such associations and distributed this model constitution within the black community. The so-called *Ohio Plan* resulted in the establishment of several associations in Ohio and spawned interest and imitation in other states as well. In addition to his work on housing and loan practices, Hall acted to reduce racial discrimination "at the gate" of employers and won agreement from the Ohio Federation of Labor to allow blacks to enter freely into labor unions.[75]

In Michigan, Forrester Washington was a very active administrator, as was William Jennifer, who followed him. Like Ohio, Michigan was a major migration magnet. The Detroit area saw explosive growth in its black population and in the resulting problems of racial tensions and overcrowded housing conditions. The Michigan Labor Department and the Detroit Urban League (DUL) were struggling to place blacks in war industry jobs and deal with social problems. These bodies welcomed the attention the Department of Labor now focused on the state. The fact that Supervisor Washington was former director of the DUL assured good cooperation with existing local efforts. In his brief stint in Michigan, Washington investigated more than a hundred munitions factories, auto plants, and other shops in the Detroit area employing large numbers of blacks. He worked out a program to help these organizations increase the productivity of their black workers by providing better working conditions, setting up advisory committees of black workers, and appointing more black foremen.[76]

William Jennifer took over as Supervisor of Negro Economics in Michigan in October 1918. He immediately embarked on a statewide tour to view local conditions and build coalitions with business groups, churches, and other organizations. In addition to investigating discrimination, helping blacks find suitable jobs, dealing with housing problems, and other typical activities of a supervisor, Jennifer organized a state conference in December, one month after the World War I Armistice in November. The conference quickly shifted its emphasis to postwar labor issues. It placed importance on dealing with the problems of black women workers. A special committee developed a program to improve working conditions for this group, investigate reasons why some industries hired only white women, and fight discrimination in wages and workplace facilities.[77]

The Supervisors of Negro Economics in other northern industrial states had similar agendas, with local variations. Their impact varied, depending on when the supervisor took office and on the effectiveness of existing programs sponsored by local NWACs, governments, and private organizations. Forrest Washington left Michigan to become supervisor in Illinois. One of the main projects in his new position was to promote, with the assistance of local NWACs, cooperative retail enterprises among blacks. Several self-help ventures set up black-run businesses as a means of retaining within the community the money black residents had available to spend. Economic self-help was one of Haynes's and the civil rights community's major national priorities.[78]

New Jersey Supervisor William M. Ashby also worked hard to place black workers in well-paying war industry jobs, persuade employers to hire black foremen, and eliminate discrimination. However, when deciding where to concentrate the limited resources of his DNE, Haynes gave less emphasis to states where problems were less acute, such as New York and Pennsylvania. Consequently, the supervisors in those states did not take their posts until the war was almost over, and when they did begin operations, they focused mainly on post-war adjustment, such as placing skilled black workers displaced from shutdown munitions plants and finding jobs for returning black veterans.[79]

The Division of Negro Economics from Wartime to Peacetime

After all the state programs were set in motion and supervisors were deployed, the DNE concentrated on serving as a watchdog for local efforts, proselytizing (both directly and indirectly) for full black participation in war labor production, and promoting racial harmony. The proselytizing was accomplished through speeches and talks that Haynes and his staff gave and through press releases that were circulated widely to both the white and black presses. The public relations blitz also included distribution of prepared speeches and articles to be used by speakers and magazines around the country. On July 4, 1918, an estimated two thousand orators delivered a speech provided by the DNE on "Labor and Victory," a speech promoting the role of black people in the "world struggle for democracy." Haynes estimated that these messages reached at least one million people a month.[80]

During its existence, the DNE had significant interaction with, and impact on, other sections of the Labor Department that housed it. In August 1918 Post, Haynes, and others developed cooperative arrangements between the DNE and other Department of Labor offices at the local level. Post circulated the DNE's annual budget around the department for comments.[81] The USES adopted a plan developed by Haynes for hiring black war workers. The Women in Industry Service (WIS), forerunner of the Department of Labor's Women's Bureau, consulted with the DNE in developing a survey on the treatment of female black workers in war industries. The DNE helped locate qualified researchers to lead the WIS effort. When the department's Inspection and Investigation Service started planning a study of black workers in northern industries, the division assisted in similar fashion.[82]

After the war ended with an armistice on November 11, 1918, the DNE reinvented itself for peacetime work, and Haynes saw a chance for African Americans to build on progress made during the war. In a speech titled "Grasping the Hands of Economic Opportunity," Haynes pointed out that "for the first time the Negro has the chance to firmly entrench himself in the better occupations," and he urged his black listeners to take advantage of *Mr. Opportunity*, as he put it. But holding on to wartime gains was only one of his priorities.[83]

Shortly after the armistice, Haynes alerted Labor Department policy makers to the problem of the large numbers of unemployed blacks who were about to be demobilized from war industries and mustered out of the military.[84] He also emphasized that, in the North, the potential for racial friction was increasing in those cities with new black populations, and in the South, employers needed to improve the often harsh working conditions blacks faced. However, the most critical postwar problem, in Haynes's view, was the challenge to improve relations between black workers and their white colleagues and employers. He saw the work of the racially mixed local NWACs as the best way to deal with these issues, and he threw the support of the DNE behind their efforts.⁸⁵

The Department of Labor and the DNE supported local efforts to improve postwar race relations in a number of ways. In February 1919 Secretary Wilson called a national conference of the NAACP, the Phelps-Stokes Fund, and other social welfare organizations with the goal of promoting better race relations and addressing black issues involving women in the workplace, farm workers, and training and education. Participants worked on facilitating cooperation among their organizations and on coordination between them, the Department of Labor, and other government agencies. Conferees called for the Department of Labor to renew efforts to improve the lot of black workers by taking such steps as continuing to survey their working conditions and training black youths for entry into industry. After the conference, Haynes authorized supervisors in states with camps for black soldiers to work jointly with the USES toward placing discharged veterans in civilian jobs. This task was made more difficult by a virtual shutdown of the munitions industry and a nationwide economic recession.⁸⁶

In an era of revolutions abroad, Red Scares, and racial unrest at home, Haynes and the DNE responded in various ways to the unstable social landscape of postwar America. The wartime rumors of German efforts to propagandize blacks morphed into a peacetime hysteria about Bolshevik propaganda. The DNE escaped attack by extremists in most areas. However, in Florida, it ran into rough waters when whites charged that radicalism was being engendered in the program by leftist journals. This accusation tainted the efforts of both the Florida NWACs and the DNE in the minds of those who equated advocacy of improved conditions for blacks with Bolshevism. Florida Governor Sidney Catts, an erstwhile supporter of the DNE during the war, succumbed to the changing winds of postwar politics. He charged that the division and local USES offices were filled with "carpetbag, negro federal officers" who advocated mixing of the races. Catts demanded that Wilson abolish the DNE and replace the head of the USES office in Florida. Wilson refused these demands, but under pressure to compromise, he temporarily suspended the Labor Department's race relations work in Florida.[87]

In the Midwest, badly housed black migrants were isolated into urban ghettoes and made unwelcome by resident whites. Haynes felt these conditions made this population "a very ripe field for critical developments of unrest, friction and disturbances" and a possible victim of efforts "to arouse the black group to radical action." He reported to Wilson that the DNE had partially countered these influences by guiding newly arrived blacks to employment offices and social service organizations. However, he insisted, "I do not see . . . how we can help the situation" unless the division could hire more black field assistants. Unlike the Florida critics, Haynes saw this program as a solution, not a problem.[88]

After bloody race riots in Chicago in July 1919, Louis Post, administering the Labor Department in place of the ailing Wilson, sent Haynes on a fact-finding mission to several Midwestern cities. Haynes found whites pitted against blacks because of the familiar syndrome of social, economic, and political disruption associated with the migration, but he failed to find any evidence of incitement by radical provocateurs. One special factor he noted was bitterness among black war veterans over harsh treatment by the army. In several of the cities he visited—especially Chicago, a city with excessive black unemployment—he found that "the racial tension is so widespread as to be in fact a matter of national concern."[89]

Haynes argued that this situation required government action. Blacks echoed that sentiment, as many were now looking to government to solve problems of racial violence and poor living conditions. Indeed, the work of the DNE, along with the state and local activities it spawned during and after World War I, seemed to have generated hope and enthusiasm among blacks and racial progressives throughout the nation. Ohio Supervisor Charles Hall reported that blacks in his state "watched with increasing interest" the DNE's activities on their behalf. They were developing an appreciation of government at all levels. As a result, blacks in Ohio, Hall said, felt that "the Government has recognized them industrially, that they now have a medium through which to voice their complaints, and that . . . they will be less subject to exploitation." An investment banker from Memphis wrote to Wilson praising Haynes and expressing the hope that the DNE would continue its postwar work of "preserving the proper attitudes of the races toward each other."[90]

Unfortunately, racial relations in the United States reached a nadir during what became known as the *bloody summer* of 1919. From Washington, DC, to Chicago and points south and west, a wave of violence raged against black people, fueled by the potent postwar mixture of unemployment, inflation, job shortages, fears of revolution and, above all, fear of black political power and social advancement. In Washington, DC, lurid newspaper accounts of alleged black assaults on white women fomented mob attacks on blacks, who retaliated in kind. Two thousand army troops had to be called in to restore order. Similar violence broke out in Chicago, Indianapolis, Knoxville, Omaha, and other cities. In rural Arkansas, an estimated 250 blacks were murdered by whites, who deeply resented and felt threatened by a perceived rise in the victims' standard of living.[91]

Just as the bloody summer started, the department sought to fund the DNE for the new fiscal year beginning July 1, 1919. Haynes remained hopeful for the division's future. He noted that "everyone who has looked into it commends the work as valuable and necessary." However, the program's timing was not good. Congress was unsympathetic to the continuation of the DNE. During proceedings on the Department of Labor appropriations bill, the DNE and two other wartime agencies were excluded from the legislation. In the enacted appropriations bill, funds were restored to the other two bodies, but not, unfortunately, to the DNE. The division was able to survive through fiscal year 1919 (ending July 1, 1919) only by borrowing resources from the US Conciliation Service and other Department of Labor offices. It was unable, however, to fund the system of state NWACs, which quickly withered away.[92]

Despite the budgetary woes, Haynes remained optimistic and continued to plan for the future. He proposed a federal-state effort led by the Department of Labor to collect data and work cooperatively on black labor issues. He envisioned a joint effort "for the investigation of black affairs and race relations in as many localities as possible . . . as a means of having information and advice to improve conditions and race relations." Unfortunately, the DNE had no better luck in Congress in 1920, and it went out of existence after the administration of Republican President Warren G. Harding took office in March 1921.[93]

The 1920s: An Age of Federal Minimalism

While the DNE disappeared during the 1920s, the social problems that it addressed—the urbanization of black workers and their assimilation into industry—only became more pressing. Spurred on by the booming economy of the 1920s, the black migration from the rural South to the cities of the North and Midwest continued at an accelerated pace. Part of the reason for increased migration was the growing mechanization in farming. These innovations reduced the demand for agricultural labor in the South, as elsewhere, and forced thousands of blacks to leave the region every year to seek work. In the 1910s, the net average increase of the black population outside the South was 34,000 per year.[94] In the early 1920s, that figure swelled to over 100,000 per year.

Partly as a result of the growing concentration of African Americans in New York City's Harlem in the 1920s, there was a flowering of creativity in black music, literature, and art known as the Harlem Renaissance, which celebrated black identity and sought to displace negative stereotypes. This, and similar flowerings of black culture elsewhere, acted as magnets attracting additional migrants from the South. Adding to the incentive to move, Ford Motor Company—partly motivated by the desire to break up unions—adopted a policy of paying black workers equal pay for equal work and placing a number of African Americans in high-wage jobs.

After the war, many black workers were able to retain their foothold within industry. Expanded black urban populations also increased the demand for black professionals and small businessmen. Consequently, many blacks were able to enter the ranks of the middle class, although the bulk of them still remained in low-skill, low-wage jobs.[95]

Several factors combined to restrain significant federal efforts to promote equal opportunity for African Americans in the 1920s. The predominant policy of Presidents Harding, Coolidge, and Hoover was to minimize government involvement in the economy. The prosperity of the 1920s only reinforced this approach. There was also widespread growth of xenophobia and an explosion of membership within the Ku Klux Klan in many areas. This expansion of formalized racism overwhelmed whatever social pressures may have existed on the federal government to adopt progressive racial policies.

Federal labor policy became focused on developing and enforcing more restrictive immigration laws. The primary successes for black groups came in winning inclusion of pro–civil rights planks in both the Republican and Democratic Party platforms in presidential election years.[96] In the area of federal employment, obstacles to the hiring of blacks that had been raised during the Wilson administration remained largely in place. These obstacles included the Civil Service Commission's requirement that photographs accompany federal job applications.[97] Throughout the 1920s, the majority of government agencies continued to hire only white applicants for work above the unskilled level. The Department of Labor reported in 1928 that most blacks who managed to get federal jobs had been relegated to the lowest-paying positions. In addition, many black workers were still routinely segregated to minimize their contact with white workers. One exception during the Harding and Coolidge administrations was the Department of Commerce. Herbert Hoover, Secretary of Commerce from 1921 until he was elected president in 1928, eliminated segregation in his department. Black employees in most of the other departments that had implemented Jim Crow under President Wilson continued to suffer discrimination.[98]

For the most part during the 1920s, the federal government ignored the public policy legacy of the Division of Negro Economics. Nevertheless, a precedent for federal intervention on behalf of black workers was in place. Federal intervention during World War I—limited as it was—had encouraged a propensity within the black community to look toward government (particularly at the federal level) for fair treatment and better opportunities.

CHAPTER 2

Depression and New Deal

Lurking under the surface of the prosperous 1920s was an economically lethal combination of factors that would soon combine to produce the Great Depression. Millions of Americans were forced into unemployment and poverty that endured almost unrelieved until World War II. The complex causes included persistent low wages, excessive speculation in real estate and securities, weakened international financial structures and, perhaps foremost, a depressed agricultural sector. Partly due to a cost-price squeeze on agricultural commodities in the 1920s, agriculture slipped into a rapid decline that, because it had become an integral factor in the national economy, soon dragged down the other sectors. By the time of the stock market crash of 1929, the country was already in deep economic trouble.[1]

African Americans felt the effects of the Depression disproportionately. The agricultural decline of the 1920s forced many of those working on farms to migrate to seek scarce industrial work, and many wound up in unemployment lines. In many cases, those lucky enough to be employed at the onset of the Depression had only recently obtained good industrial jobs and fell victim to the traditional rule of "last hired, first fired." As the economic tide ebbed, those already below the surface sank further. Black unemployment rates eventually exceeded 50 percent in many areas, double the maximum general rate of 25 percent. By the early 1930s, 17 percent of whites were unable to support themselves, but 38 percent of blacks were in a similar predicament.[2]

During the administration of President Herbert Hoover, the federal government attempted to alleviate unemployment through limited public works programs. However, there was no effort to compensate for the disparate impact of the Depression upon black workers. When Hoover ran for reelection in 1932, his opponent was Franklin D. Roosevelt, Democratic governor of New York. Roosevelt had instituted extensive anti-Depression programs in his state, and he promised to do the same for the nation as president.

However, FDR had never shown much interest in racial matters, and his campaign was not strongly supported by blacks. Like Woodrow Wilson—in whose administration he served as assistant secretary of the navy—FDR deferred, during the campaign, to the southerners who still dominated the Democratic Party. While the Republican Party platform contained a mild civil rights plank, the Democratic nominating convention failed to adopt one. Many blacks worried that a victory by FDR would put southern segregationists back in power. As a result, black voters maintained their traditional loyalty to the Republican Party and voted overwhelmingly for Hoover.

The Roosevelt Administration and the "First New Deal"

While Roosevelt carried only four of the fifteen largest black wards in the northern states and won black majorities only in New York City and Kansas City, he won the election in a landslide. The country turned to a new president to lead it out of the Depression.[3] Roosevelt took the presidential oath of office on March 4, 1933, vowing to inaugurate a "New Deal" for America. He immediately commenced a historic national mobilization designed to relieve the economic and psychological suffering from the Depression and bring about the return of prosperity. In the 1930s, Roosevelt and the now heavily-Democratic Congress greatly expanded the size and scope of the federal government and developed a number of programs that, while not aimed specifically at African Americans, aided them greatly. In practice, these programs were not always racially fair in their distribution of relief and employment benefits, but racial equality was always the goal. The participation of unprecedented numbers of blacks in policy-making positions in Washington increased the chances that African Americans would be treated fairly during the greatest economic crisis in the nation's history.[4]

Roosevelt's entire cabinet was confirmed by the Senate and sworn in on Inauguration Day. Despite FDR's weak stance on civil rights, the make up of his administration's leadership boded well for blacks. One of the leading racially progressive appointees was Harold Ickes, the secretary of the interior. Ickes, a white, had served as head of the Chicago branch of the NAACP and became a champion of Native American rights in the 1920s.[5] Frances Perkins, FDR's New York State labor commissioner, was his choice for secretary of labor.[6] As a young social worker in Philadelphia, she helped black girls arriving from the South avoid the clutches of prostitution rings.[7] Another Albany, New York, alumnus was Harry Hopkins, who served initially as a presidential adviser before moving on to head major New Deal programs. Like Perkins, Hopkins had been a social worker with private welfare organizations. Then he joined FDR's successful 1928 gubernatorial campaign, won Roosevelt's trust, and was appointed director of the state's Temporary Emergency Relief Organization.[8] This trio of social progressives brought in a small army of like-minded aides, many of them black. First Lady Eleanor Roosevelt, who had become personally involved in a number of social issues in the 1920s, became a major ally of the racial progressives and an influential supporter of black causes. In terms of racial attitudes, Roosevelt's White House differed sharply from Wilson's, and despite FDR's personal lack of involvement in racial matters, the new administration was poised to build on the legacy of the Division of Negro Economics.[9]

A privately sponsored Washington "Conference on the Economic Status of the Negro" in early 1933 sought to direct national attention to the impact of the Depression on black incomes and the black family.[10] FDR, however, was totally focused on the broader goal of overcoming the Depression through aggressive federal action. Like Wilson, FDR badly needed the support of Southern Democrats in Congress, and he was willing to accommodate (to some degree) their racial views to win their backing for his economic recovery program.[11]

With the help of this key bloc, Roosevelt was able to quickly initiate his New Deal. In its first one hundred days, he sought to stimulate recovery through such measures as stabilization and control of banking and the currency, extensive federal loans to private industry and property owners, unprecedented regulation of private enterprise, and massive relief efforts for farmers and the unemployed. Frances Perkins and Harry Hopkins met with FDR early on and persuaded him to also support a strong relief effort to help working people and their families.[12] Thus was set in motion a cluster of laws and programs that became known as the First New Deal (1933-1935).

To relieve hunger and homelessness, Congress created the Federal Emergency Relief Administration (FERA) in May 1933 to fund state relief efforts. The FERA provided hundreds of millions of dollars in grants to state relief agencies. Roosevelt appointed Harry Hopkins to direct the massive program. Hopkins believed that work was superior to the "dole" and always sought to convince the states to provide public service jobs rather than handing out checks or goods. A few areas, such as New York City, followed the jobs approach under the FERA, but most of the country opted for welfare because it provided quicker relief at a lower cost. Hopkins went to great lengths to assure that blacks across the country would receive their fair share of benefits. This goal proved difficult to achieve in the South, however, because welfare benefits were lower there, and blacks were often denied a fair proportion of the meager relief that was available. Partly because of this lack of access to welfare, migration out of the South jumped during the 1930s, and the black population in the North grew by 25 percent. Another problem was that migrant farm workers, a disproportionate number of whom were black, were totally excluded from relief under the FERA on the phony basis that aiding them amounted to a federal subsidy of their employers.[13]

To help restore prosperity, on June 16, 1933, Congress passed the National Industrial Recovery Act (NIRA), which created the National Recovery Administration (NRA). This program operated on the theory that ruinous competition had brought about low prices and overproduction—factors that helped cause the Depression. The NRA sought to limit production and raise prices by imposing mandatory controls or codes in each industry. To gain the support of organized labor, the NRA affirmed the right of workers to organize and bargain collectively under Section 7a of the NIRA. The NRA also required that all codes include a minimum wage of up to forty cents per hour and overtime pay after thirty-five to forty hours per week, depending on the industry. Participating businesses displayed the distinctive NRA Blue Eagle emblem, and consumers were urged to sign pledges to only patronize NRA businesses.[14]

Committees representing business, organized labor, and consumers drafted NRA codes for most industries by September 1933. Unfortunately, representatives of black workers were absent from the deliberations. Not surprisingly, the codes that emerged tended to work to their disadvantage. The Joint Committee on National Recovery, a black watchdog group, reported a system of discrimination in the codes that resulted in lower incomes for blacks. Traditional "Negro occupations," such as janitorial and household help, were often excluded from minimum wage and maximum hour requirements. Industries concentrated in the South, that still housed the bulk of the black workforce, were allowed to pay lower wages than other industries. For many other industries and occupations, pre-existing wage differences (often based on race) were frozen in place by a wage differential. When blacks received higher wages under the codes, southern employers often replaced them with white workers. Echoing similar concerns expressed during World War I, employers complained that high wages—dictated by what some of them dubbed the *Negro Relief Association*—deprived them of cheap labor for picking and chopping cotton. Weak and biased enforcement allowed many employers to get away with paying subcode wages to black workers. Reflecting widespread dissatisfaction, black newspapers came to refer to the NRA as *Negroes Ruined Again* or *Negro Run Around*. Few blacks mourned when in 1935 the Supreme Court ruled that the NIRA was unconstitutional and closed down the NRA.[15]

Born of the NIRA and long surviving its nullification was the Public Works Administration (PWA), established in June 1933. Congress appropriated the unusually large sum of $3.3 billion to fund the PWA to build public structures of all kinds to provide jobs, stimulate the economy, and provide badly needed new facilities and infrastructure. The PWA was intended to address the anomalous combination of hundreds of thousands of idle laborers and skilled workers, business inventories overflowing with construction materials; and schools, housing, roads, and sewer systems crumbling because of the lack of public revenues. Roosevelt chose Harold Ickes to head the PWA, while Ickes also continued to serve as secretary of the interior.[16]

To assure fairness to workers, Ickes arranged (whenever possible) to use the new version of the US Employment Service, which had been reincarnated and strengthened by the Wagner-Peyser Act of June 1933. The new USES was to refer workers to job sites and to do so regardless of race. Ickes believed that hiring through the USES would help counter the tendency of employers to give preference in hiring to former employees, who were often disproportionately white, rather than considering new applicants. The USES also helped open PWA jobs to blacks in unionized firms that normally hired through union business agents (except in the case of the industrial unions). This move resulted in favoritism to whites because of past union discrimination. Consequently, many unions resisted the PWA's use of the USES. A compromise was worked out whereby business agents were given forty-eight hours to place a union member in a new position. If the union hall could not fill the position, the local USES office took over. The USES also handled all nonunion placements. To get the USES system operational as quickly as possible, the PWA agreed to finance the agency's operating costs. By the end of 1934, the USES and other bodies had placed two million workers in PWA jobs.[17]

Like the NRA, the PWA set minimum wage levels. The PWA system was more elaborate than the NRA's, however. It took local variations into account, with a separate structure for each region. Nationwide, wages ranged from $1.00 to $1.20 per hour for skilled workers and $0.40 to $0.50 for those classified as unskilled, with workers in the southern region at the bottom of the scales. Unions opposed minimum wages in principle at that time, but they were mollified by a proviso allowing PWA to accept local prevailing union rates under certain conditions. Classification of workers as skilled or unskilled labor, a classification which had a major impact on a worker's income, was a touchy issue for both union and nonunion workers alike. Ickes established a Board of Labor Review to assure fairness and to settle any disputes in this area.[18]

Even before organizing the PWA, Ickes had established himself as a major champion of black workers' rights in the Roosevelt administration. In an order dated September 1, 1933, he specifically banned discrimination based on either race or religion in hiring for PWA contract work. To clarify and enforce the rule, Ickes adopted a recommendation from his staff to set racial hiring levels (in effect, quotas) and make them proportional to population. He ruled that the number of blacks hired in a given trade had to be proportional to the total number of blacks in the workforce for a given area who plied that trade based on 1930 census data. Failure to meet this standard was interpreted as prima facie proof of discrimination.

Conversely, meeting the quota was considered prima facie proof of compliance. The PWA was largely successful in implementing its quotas and did not encounter any legal challenges. While the proportional hiring requirement was sometimes disregarded by individual contractors, blacks overall held their fair portion of PWA construction jobs and received 31 percent of total wages by 1936. With this policy, Ickes became the first federal official ever to set racial quotas for federal programs. Thereby, he set a precedent for proportional representation that was widely adopted throughout the New Deal agencies that followed and helped lay the basis for affirmative action in the 1960s (see chapter 9).[19]

Backing up Ickes's equal treatment orders was the PWA's Division of Investigations. Ickes selected Louis Glavis, an attorney who actively supported minority rights, to head the division. A staff of 150 agents looked into issues of fraud and corruption, as well as unfair treatment of employees. The most common violations involved wages. To protect against unfair wage practices, the PWA required that employers publicly post wage rates in workplaces and pay workers by cash or check.[20] This enforcement eliminated the practice of payment in company-issued scrip which could only be spent at company-owned stores.[21]

Despite its efforts for racial fairness, the PWA drew some criticism from the African American community. In the summer of 1933, Roy Wilkins of the NAACP complained that out of four thousand workers at the Boulder Dam site, only eleven were black, and they were not fairly treated. Ickes could do little about hiring, in this case, because the contracts predated the PWA. However, he was able to improve the living arrangements of the black workers. When Glavis turned up instances of discrimination in Illinois's PWA projects, Ickes ordered the state engineer to "see to it that the existing discrimination against blacks is remedied at once."[22]

In the long run, the PWA significantly benefited both blacks and the economy. However, it started up very slowly because of the painstaking project-approval process Ickes had established. By the end of 1933, the PWA had spent only a fraction of its initial funding. As unemployment soared, PWA jobs were not being generated rapidly enough to satisfy the Roosevelt administration. By November 1933 there were only 250,000 workers on PWA-funded payrolls.[23]

At that point, the administration decided to look into a new approach to job creation. Harry Hopkins persuaded FDR to allocate $400 million from PWA funds for a short-term jobs program to help the unemployed survive the winter of 1933-1934. On November 8, 1933, the White House announced the initiation of this new program—which was to be administered by the Civil Works Administration (CWA)—with Harry Hopkins as head. Hopkins appointed Aubrey Williams, a racially progressive, white southerner, to assist in administration.[24]

With the goal of establishing useful jobs that provided both dignity to the unemployed and income for their survival, Hopkins used the

FERA's administrative machinery to establish and oversee work projects. Labor policies were closely modeled on the PWA, with an identical wage scale and the same dual reliance on unions and the USES for hiring. Over its brief course, the CWA spent $934 million, with 80 percent of the money spent in wages for 4 million recipients. Its 177,000 projects included construction or repair of hundreds of libraries, schools, and other public buildings, paving of hundreds of miles of streets, and cultural projects to employ the growing army of unemployed white-collar and creative workers. New York City used CWA funds to help black artists such as sculptress Augusta Savage, who established the Harlem Community Arts Center to train budding artists.[25]

While data on the participation of African Americans in the CWA is scanty, they appear to have been included, at least in proportion to population. There is some evidence of discrimination in hiring, but most failures to employ individual blacks were due to inefficiency and the rushed pace of hiring. The CWA established a grievance system and complaint process, but few complaints of discrimination were reported.[26]

A quick termination of the CWA was a foregone conclusion, given the resistance of FDR to funding long-term government work relief jobs. By March 31, 1934, the CWA had shut down most of its projects and released most of its employees. In its short life, the CWA pumped substantial income into the economy, enhanced the public infrastructure, and reduced the stigma of relief by providing employment at a decent pay. It also provided a precedent for later federal programs that served blacks and other victims of the Depression on a longer-term basis. As if to underscore the arguments of Hopkins and others who wanted to continue the CWA, immediately after its shutdown, the relief rolls swelled by 1.3 million. By late 1934, the economy exhausted the pump-priming benefit of the CWA and fell to its lowest level of the year.[27]

A much longer-lived work-relief program was initiated even before the CWA was fully functional. Alarmed by the exceptionally high rate of unemployment among young people, FDR proposed the idea of putting them to work to preserve natural resources in the nation's public forests. A cabinet group consisting of Harold Ickes, Frances Perkins, Secretary of Agriculture Henry A. Wallace, and Secretary of War George Dern was asked to develop a bill based on FDR's idea. As a result, on March 31, 1933, Congress enacted the Emergency Conservation Work Act. It created a program for young men (women were not included) aged seventeen to twenty-three to do forestry work, flood control, fire fighting, and trail construction in national forests and parks. Dubbed the Civilian Conservation Corps (CCC), it was jointly administered by the Interior, Labor, Agriculture, and War Departments. The corpsmen, who served up to eighteen months, were housed in special camps and provided room and board and a thirty dollars per month allotment, twenty-five dollars of which went directly to their families. The AFL had opposed the bill because it considered the pay inadequate. To mollify organized labor, FDR appointed Robert Fechner, a vice president of the International Association of Machinists, as director. This appointment would prove to be unfortunate, at least in regard to racial policy in the CCC.[28]

Fechner, who was born in Chattanooga, Tennessee, and served as director until his death in 1939, oversaw the quartet of agencies that operated the CCC. To those who expressed concern over the fourfold division of authority, Roosevelt responded, "The Army and the Forest Service will really run the show and Fechner will 'go along' and give everybody satisfaction and confidence." The US Army served the vital role of administering and maintaining the camps. The USES enrolled men for the camps, Interior supervised projects in national parks, and Agriculture oversaw work in the national forests. Eventually, over two million young men—two hundred thousand of them blacks—served in the CCC. It was one of FDR's most popular programs. However, it was a mixed blessing for African Americans, representing for them, both the best and the worst of the New Deal.[29]

After the army enrolled the initial contingent of corpsmen in April 1933, the USES took over the job and established recruiting quotas for each state based on population. While black participation was low at first, the number eventually reached the national benchmark proportionality level of 10 percent. Nominal parity was misleading, however, as black youths were disproportionately represented in the ranks of the economically disadvantaged.[30]

The low black participation rates in the early stages of the program were largely a result of discrimination. Georgia, with a 36 percent black population, sent no blacks at all to the corps in the early weeks. Mississippi included less than 2 percent blacks in its June 1933 contingent, despite a statewide black proportion of 50 percent. In Dallas County, Alabama, white enrollees outnumbered blacks 2 to 1 despite the fact that the population was 75 percent black. In California, black participation was initially low because of a failure to publicize the CCC. Most blacks there learned about it through word of mouth.[31]

The existence of discrimination in recruitment generated countermeasures, some more effective than others. The CCC's establishing law decreed that "no person shall be excluded on account of race, color, or creed." To enforce this requirement, Fechner instituted mandatory quotas based on proportional enrollment of blacks in each state. However, local administrators could get around these measures and deny blacks admission, claiming falsely that the state had already met the quota. To counter these deceptions, Frances Perkins instructed state employment agencies to avoid discrimination in recruitment. She telegraphed one governor to observe the antidiscrimination clause of the law and to look into allegations that it was not being observed.[32]

On another occasion, however, Perkins consented to discrimination at the CCC. In July 1935 Fechner asked USES Director Frank Persons to cut off the number of black recruits in Texas at 3,200 for the year. He argued that a limited number of projects existed in Texas to which black CCC corpsmen could be assigned without provoking strong objections from local white populations. Persons drafted a letter to Fechner objecting to this request as a violation of the CCC law. Secretary Perkins, for reasons unknown, supported Fechner and informed Persons, "I prefer that this letter not be sent." The limitation on Texas enrollments stood.[33]

The treatment of black recruits in the CCC camps was often unsatisfactory. In the South, black corpsmen were assigned to separate camps. Elsewhere, the races were initially assigned to mixed camps. However, the existence of camps with black corpsmen bothered nearby communities, particularly in areas of the West where few African Americans lived. Because of such community concerns, and also in response to allegations of racial strife within the camps, Fechner toured the western CCC region in the summer of 1935. He presumably saw what he wanted to see since he concluded that race relations were a problem and immediately asked the army to segregate the races into separate camps. The army complied and ordered complete segregation, except when there were not enough African American corpsmen to complete a full CCC company. To deal with community complaints about black corpsmen from out of state, the order required that blacks be assigned only to camps in their states of residence. Thereafter, Jim Crow conditions prevailed throughout the CCC. To further assuage the sensitivities of white communities, Fechner relocated black camps from Gettysburg, Pennsylvania; Springfield, Illinois; and the vicinities of various cities in New York and New Jersey to more remote sites. In its zeal to limit contact with local whites, the army established isolated black camps deep in federal lands.[34]

Discrimination was also rife in the staffing of the camps. The need for a complement of camp officers in the black camps—army doctors, teachers, clerical staff, and service workers—seemed like an opportunity for blacks, both military and civilian. However, the army held a long-standing policy of never putting black officers into positions where they might be able to issue orders to, or minister to, whites. Fechner supported the army, and black officers were initially ruled out in the camps. Walter White of the NAACP and Emmett Scott, the black World War I–era War Department official (see chapter 1) now at Howard University, led a movement to force the CCC to allow black officers and military doctors to serve. FDR ordered the army to permit this suggestion, but only a handful of black officers were eventually called to duty at only two all-black camps.[35]

The CCC provided an extensive education and training program, with general educational and vocational classes in a wide range of subjects for corpsmen. However, the Interior Department's Office of Education, which administered the educational programs, did not oppose the army's discriminatory racial policies. As a result, blacks were initially excluded from staff positions in the training program. After Harold Ickes protested vehemently to Army Secretary Dern, the army relented and allowed the appointment of black educational advisers in most of the all-black camps.[36]

Despite the existence of a significant degree of discrimination, a substantial number of young black men were allowed to receive the benefits of the CCC. The program eliminated a significant amount of illiteracy and probably reduced the level of juvenile delinquency in the black community. Except for training provided only to blacks in so-called *Negro occupations*, such as cooking and serving, both races received the same training, which focused on high-skill occupations. Training did not always translate into appropriate employment for blacks, however. Most black alumni in the California CCC found jobs as laborers. Blacks were appointed to positions of responsibility as officers and educators, although they were limited to service in the black camps. At the intangible level, the program buoyed the spirits of the young black enrollees and provided them with a measure of social and economic security.[37]

In the Federal Departments

While the alphabet soup of agencies born of the First New Deal was wrestling with issues of racial fairness, the cabinet departments began to deal with long-standing fairness issues of their own and to involve blacks in policy-making. As he had in the PWA, Harold Ickes strove to make the Interior Department a model of nondiscrimination. Aside from Ickes's personal interest in racial justice, it made historical sense for his department to take the lead on this issue. Besides being responsible for Indians on their reservations and for other minorities on island territories, Interior had long managed several institutions that specifically served blacks. The institutions included Howard University, Freedmen's Hospital, and St. Elizabeth's Hospital for the Indigent, all in Washington, DC. Ickes appointed several white racial progressives to top staff positions in the department. Notable among them was Louis Glavis, who headed the Inspection Division. Glavis was already performing a similar duty at the PWA. Nathan Margold, a former US Attorney who had done a study for the NAACP on the denial of citizenship rights to blacks, was appointed Departmental Solicitor.[38]

In March 1933 Ickes ordered removal of "Whites Only" and "Colored Only" signs at cafeterias, restrooms, and drinking fountains in the Interior Department. He also banned discrimination in hiring practices. When the park system in Washington, DC came under his jurisdiction in June 1933, he desegregated all public parks. Ickes was, however, forced to bow to public sentiment and did not integrate swimming pools or golf courses.[39]

The Department of Interior rose quickly from role model to policy leader on racial affairs with the summer of 1933 appointment of a "special assistant on the economic status of Negroes." This appointment came about after the NAACP pressured FDR to take action on behalf of the African American population. Simultaneously, Julius Rosenwald, who headed a fund he established in 1919 to aid minority groups, recommended to Roosevelt that he appoint an adviser to the administration to represent blacks in the planning and management of the program for economic recovery. Roosevelt, however, feared that appointing such an adviser would alienate congressional Southern Democrats.

Ickes and Rosenwald worked out a way to set up the new position.[40] Prompted by Rosenwald, as well as by his own racial sympathies, Ickes offered to house the function in his department. FDR did not object, but there was a problem with funding this new position. Roosevelt had drastically pared back the regular budget to find money for the economic recovery program. Ickes had to cut his own department's budget in half while he administered the massive PWA. It would have been difficult to obtain funding from Congress for the position. Rosenwald solved the dilemma by agreeing to pay for the position out of his own pocket.

Rosenwald recommended Clark Foreman, the Rosenwald Fund's research director, for the post. Ickes welcomed the idea and appointed Foreman as his "Adviser on Negro Affairs." Foreman was a young white southerner who had worked with the Georgia Commission for Interracial Cooperation. Roy Wilkins of the NAACP responded negatively when Ickes did not appoint a black to the most important position in the government dealing with race. Ickes defused the NAACP's opposition by creating two additional positions (also paid for by Rosenwald) under Foreman, specifically to be filled by blacks. One was for an assistant and the other, a secretary. Ickes appointed Robert Weaver, a young Harvard economist who went on to a distinguished public and academic career, to the assistant position.[41]

The first concrete accomplishment of Foreman's group was to convince other agencies to appoint black advisers. Among those who were then brought into the government were Robert L. Vann, editor of the *Pittsburgh Courier*, in the Justice Department; Eugene Kinckle Jones, executive secretary of the National Urban League, at the Department of Commerce; and Lawrence A. Oxley, an experienced social worker and labor mediator, at the Department of Labor (see below). Working with the Interior Department group, these advisers pressed for fair consideration of the needs of blacks in the recovery program.

With the advisers providing leadership, treatment of black career federal employees in many agencies, besides Interior, began to improve. More "Colored Only" signs came down, and entire agencies were integrated, some of them demolishing racial dividing walls dating back to the Wilson administration. The Civil Service Commission ruled that applicants for federal employment no longer had to submit a photograph with their application. However, the CSC retained the "rule of three" whereby employers interviewed three qualified job candidates at a time. An employer was free to hire any one of them, or reject all three, without explanation or recourse. Despite this regressive rule, black employment in FDR's first two terms grew from 50,000 to 150,000. The black percentage of the rapidly expanding federal workforce doubled from 5 to 10 percent, thereby attaining rough proportionality in relation to the white population. The bulk of these jobs were in Negro occupations—janitors, chauffeurs, and elevator operators, for example—but many blacks also worked as clerks and secretaries. A number were hired at the professional level as architects, engineers, lawyers, and librarians. In addition, FDR appointed over one hundred blacks to administrative and patronage posts, a number far exceeding that of any previous administration.[42]

Reflecting the unprecedented role of African Americans in making national policy in January 1934, Ickes established the "Interdepartmental Group Concerned with the Special Problems of Negroes," composed of the growing body of special advisers in the various departments. It was led by Clark Foreman and Robert Weaver. Previously, the two had suggested the establishment of a "National Advisory Board on Negro Welfare." Ickes had vetoed that proposal because he feared that the name would make it a red flag to segregationists. He believed an "Interdepartmental Group" would sound much less threatening. The purpose of the group was to organize and rationalize federal policies affecting blacks and to promote programs on their behalf. Members began meeting with white representatives from numerous departments and New Deal agencies, but the innocuous name of the group did not shield it from significant resistance to its ideas. Most agencies soon dropped out, and it held its fourth and last meeting on June 1, 1934. However, a precedent had been set for the eventual emergence of a more influential body—the "Black Cabinet" (see below).[43]

One agency that gave full cooperation to the Interdepartmental Group and fully shared its goals was the Labor Department. Secretary Perkins desegregated the department's cafeterias, where white and black employees had been kept apart by having one area for manual laborers, who were mostly black, and another for white-collar workers, who were mostly white. Perkins canceled a plan by the department to fire black elevator operators and replace them with whites. She noted that in the 1920s whites had scorned jobs of this nature. She added a total of 129 black employees to the Department of Labor's rolls, many of them not in Negro occupations.

Perkins also attempted to see that the USES treated black job applicants fairly. Early on, she ordered that in states with large black populations, there should be blacks on the USES staff in local offices. Southern members of Congress closely monitored the operations of the USES, particularly its offices in their region. From its inception in 1933, these Congresspersons constantly pressured the USES to accept Jim Crow practices in the South. As a result, and despite Perkins's call for equal treatment, the USES bowed to pressure and began accepting employer requests that it refer only white candidates for a given position. Blacks objected strenuously to this practice, which became a bone of contention between civil rights groups and the USES until the 1960s.

In an effort to shed light on the situation of black workers in America, Perkins had the department undertake and publish a number of special studies. One of the first products was an article by Robert Weaver, published in the *Monthly Labor Review* (*MLR*), the journal of the Bureau of Labor Statistics (BLS). In his article, Weaver contradicted the common notion that relief rolls were overloaded with blacks because these workers lacked ability and initiative. Throughout the 1930s, the *MLR* published a series of articles and reports on black labor, covering such topics as migration, restrictions on black employment, problems of black youth, and blacks in federal relief programs.

While the PWA was primarily Harold Ickes's responsibility, the Labor Department had an interest in assuring fair hiring practices in that program. Regarding a PWA-sponsored construction project for housing in the largely African American south side of Chicago, Perkins was made aware that black workers were not obtaining a fair share of employment. To see that the situation was rectified, she sent BLS Commissioner Isador Lubin to meet with the Chicago building trades unions and contractors association. Lubin presented them with a fair hiring plan that Ickes had seen and approved. It was based largely on Ickes's fair hiring policy of 1933 which represented a relaxation of straight proportional hiring, and specified black employment in the project in relation to black participation in specific trades. These rates were usually lower than the black percentage of the general population in toto. This formula resulted in fewer construction jobs for blacks. Lubin summarized the Labor Department's plan in a March 27, 1935, letter to Ickes:

> [The formula] provided for the allocation of jobs for Negroes according to the ratio that prevailed between white and Negro artisans in the Building Trades in Chicago as shown by the census of 1930. That ratio showed that 13 percent of the unskilled jobs and 3.5 percent of the skilled jobs should go to Negroes. The Building Trades representative undertook to arrange that in the event the contact was awarded to a contractor who had an agreement with organized labor, the above mentioned percentages of the payroll should be paid to Negroes. They further agreed that the proportion of the jobs to be given to the various crafts should be related to the ratio of Negroes to whites in the various skilled crafts. This ratio varied from 1.3 percent for electricians to 11 percent for plasterers and cement finishers. In those instances where there are no Negro employees in a given craft union, an arrangement would be made for the granting of working permits to a number of Negro workers sufficient to make possible the employment of the necessary percentage of persons.

Lubin won agreement from both labor and management to carry out a fair hiring plan along these lines, and he also won the support of key black leaders who had been involved in the discussions.[44]

At the request of the black community, Perkins appointed an African American to advise the Labor Department on black issues. Previously, she had sent a white representative to several black labor conferences and had appointed a departmental committee to study the health and welfare of blacks. In early 1934 she appointed Lawrence A. Oxley to serve as a black issues adviser and gave him the official title of Director of the new Division of Negro Labor (DNL). Oxley was a former social worker employed at that time as a labor mediator with the department's Conciliation Service. As DNL director, he reported to Isador Lubin.

Modeled partly on the World War I Division of Negro Economics, but less extensive in scope, the DNL had several tasks. One was to serve as liaison with black groups and unions and maintain communications with the large body of unorganized black workers. Oxley advised the BLS, USES, Women's Bureau, and other departmental agencies. His "Weekly Progress Reports" to Lubin indicated frequent meetings and contacts throughout the government on civil rights issues, as well as numerous speaking engagements at black schools and conferences. He also continued to work on special assignments for the Conciliation Service, conducting an extensive investigation into black participation in organized labor, focused on the construction trades.[45]

Like the World War I–era DNE, the Division of Negro Labor organized numerous state conferences on black labor problems. The goal was to encourage the states both to develop plans for assuring that blacks would receive their fair share of jobs, and to devote special attention to the racial attitudes and misunderstandings that might interfere with this goal. In a letter inviting the governor of

Alabama to participate in a conference, Oxley noted: "These facts [of racial friction] must be recognized locally as well as nationally, and they must be dealt with in a statesmanlike manner." An indication of the impact of the conferences can be seen in a newspaper report on a 1939 North Carolina conference of black and white leaders and officials, and organized by Oxley and the governor. Reporter William Howland wrote that, although it was too early to know specifically what the conference accomplished, "It is certain that it focussed ... the thought of leaders of both races on an ever-growing problem."[46]

The "Second New Deal"

During the off year, Congressional elections were held in the fall of 1934. Instead of losing seats, as was normal for the incumbent party after winning the White House, the Democrats gained ten seats in each house. Part of the reason for this gain was a shift in the black vote away from the Republican Party. FDR's dramatic actions and engaging manner as president attracted blacks' interest and support. His inaugural address, which asserted that "the only thing we have to fear is fear itself," resonated with African Americans suffering from an ongoing wave of lynching and other terrorism. They were also encouraged by being included in New Deal programs. For the first time, Democratic candidates made a major effort to win black votes, and Democratic political machines courted black leaders. As a result, Democrats gained a majority of the black vote for the first time in history. They even elected the first black Democrat to the House of Representatives when Arthur Mitchell defeated the incumbent black Republican Oscar DePriest in Chicago. The election gave blacks much greater influence in Washington.[47] It also weakened the hold of the Southern Democrats on the Congress, enhancing both the prospects for stronger relief and recovery efforts, and the chances of blacks for fairer treatment and greater benefit from federal programs.

Strengthened by the 1934 election, the Roosevelt administration pursued the Second New Deal which, in many ways, turned out to be more beneficial for African Americans. This was fortunate because the numbers of blacks in need had been augmented by thousands of displaced tenant farmers. They were victims of the well-intentioned efforts of the Agricultural Adjustment Administration (AAA), a New Deal program that sought to protect American farms by preventing overproduction and by shielding them from ruinously low commodity prices. The subsidies paid by the AAA were intended for farm owners and tenant farmers alike, but the unintended consequence was that a large number of owners replaced their tenants with hired hands so they could retain all the benefits for themselves. Many of the former tenants were then forced onto the relief rolls.[48]

By 1935 New Dealers had decided to take more forceful steps to stimulate the economy and provide jobs. Beginning that year, the government engaged in a massive and historically unprecedented intervention, eventually spending $14 billion to help the needy unemployed. Roosevelt's goal became to "weed . . . out the overprivileged" and "lift . . . up the underprivileged."[49]

First Lady Eleanor Roosevelt began paying even closer attention to black issues. Through friendships with Mary McLeod Bethune, president of the National Council of Negro Women, and Walter White of the NAACP, she learned more about their concerns and became an advocate for their causes. Bethune and White became frequent guests of hers at the White House. She developed a particularly close friendship with Bethune and reportedly "would run down the drive to meet her."[50]

Eleanor Roosevelt fully utilized her unique status in Washington and became an influential friend of black Americans. Through her, black leaders made their views known to the president. She allied herself with Ickes, Hopkins, and Perkins, and pressured other officials to promote equal rights in their programs. She also won a number of federal appointments for prominent blacks, including Bethune, who served in the National Youth Administration (see below).[51]

The Works Progress Administration

Armed with the mandate of the 1934 elections, FDR proposed to institutionalize work-relief spending and fund it on an unprecedented scale to overcome the stubborn Depression. In Roosevelt's January 1935 State of the Union address, he proposed a $4.88 billion program to help the needy unemployed.[52] In April 1935 the overwhelmingly Democratic Congress gave him the requested amount in the Emergency Relief Appropriations Act (ERAA). It was then the largest single federal spending bill in history. While most of the money went to existing programs, such as the PWA, CCC, and various rural-aid agencies, $1.4 billion was allocated to a new agency—the Works Progress Administration (WPA). Conceived and headed by Harry Hopkins and established by Executive Order (E.O.) 7034 in May 1935, the WPA was originally intended to oversee and assist in the "progress" of the other programs funded by the ERAA, and also to develop "small useful projects" of its own.[53]

Almost an afterthought, the "small useful projects" quickly came to dominate the WPA. Under Harry Hopkins the agency (in its first five years) spent almost $8 billion on a wide variety of labor-intensive public works, as well as on educational and cultural projects. It employed an average of 2.2 million men and women at any one time, with peaks as high as 4 million. Ninety percent of those hired had to be from relief rolls to assure that benefits went to the neediest and also to bring about a shift that the administration was seeking—from relief to employment programs. Discrimination was banned in the WPA, and blacks benefited significantly from its programs, especially in places like Harlem, where it was one of the main providers of income. Black poet Paul Laurence Dunbar wrote about a song he heard in the streets of Harlem in those years:

> "You buy my groceries / and pay my rent. /
> Mr. Roosevelt, you're my man!"

The cumulative result of thousands of local WPA projects was a massive upgrade of the nation's public facilities. By June 1940 WPA workers had constructed over half a million miles of roads and streets; built over 4,000 school buildings, expanded 30,000 more; created 132 new hospitals, improved 1,670 others; laid 18,000 miles of sewer lines; and built 39 electric power plants.[54]

A WPA program known as Federal Project Number 1 contributed to an ongoing cultural and intellectual renaissance in the African American community by putting thousands of unemployed musicians, artists, actors, writers, and historians to work. Through research, writings, performances, and works of art relating to American history and culture, they documented and preserved diverse ethnic folkways that were rapidly fading in many regions. The WPA also provided a training ground for young artists, performers, and writers.[55]

The thousands of white-collar and millions of blue-collar workers recruited to the WPA were generally hired without regard to race. Each state's allotment of WPA jobs was proportionate to its number of able-bodied workers on relief, and 90 percent of new hires had to show financial need. On May 20, 1935, FDR issued E.O. 7046 setting rules and standards for the WPA. This executive order guaranteed that qualified applicants "shall not be discriminated against on any grounds whatsoever." Hopkins elaborated on the order in 1936 when he barred discrimination against qualified and eligible WPA job candidates "on any grounds whatsoever, such as race, religion, or political affiliation."[56] Congress codified the

WPA antidiscrimination policy into law in 1939, making violation a felony punishable by a $1,000 fine or one year in prison.[57] In a number of projects, the WPA went beyond racial proportionalism and hired blacks and whites in equal numbers. The WPA was so adamant about equal treatment that it omitted information on workers' race, religion, and politics from reports and personnel records. While well-meaning in its intent, these omissions made it difficult for researchers to accurately gauge the effectiveness of the WPA's nondiscrimination policies.[58]

Like other New Deal job programs, the WPA prescribed a wage schedule and set restrictions on the hours of work and duration of employment. In line with the WPA's dual goal of reducing relief rolls without competing with private industry for workers, it developed what it called a *security wage* structure. The average monthly wage was set at $50, double the average relief payment but well below the wages offered in industry. E.O. 7046 set the maximum hours of work at eight hours per day and forty hours per week. In addition, Hopkins set a monthly maximum of 140 hours and a maximum term of service of 18 months.

E.O. 7046 also established schedules of earnings for four skill classes, ranging from unskilled to professional, in each of four national regions. There were demographic sub-schedules for each region to allow for local rural-urban variations in the cost of living. As was the case with the CWA and PWA, the Deep South (Region IV) had the lowest wage scales in the program. The greatest pay disparities between the South and other regions existed in the category of unskilled jobs in rural areas. This distribution had a disproportionately negative effect on African Americans. To reduce the wage gap, Region IV was abolished in 1936 and merged into the higher-paying Upper South (Region III), adopting the latter's higher wage scale.[59]

The WPA helped African American workers and the black community both financially and psychologically. Hundreds of thousands were taken off welfare rolls every year and given useful, if short-term, employment at decent wages. The range of projects and services that helped blacks was broad and varied. Most of the jobs for blacks and whites alike were as laborers in infrastructure improvement. But there were numerous skilled and creative positions as well. For example, in addition to upgrading the physical plant in school systems, the WPA developed a national adult education system that trained tens of thousands of blacks, many of them acquiring literacy in the process. Thousands of blacks were employed as teachers. In Harlem alone, there were thirty-four WPA education centers. WPA-run housekeeping services employed single female heads of household to help the elderly and the incapacitated with their domestic chores and provide basic nursing services.[60]

The Federal Arts Projects of the WPA assisted many African Americans involved in cultural activities. In New York City, the Federal Music Program—under famed conductor, Nikolai Sokoloff—hired talented black musicians and sponsored performances of works by William Grant Still, Clarence Cameron White, and other black composers. Black writer Ralph Ellison, later the Pulitzer Prize-winning author of *The Invisible Man*, worked in the Federal Writers' Project researching black history and culture. While the New York Writers' Project never published a book specifically on black life, it did include material on this subject in its series of local area guides. In addition, the Federal Writers' Project enabled Ellison and other black writers to survive and to develop material they used later in their own works. The Federal Arts Project hired thousands nationwide and, under pressure from the Harlem Artists' Guild, set proportional quotas for blacks.

Participating black artists like Jacob Lawrence, creator of an epic series of sixty paintings depicting the Great Migration, produced many more works illustrating and celebrating black history and identity. Art schools in Harlem and Chicago's south side trained a generation of black artists and sculptors. The Federal Theater Project produced eighty-one new plays, fourteen dealing with racial issues. The Negro Theater Project in New York produced works by black playwrights and an all-black version of Shakespeare's *Macbeth*. Federal Theater Project pageants depicted figures important in black history, such as John Brown, Nat Turner, and Harriet Tubman. However, vociferous congressional opposition and allegations of Communist influence led to the cancellation of several productions and ultimately killed the Federal Theater Project in 1939.[61]

To help assure fair treatment for African Americans in the WPA, Harry Hopkins saw to it that significant numbers of black professionals were involved in the oversight and administration of the effort. He appointed blacks to key WPA positions across the country to counteract the tendency of local government officials toward bias in the distribution of WPA jobs. Ninety-one blacks were employed in the national WPA office, including an administrative assistant and several other top staff. To oversee its own national equal-treatment effort, the WPA placed black advisers in the field and established a network of national, state, and local advisory boards.[62]

By 1939 approximately one million black workers and dependents had received significant income through the WPA.[63] Approximately 14 percent of all workers certified for continued WPA employment were black. The WPA was truly seen by many black people as a godsend. It not only provided economic benefits but empowered blacks to feel more included in the mainstream of national life.[64]

However, masked by the favorable nationwide data on WPA, recruitment of blacks was significant in regional differences. New

York City was among the leaders in meeting or exceeding WPA hiring goals for blacks, an expected finding since northern states generally had the highest black participation rates. In 1943 sociologist Richard Sterner's book *The Negro's Share* provided detailed findings on black and white employment in the WPA. Sterner found that in northern states with large black populations, the percentage of blacks in WPA employment was far higher than their percentages either of general population, or of all unemployed workers. However, in the southern states, black WPA and unemployment percentages were fairly close, and the percentage of blacks in WPA jobs was usually far below their proportion of total unemployed. Rural blacks were the hardest-hit group.[65]

Black female heads of household in the rural South were less able to obtain WPA jobs than their male counterparts. This discrimination was partly the result of local Jim Crow laws that allowed black and white men to work together but did not allow racial integration among women. Also, local whites often opposed offering WPA jobs because these might lure black women away from employment as domestics.[66]

Nationally, average wages for blacks in the WPA were lower than those of whites, a disparity partly the result of demographics. Blacks were concentrated in the South, the area with the lowest wage scale. In addition, blacks were disproportionately classified as unskilled workers, a group which was always at the bottom of the pay scale.[67]

Some relief agencies applied different standards of eligibility to the races when referring candidates for WPA jobs. They sometimes denied jobs to qualified blacks on the spurious grounds that black workers were accustomed to a lower standard of living than qualified whites. Similarly, blacks who refused low-paid private sector jobs were more likely to be denied a WPA job than whites in the same circumstances. Under WPA eligibility rules, workers, who refused private employment at local prevailing wages for a given type of work, were not supposed to be hired by the WPA for the same work. Whites were often excused from this requirement and, when they turned down private jobs, were placed in WPA jobs that might otherwise have gone to blacks.[68]

Local governmental bodies were frequently able to ignore Washington's antidiscrimination policy because the WPA had a limited ability to enforce its rules. The WPA was largely focused on getting considerable numbers of people into jobs; oversight of relief agencies and project sponsors was not a major concern. When the WPA did pry into these bodies, the attention was often received with hostility. As a result, it tended not to interfere in the business of these local governments.[69]

Throughout its existence, the WPA had to deal with public hostility, congressional criticism, and constricted budgets. Dubious about long-term relief employment and under pressure to balance the federal budget, FDR authorized a huge cut in the WPA budget in 1936.[70] Fiorello LaGuardia fruitlessly implored FDR to roll back the cuts as criticism mounted and thousands of enrollees organized protests. A nineteen-year-old black woman named Catherine Brunson shocked the nation when she jumped five floors to her death after she learned that her husband had lost his WPA job. Some saw the WPA and its network of local government agencies as a huge Democratic political machine. Civil rights groups criticized discrimination in the WPA in the South. Conservatives lampooned nonproductive "leaf-raking" jobs and charged that arts projects dwelled excessively on social unrest and promoted radical causes. In 1939 Congress reoriented the WPA toward large-scale public works projects and cut its budget sharply. As was the case with most other New Deal programs, the WPA and its mission of recovery and relief became irrelevant during the World War II emergency, and it soon went out of existence.[71]

Mary McLeod Bethune, the NYA, and the "Black Cabinet"

A companion agency to the WPA, that also incorporated aspects of the CCC, was the National Youth Administration (NYA). Created on June 26, 1935, under E.O. 7086, its purpose was to serve in-school and unemployed youths. The NYA owed its existence, in large part, to Eleanor Roosevelt. She wanted to establish a broad program that would help all young people, not just males (e.g., the CCC), as they sought to complete their education while struggling to survive the Depression. Five million youths were out of work in 1935, representing 25 percent of the out-of-school group. Around three million were on relief. Harry Hopkins, Aubrey Williams, Frances Perkins, and others were thinking along similar lines as Mrs. Roosevelt and presented their ideas to FDR in the spring of 1935. While the exact nature of Mrs. Roosevelt's role is not clear, she certainly was deeply involved in the planning for the NYA and played a key role in convincing FDR to approve its establishment.[72]

FDR appointed Aubrey Williams to head the new agency. The NYA took over the FERA program to aid college students, initiated assistance to high school students, and provided public works jobs for youths who were not in school. The NYA also supported apprenticeships, vocational guidance programs, and recreational opportunities for youths. Buttressed by a national advisory committee and a national network of fifteen hundred state and local committees, the NYA ultimately provided over four million youths with jobs and educational assistance.[73]

Not only did the NYA serve more young people than the CCC, which helped just two million, it was preeminent among all New Deal agencies in its effectiveness in serving African American youths. Much of its success was attributable to Aubrey Williams and Eleanor Roosevelt. Williams worked to assure that black youths would be equally compensated and fully included in training that would enable them to move into skilled and nontraditional jobs. He directed local administrators in all regions to be scrupulously fair to all applicants and installed black administrators in heavily black districts.[74] Eleanor Roosevelt worked closely with Williams, who maintained dual involvement with the WPA until 1938. She made a point of knowing as much as possible about the agency and regularly passed information and suggestions along to Williams. In addition, she worked to defend the NYA from charges of radicalism and helped maintain smooth relations between the operating staff and the sometimes difficult Williams.[75]

The primary credit for the NYA's success on behalf of blacks, however, goes to Mary McLeod Bethune.[76] She was initially appointed to the NYA's advisory committee and then, with the support of Eleanor Roosevelt, as director of the Division of Negro Affairs (DNA). Born in 1875 in South Carolina and one of seventeen children of two former slaves, Bethune was the only child in her family to attend college, earning her way to graduation from the Moody Bible Institute in Chicago. Starting out as a teacher in bible schools, she became a leading educator and founded Bethune-Cookman College, a black teachers and industrial education school in Daytona, Florida. Active in the NUL and the NAACP, and the founder of the National Council of Negro Women, she was the most famous and highly regarded black woman in the country by the time of FDR's election.

Under Williams's and Bethune's leadership, the NYA performed its mission by means of two operational divisions. The larger of the two was the Student Work Program. It provided part-time jobs for students sixteen to twenty-four years of age who needed assistance in order to stay enrolled in high school or college. The jobs for college students were related as closely as possible to their interests and coursework. Almost all of the 120 existing black colleges participated in the program. Out of 440,000 youths employed, 42,900

(9.7 percent) were black. While not applying a quota, the program still achieved rough racial proportionality.[77]

The smaller division of the NYA was the Out-of-School Work Program. It provided income and work experience for unemployed youths through part-time jobs in a wide range of occupations, from construction and production work to clerical, professional, and technical assistance. Of 312,000 employed in January 1940, 40,200 (12.9 percent) were black. In addition to providing regular part-time jobs, the NYA developed a program of resident work centers, largely in the South. A total of 29,000 youths, 13 percent of them blacks, lived in these centers, where they also worked and received vocational training. In a reflection of Jim Crow practices in the South, black participants in the work centers were segregated into separate Negro Resident Training Centers. This was one of the few racial blemishes in the history of the NYA.[78]

Over eighty thousand black students and unemployed youths benefited from the NYA. Blacks participated at rates equal to or exceeding their proportion of the local youth population in most locations. Unlike the PWA, the NYA's wage scales were absolutely identical in all parts of the country, and blacks were paid exactly the same as whites. Bethune's goal for the DNA was "the adaptation of the program to the needs of Negro people and the interpreting of the program to them." Her staff of seven implemented and reported on the program and served as liaisons with local NYA programs. Blacks were well represented throughout the DNA. Augmenting the division's work in Washington, supervisors of Negro Affairs operated in twenty-seven states, blacks served on advisory committees in twenty-three states and on numerous local planning boards, and there were more than five hundred black project managers.[79]

The combination of Bethune's position in the NYA—which made her the highest-ranking African American in the Roosevelt administration—and her access to the White house, enabled her to be a highly effective advocate for the African American population in the New Deal. Bethune saw to it that black workers were both beneficiaries and also administrators and policy makers in New Deal programs. According to her associate Dorothy Height, a black civil rights activist who later headed the National Council of Negro Women, Bethune was bold about seeking meetings with President Roosevelt. When she wanted to see him, she would simply tell Eleanor Roosevelt, "The president really needs to see me," and Bethune would usually get her meeting, if not her way.[80]

With Bethune's help, the number of black advisers in the Roosevelt administration eventually swelled to over one hundred. Bethune began to gather this young professional group at her home on Friday evenings to discuss black issues. The press called them the *Black Cabinet*, after similar bodies that had advised presidents beginning in the late nineteenth century. The main difference from the past was that now there were far more blacks in high appointive positions than ever before. It was also known as the *Black Brain Trust*, echoing FDR's Brain Trust of New Deal planners.[81]

The Black Cabinet brought about greater awareness of black problems on the part of both the government and the public. Although the Black Cabinet initially lacked official status and kept no minutes, it provided a valuable forum and breeding grounds for policy ideas. Based on its deliberations, members developed ideas for further discussion, presented ideas in their departments, and worked with the press to get information out to the public. The black *Cabineteers*, as they were dubbed, vetoed a proposal in the administration to create a federal Negro Bureau to centralize all initiatives regarding race. They may have seen it as a potential rival to their own influence in Washington. In 1936 they were officially recognized as the Federal Council on Negro Affairs, but Black Cabinet remained the unofficial name.[82]

The council (i.e., the Black Cabinet) served as a liaison between the administration, civil rights organizations—such as the NAACP and NUL—and labor leaders like A. Philip Randolph, founder of the all-black Brotherhood of Sleeping Car Porters (BSCP). Besides helping the White House keep in touch with the black community, the council also transmitted a detailed picture of operations in the White House to the black leadership. The Cabineteers worked closely with colleagues outside of government and joined with them when needed to protest particular policies and bring pressure against the appropriate officials.[83]

With support from the Black Cabinet and the NYA, Mary McLeod Bethune organized two government conferences on black welfare and black youth. A precursor to these efforts came in 1935 when the Joint Committee on National Recovery organized a conference at Harvard University on the economic status of black people that presented dramatic testimony from black and white workers to five hundred scholars and students. This conference publicized the plight of African Americans during the New Deal and helped set the stage for the later federal conferences. Held in 1937 and 1939, the Conferences on the Problems of the Negro and Negro Youth covered employment and training problems and issues, relations with labor unions, black education, and federal employment opportunities. The conferences made numerous recommendations to benefit black workers. For example, the 1937 conference called for establishing a thirty-hour workweek to increase employment of blacks; eliminating discrimination in labor unions; barring federal contracts which involved discrimination; eliminating abuses interfering with fair employment of blacks by the federal government; hiring black supervisors and managers in every federal department and every region; and appointing blacks to federal and state committees on apprentice training.[84]

Second New Deal Legislation, the Courts, and Blacks

Among the more significant accomplishments of the Second New Deal in relation to working blacks were several important laws that, while not aimed at them, nonetheless provided direct or indirect benefits. The 1935 National Labor Relations Act, also known as the Wagner Act, guaranteed all workers the right to form unions and bargain with their employers. At the time, it was doubtful that the law would be of any help to blacks. It specifically excluded agricultural and household workers, representing 65 percent of black workers, and a provision to prohibit unions from discriminating against or excluding blacks had been defeated. However, the Wagner Act empowered the new Congress of Industrial Organizations (CIO), established in 1935 as the Committee on Industrial Organization, to aggressively organize whole industries into single unions, rather than following the model of the AFL and organizing each craft into its own union. The CIO concentrated on the automotive, steel, meatpacking, and other relatively nonunionized industries. In most of these industries, blacks had become a significant part of the workforce. Generally speaking, they were welcomed into and treated fairly by the new CIO unions.

To compete with the CIO, the AFL urged its affiliates to also organize blacks and accept them as equals. Even before the Wagner Act, in early 1935 the AFL had admitted the all-black BSCP as an affiliate. The result of the competition between the AFL and the CIO to organize workers was that, especially in cases where union representation was determined by elections, thousands of new black union members benefited from good union wage scales, improved benefits, and better working conditions.[85]

A landmark law for all Americans, but especially important for those with limited means, was the Social Security Act of 1935. By providing old-age pensions, unemployment insurance, and other benefits, it established a safety net that served the large mass of blacks who had limited resources to carry them through economic hardship and old age. The law was crafted and administered in a generally fair manner, but Social Security had its limitations. Before enactment, Senator Harry Byrd and other Southern Democrats had objected to Title I, which provided for federal oversight of the states as they determined who would receive Social Security payments and how much they would be paid. Byrd and his colleagues saw this language as a threat to state control and feared that it would lead to federal interference with discriminatory southern racial policies. They feared that Washington would be able to deny Social Security funds to any state program that it believed was discriminating against blacks. As a result, the clause in Title I that governed federal control over states was watered down.[86] In addition, the law excluded most farmworkers, a disproportionately large number of whom were black. Mary McLeod Bethune and others succeeded in broadening the coverage of the law in other areas. Bethune also objected to the small percentage of blacks employed within the Social Security Administration and worked to improve black hiring.[87]

Like the Social Security Act, the Fair Labor Standards Act of 1938 (FLSA) was a broad law that benefited many blacks. The FLSA set an initial minimum wage of twenty-five cents per hour, required payment of time and a half for time worked beyond eight hours in a day and forty hours in a week, and eliminated abusive child labor. Restricted to workers engaged in interstate commerce, the law initially excluded farmworkers, domestic help, certain transportation workers, and many others. Some white employers protested having to pay blacks a minimum wage and indicated they preferred to hire only white workers for minimum wage jobs. Initially, the law covered about a million blacks, with several million others among the excluded groups. Over the years, Congress steadily broadened the

FLSA to cover most of the lowest-paid wage groups, and it became a wage floor for black workers.[88]

A major shift in the Supreme Court in favor of a greater role for the federal government and in support of the rights of individuals, particularly benefited black Americans. Federal courts had blocked earlier attempts to establish labor standards, and the subject was a campaign issue in the 1936 election. When FDR won reelection, he tried to pack the anti-New Deal Supreme Court by appointing extra justices. FDR failed, but the court subsequently provided several important victories for the New Deal and working blacks. The New Negro Alliance (NNA)—a black activist group formed in 1933 by a group of young college graduates aided by the distinguished lawyer William C. Hastie—had initiated a campaign to picket employers in Washington, DC, who refused to hire blacks. When a federal court issued an injunction against the NNA, in a dispute with the Sanitary Grocery Company over black employment, they appealed the case to the Supreme Court. Among the range of arguments the NNA made was that the proportion of minorities working for a given employer should be close to the proportion of minorities in the local workforce. The Supreme Court ruled in favor of their actions on the grounds that such picketing against employers was protected under the Norris-LaGuardia Act, which banned the use of federal-court restraining orders in labor disputes. In 1936 Thurgood Marshall—a lawyer with the NAACP and later the first African American appointed to the US Supreme Court—devised a strategy of attacking segregated public schools. He sued to force school districts to provide equivalent salaries to both black and white teachers. The NAACP won several cases in lower federal courts, including a favorable decision eliminating serious underpayment of black teachers in Norfolk, Virginia. The Supreme Court refused to hear an appeal, and these decisions became settled law.[89]

Paralleling the court's racial progressivism, in 1939 Attorney General Frank Murphy established a Civil Rights Section in the Department of Justice. Murphy vowed to initiate "a program of vigilant action in the prosecution of the infringement of [legal] rights." The Civil Rights Section focused initially on protecting black voting rights in the South, for the first time directing the power of the federal government toward eliminating legal sanctions of discrimination.[90]

When Nazi Germany invaded Poland in September 1939, Washington's attention turned to Europe and war. The New Deal effectively came to an end, concluding a period in which the federal government provided significant economic aid to blacks. The agencies charged to provide jobs and relief from Depression–era poverty had made an unprecedented effort to do so in a way that was fair to all. Because most of these agencies were discontinued due to the war, the jobs and benefits they provided ended when the agencies did. The coming war, however, created conditions that spawned a historic shift to a permanent government effort to promote equal opportunities for blacks and all minority workers.

Part II
Institutionalization of Executive Action, 1940–1960

The second part deals primarily with the emergence of long-term executive action through presidential executive orders rather than ad hoc action by individual administrators. Chapter 3, "World War II and the Fair Employment Practice Committee," takes as its main subject the FEPC. This body was created by an executive order under threat from African American leaders to mount a massive march of blacks on Washington. The FEPC enforced equal opportunity in federal employment and defense contract work. Due to congressional opposition, it died after the war. However, as discussed in chapter 4, "Truman Administration, 1945-1952," new executive orders reestablished fair treatment policies in the two areas covered by the FEPC and also included the armed forces. Harry S. Truman was the first president to speak out clearly for civil rights, and he took numerous actions to promote equal opportunity. Chapter 5, "Eisenhower Administration, 1953-1960," shows how executive action continued in a form modified to fit the policy approaches of an administration that favored limited government. Secretary of Labor James Mitchell was an eloquent spokesman on civil rights throughout these years.

CHAPTER 3

World War II and the FEPC

When Germany initiated World War II in 1939, the Roosevelt administration had already begun developing war production capacities to support Great Britain and other nations threatened by the dominant European power. Even before the United States entered the war against the Axis Powers (Germany, Italy, and Japan) in 1941, the stimulative effect of defense production was creating millions of jobs and setting the stage for the end of the Depression. On the threshold of war, a huge reserve of unemployed African Americans (6.5 million by 1940) was available in the nation's industrial centers to help fill the vast numbers of new jobs being created.

Good defense jobs were not quickly, nor easily, realized for hopeful blacks. Several factors constricted their share of new jobs. Unlike the situation at the beginning of World War I, in 1939 there was a massive reserve of unemployed whites. In addition, there were forty-four million potential workers not in the labor force, many of them women. Because they had seniority, many whites returned to previous jobs when their employers began rehiring; these white workers were rehired before less senior blacks. Women started entering the workforce in droves, competing with blacks for defense jobs.

Racial discrimination inevitably reared its ugly head and made it even more difficult for blacks to participate fully in the explosion in hiring. Many employers sincerely feared that white unionists would strike if they began hiring blacks, but other employers used this diversion as a smoke screen to mask their own prejudices. Some employers went to such extremes to avoid hiring African American workers that production bottlenecks were created when they lured white workers away from other defense plants. The Standard Steel Corporation of Kansas City announced, "We have not had a black worker in twenty-five years and do not plan to start now." The president of North American Aviation stated flatly that blacks "will be considered only as janitors" and laborers. "Under no circumstances," he said, would they be hired for aircraft manufacture, even if they were fully trained. At one point, seventy-five thousand experienced black construction workers remained unemployed as a result of discrimination in the construction industry.

African Americans fared almost as poorly in the military. The Selective Service Act of 1940 allowed the drafting of blacks into the army and required that the numbers of draftees meet the test of racial proportionality. However, all the services remained strictly segregated, and opportunities for blacks to serve as commissioned officers were limited. The perception of unfairness in the military stimulated black activists to seek redress. Even before the war, *Pittsburgh Courier* editor Robert L. Vann, a member of the Black Brain Trust, called on Roosevelt to appoint blacks to West Point on a regular basis. A group of black officers formed a committee to promote the participation of blacks in the military. In 1940 the Brotherhood of Sleeping Car Porters (BSCP) joined the mounting call to eliminate discrimination in the military. A major victory in these efforts was the promotion of Army Colonel Benjamin O. Davis in October 1940 to become the first African American general officer in history.[1]

That same year the NAACP began a campaign against exclusion of blacks from the aircraft industry, publishing a photo of an aircraft plant and the title "For Whites Only" on the cover of the July issue of its journal *The Crisis*. Mary McLeod Bethune provided Eleanor Roosevelt with detailed documentation of discrimination in the defense industry. Black organizations published lists of industry and governmental officials accused of discrimination, and the white press began to report on the issue. The *Saturday Evening Post* published an article titled "It's Our Country, Too" by Walter White of the NAACP. White leaders joined blacks in a November 1940 conference at Hampton, Virginia, on "Participation of the Negro in National Defense."[2]

FDR, who was running for an unprecedented third term in 1940 and was aggressively courting black votes, appointed a number of additional black government advisers and sought in various ways to reduce discrimination in the federal government. For example, he appointed black federal judge William H. Hastie as a special civilian aide to Secretary of War Henry L. Stimson.[3] Hastie's job was to investigate complaints of discrimination in both the military and among civilian employees of and contractors to the War Department. At FDR's behest, the US Office of Education (USOE) required nondiscrimination in federally funded training programs for defense workers, a policy backed up by a nondiscrimination clause Congress placed in defense training legislation.[4]

Roosevelt established the National Defense Advisory Commission (NDAC) in May 1940 to coordinate industrial and manpower resources. The NDAC included a Labor Division headed by CIO unionist and New Deal proponent Sidney Hillman, who was determined to supply a sufficient flow of workers to produce everything needed to win the war. To accomplish this task, Hillman sought to tap all sources of labor, including African Americans. Accordingly, on September 1, 1940, Hillman issued a policy statement warning against discrimination based on race, age, or sex in hiring in the defense industry. Robert Weaver, a former Black Cabineteer, was appointed to spearhead the Labor Division's efforts to mobilize the black labor force.[5]

In December 1940 after winning reelection, FDR replaced the NDAC with the Office of Production Management (OPM) but continued the Labor Division. Sidney Hillman, who now jointly headed OPM with William Knudsen, established a Negro Employment and Training Branch (NETB) and put Weaver in charge. There was also a Minority Groups Service, supervised by white southerner Will Alexander, which dealt with discrimination against other groups. While this antidiscrimination machinery was being established, pressure mounted on Knudsen and Hillman to take stronger action at OPM against discrimination. On April 11, 1941, they issued a formal letter calling on defense contractors to cease discriminating against blacks who applied for work. However, the letter was never published in the *Federal Register*, limiting its impact. Weaver's NETB, lacking investigative or enforcement powers, sought to persuade and negotiate with employers to hire more blacks and reduce the burden on the relief system. Weaver focused on defense construction and was able to achieve modest gains in black employment in that sector.[6]

Roosevelt had won reelection with the help of strong support from black voters. The National Negro Congress wished to cash in on that support and proposed that Roosevelt go beyond OPM's limited antidiscrimination efforts and issue an executive order prohibiting employment discrimination within the federal government. A "Fight for Freedom Committee," organized by racially progressive whites, telegraphed OPM demanding enforcement of fair employment for blacks. In May 1941 Mary McLeod Bethune, Walter White of the NAACP, and others met with Hillman to call for an executive order banning discrimination, not just in the federal government, but in the entire defense-military establishment.[7]

Meanwhile, black labor leader A. Philip Randolph, the founder and president of the BSCP, was preparing to take more direct action. At a meeting with FDR in September 1940, Randolph asked for immediate and full integration of the entire national defense effort, both civilian and military. Roosevelt rejected this proposal, and Randolph decided to mount a march of ten thousand blacks on Washington to demand equality in the defense effort. The NAACP and the Urban League endorsed the idea, plans for a march in the summer of 1941 firmed up, and to the administration's alarm, the projected number of marchers swelled to one hundred thousand.[8]

The White House was concerned that a march could touch off racial violence in the nation's capital, which was already nerve-wracked from a sensationalized crime wave. They were also worried that such a march would confuse and distract an American public poised to support the White House's call to aid the United Kingdom, then under attack from Hitler's Germany. In an effort to meet Randolph's demands, FDR sent a memo to Hillman and Knudsen, officially placing the weight of his office behind their April 11, 1941, letter. FDR specifically directed OPM to see that the nation's workforce was used productively and without discrimination. He also arranged a meeting in New York City on June 7 at which Eleanor Roosevelt, Mayor Fiorello LaGuardia (a friend of Randolph), and Aubrey Williams, head of the NYA, tried unsuccessfully to persuade Randolph and White to abandon their plans for a march.

Roosevelt met personally with Randolph and White on June 18, joined by LaGuardia and others. FDR, who was open to the idea of change, asked, "What do you want me to do?" Randolph gave the president a memo from the March-on-Washington Committee (MOWC) he headed, outlining a number of necessary actions. The memo demanded issuance of executive orders that would bar awarding government contracts to firms known to discriminate; end segregation in the military; ban discrimination in federal defense-work training programs (that FDR had already done, but not by executive order); order the USES to refer workers to jobs regardless of their race; and abolish discrimination within the federal government. The MOWC memo also called on Roosevelt to seek legislation denying the benefits of the Wagner Act to any unions that discriminate.

FDR balked at accepting the entire package, and the discussion ground to a temporary halt. LaGuardia broke the ice. He noted that "it is clear that Mr. Randolph is not going to call off the march" and suggested that "we all begin to seek a formula." Roosevelt agreed and appointed a committee, chaired by LaGuardia, to draw up a response to the MOWC demands. The LaGuardia committee quickly recommended that FDR issue an executive order banning discrimination in defense contracting. The committee made that recommendation despite objections from the War Department that contractors in the South might refuse to bid for contracts and that the order would be unenforceable anyway. Roosevelt accepted the idea and began negotiations with Randolph and the MOWC. He balked at their call to include desegregation of the military in the order but agreed to their demand to include federal employees. When a final agreement was reached on June 24, Randolph called off the march.[9]

Executive Order 8802 and the FEPC

The next day, June 25, 1941, President Roosevelt issued Executive Order (E.O.) 8802 establishing the president's Fair Employment Practice Committee (FEPC). The black press hailed the order as a second emancipation proclamation, but segregationists immediately objected to the agency it created. As a result, the FEPC became the most controversial World War II agency of the federal government.[10] E.O. 8802 marked a significant expansion of federal antidiscrimination policy. For the first time there was a federal body specifically responsible for administering equal employment opportunity requirements. While the FEPC's powers were few, its budget small, and its life span limited to the World War II period, it marked the beginning of a quarter century of almost continuous executive action promoting fairness in employment funded by the federal government.

The overall goal stated in E.O. 8802 was "to encourage participation in the national defense program by all citizens . . . regardless of race, creed, color, or national origin." It required an end to discrimination by the federal government and by defense contractors. It also called upon unions and all other private employers to make a voluntary effort to eliminate discrimination.

The order established two main requirements. First, federal training programs for defense production were to be administered free of all discrimination. Second, and more importantly, all federal defense contracts were to include a nondiscrimination provision. The order placed the FEPC under OPM. The committee could investigate any complaints of discrimination it received, though it was not empowered to initiate specific investigations on its own. It would then "take appropriate steps" to remedy discriminatory situations and make specific recommendations to federal agencies and the president on how best to implement the order. However, the FEPC did not enforce any laws, and it lacked the power to subpoena witnesses or sue violators in court. It did have the right to call for cancellation of contracts as a remedy, but it could not require this action.[11]

Initially, the committee was to have five members. Shortly after the order was issued, Randolph and White met with Sydney Hillman to discuss the committee's membership. Randolph and White agreed with Hillman that the AFL and the CIO should each have a representative, but they wanted the committee enlarged to seven members to assure that organized labor, whom the black leaders did not trust, would not dominate it. A compromise was reached at six members, and E.O. 8802 was amended to reflect the change.[12]

In July 1941 Roosevelt appointed Mark Ethridge, a white liberal and publisher of the *Louisville Courier-Journal*, as chair of the committee. Two black members were appointed: Milton Webster, vice president of the BSCP, and Earl Dickerson, a Chicago alderman. Other members included William Green, president of the AFL; William Murray, president of the CIO; and, representing the business community, David Sarnoff, president of the Radio Corporation of America.[13]

The committee formally organized in August 1941. One of its first actions was to appoint Lawrence Cramer, the white former governor of the largely black US Virgin Islands, as executive secretary, and George M. Johnson, the black dean of the Howard University Law School, as Cramer's assistant. The subordination of Johnson, a distinguished legal scholar, did not please the black community. Due to budget limitations, the FEPC hired very few employees initially and was forced to rely on OPM staff for additional support. From the outset, the members were concerned that federal government workers, while technically covered under E.O. 8802, were mentioned only in passing. By contrast, several provisions were devoted to antidiscrimination enforcement in defense contract work. To alleviate the committee's concerns, Roosevelt specifically directed the heads of all federal departments to treat their employees with fairness.[14]

Another early problem was the public's lack of knowledge about the committee. Therefore, it initiated a publicity and educational campaign and distributed seventy-five thousand posters on E.O. 8802 to federal agencies and contractors. The members decided to hold a series of four public hearings on fair employment, one in each region of the country, in order to publicize the order and investigate discrimination. The first hearing was held in Los Angeles in October 1941. Subsequent hearings occurred in 1942 in Chicago, New York, and Birmingham, Alabama. The hearings focused on the employment policies of local defense industries and the associated unions. Evidence turned up proving that, from New York to Los Angeles, discrimination was a serious barrier to minorities in war work. Venturing beyond E.O. 8802's mandate to investigate specific complaints only, the committee made general recommendations to the private sector on abating discrimination. These early actions were largely ignored by the mainstream press, but black newspapers such as the *Chicago Defender* praised it for "[giving] hope to millions of black workers."[15]

The FEPC had to find a new home when OPM was disbanded in late 1941 due to a reorganization of the government's war production effort. The FEPC was transferred to the new War Production Board (WPB) in January 1942. Shortly after that, Ethridge—partly due to frustration with the extremely limited staff and budget allowed to the committee—resigned as chair, although he remained a member. Malcolm McLean, president of Hampton Institute, took over as chair. With organizational matters settled for the time being, the committee completed its hearings. The White House praised the work of chair McLean. As the FEPC celebrated its first anniversary on June 25, 1942, it was slated to receive a substantial budget increase and was planning to set up regional offices in twelve cities.[16]

Unfortunately for the committee, these plans had to be put on hold just one month later. The committee's troubles began with the last of its four hearings. This final hearing was held in Birmingham in June 1942 and highlighted revelations of extensive discrimination in defense work in the South. Many southerners now came to see the committee as a threat to the Jim Crow system, and southern politicians pressured FDR to restrain the FEPC. The Democratic Party badly needed southern votes in the fall elections. On July 30, 1942, FDR gave in to political pressure and transferred the committee to the War Manpower Commission (WMC). This body had been created in April 1942 to deal with labor shortages that were beginning to interfere with war production. The FEPC, whose members considered WMC head Paul McNutt to be unsympathetic to the mission, had hoped to be transferred to the White House's Office of Emergency Management. The move to the WMC, besides placing it under an unfriendly administrator, meant that the FEPC would now be funded through regular congressional budgetary procedures that gave Congress direct control over its budget.

Confirming the worst fears of the committee's supporters, the FEPC quietly languished in its new home. McNutt delayed for three months, after the transfer, before approving a procedure for merging the two agencies. He cut the committee's budget, denied it access to WMC offices in the field, and refused to appoint needed staff members. Furthermore, he placed the FEPC under his direct supervision, depriving it of the relative autonomy under which it had been operating. In one bright spot, in October 1942 Robert Weaver's NETB and Will Alexander's Minority Group Branch were consolidated into the FEPC, significantly strengthening its staff.[17]

The last straw for the supporters of the committee came in January 1943 when McNutt, responding to pressure from critics of the FEPC, indefinitely postponed scheduled hearings on discrimination in railroad employment in the South. Black groups, sympathetic labor unions, civic and church leaders, and others petitioned the president to order that the hearings be held. At the same time—because of the weakening of the commission under the WMC—McLean, Ethridge, David Sarnoff, and Executive Director Cramer resigned with numerous staff members.[18]

The "Second FEPC"

The Roosevelt administration, concerned about growing labor shortages on the one hand and the difficult status of the committee on the other, had already begun exploring ways to better accomplish the mission of E.O. 8802 and mobilize a larger portion of the African American workforce for the war effort. In February 1943 at Roosevelt's request, McNutt and Attorney General Francis Biddle met with twenty-four leaders of the pro–FEPC community. The black supporters demanded that the committee be removed from the WMC and report directly to the president, but the administration made no commitments at this time. In fact, FDR made no decision at all for several months. During this time, the FEPC, White House, Bureau of the Budget, and Department of Justice considered a wide variety of options. These options ranged from the extreme of abolishing the committee to strengthening it and removing it from the control of the WMC.[19]

In this period of limbo, the committee aggressively resumed its antidiscrimination work, partly in the hopes of pressuring the administration into a favorable decision on its fate. Without McNutt's approval, the committee announced a new series of hearings on discrimination in the defense industry, beginning in Detroit on May 24; it also rescheduled the postponed hearings on the southern railroads. These steps probably had some impact on the White House. More important was Attorney General Biddle's support for the FEPC and his recommendation that it be reestablished and strengthened.[20]

Heeding Biddle's advice, on May 27, 1943, Roosevelt issued E.O. 9346, replacing the old FEPC with what became known as the *Second FEPC*. It was located, as FEPC members had originally sought a year earlier, within the Office of Emergency Management and reported directly to the president. Monsignor Francis Haas, a social scientist at Catholic University in Washington, DC, was appointed chair, and vacancies on the committee were filled. Then, in October 1943 Haas suddenly resigned when he was appointed Bishop of the Diocese of Grand Rapids, Michigan. However, in his short tenure he brought greater racial and religious diversity to a staff that was 90 percent black when he took over. This diversity reflected his goal of seeing that the FEPC met its mission to serve all minority groups, not just the predominantly black population. He was replaced by Malcolm Ross, the former public affairs officer at the NLRB. Under Haas and Ross, the committee received better support and was able, at last, to establish the twelve regional offices it had long wanted, plus three additional subregional offices.[21]

E.O. 9346 did not dramatically reorganize the committee, but it did enlarge the scope. Now the FEPC's jurisdiction extended to work that was not performed under federal contract, provided it was considered essential to the war effort. The antidiscrimination clause that E.O. 8802 required in defense contracts was extended to all federal contracts. Since E.O. 9346 did not drastically alter the FEPC, reactions from most interested parties (whether critics or supporters) was mild, and the mainstream press gave it little attention.[22]

There was, however, a quiet transformation in policy. Although the committee finally held the delayed railroad industry hearings, its primary emphasis shifted from investigating whole industrial sectors to focusing on resolving individual discrimination complaints.[23] Under FEPC rules—in order for a case of alleged discrimination in hiring, placement, or training to merit investigation—an affected individual had to submit a signed complaint against a specific employer, government agency, or union. By adhering to this approach, the committee avoided charges of going on "fishing expeditions" in various workplaces and industries. However, it interpreted E.O. 9346 broadly enough to allow it to accept complaints from anyone who had evidence of possible discrimination, not just complaints from aggrieved persons themselves. It also investigated discriminatory job advertisements, job placement orders, and application forms.

Investigation of a complaint typically began in the region where the alleged discrimination took place. If the FEPC's Fair Practice examiner assigned to the case determined it to be legitimate, he or she first sought to negotiate an informal settlement between the employer or the union and the aggrieved party. Settlements took many forms: an employer might promise in writing to "cease and desist" discriminatory practices; a complainant who was denied a job might be hired; an employer might agree to drop racial requirements for job openings; or the employer might eliminate questions about race from application forms. Most cases were resolved in this manner with only 15 percent handled above the regional level. If the regional examiner did not resolve the case, he or she referred it to the FEPC's Office of Field Operations in Washington. In rare cases when the ensuing visit from a national office examiner did not clear up the matter, it went to the Legal Division for further investigation. In some cases a public hearing was held.[24]

For cases that remained unresolved after these steps had been exhausted, there was not a great deal the committee could do. It lacked the authority to enforce directives in the courts or to collect fines for willful violations. It could recommend cancellation of the contract in question, but in fact, no contract was ever cancelled due to discrimination. The administration discouraged cancellation of contracts, fearing that such a drastic action would interfere unduly with the war effort.

Given its limited enforcement powers, the FEPC was heavily dependent on employers, unions, and community groups to voluntarily improve the racial climate and reduce, or eliminate, discrimination. Accordingly, it emphasized education, cooperation, and non-adversarial relations. The field staff was trained to be friendly, evenhanded, and tactful. The director of Field Operations advised staff to avoid cold, formal phrases such as "It is hereby requested" in favor of the more conciliatory "Will you be good enough to . . ." types of requests. Examiners were expected to thoroughly review and verify evidence of complaints and look for mitigating factors in apparent acts of discrimination. Complaints were kept confidential to avoid embarrassing, or alienating, employers or unions. Examiners were also expected to avoid questioning the good faith of an accused party. Rather, they were to make sure the party understood that FEPC staff wanted only to help resolve problems. While supporters of the committee lamented the lack of strong enforcement tools, there is evidence that the voluntary approach had an impact.[25] For example, in Detroit the local FEPC officials were credited, particularly, with fostering racial harmony in industry at large and, generally, throughout the city after extensive race riots in 1943.[26]

The FEPC also emphasized cooperation with federal agencies. The committee worked closely with the WMC, which had an extensive network of offices around the country. Under a special operating agreement, the WMC provided staff and other assistance for complaint cases that the committee was investigating. The WMC handled all complaints that it received that was of significant help to the committee because the WMC received 20 percent of all discrimination complaints.[27]

The FEPC worked with a number of other agencies under both E.O. 8802 and E.O. 9346 with varying success. The Navy and War Departments made a substantial effort to implement the order, but their effectiveness was impeded by the overriding goal of promoting production and winning the war. When employees of contractors resisted efforts to hire or promote blacks, the contracting agency often tolerated discrimination rather than risk a strike or lose production.

The Maritime Commission successfully promoted minority rights in shipyards in the Northeast and on the West Coast, but they met resistance in the South. The War Shipping Administration (WSA) followed equal treatment policies in referrals for maritime jobs, but it did not have much cooperation from the Seafarers International Union. Often, by the time it came to the attention of the WSA that a ship's crew had been hired in violation of E.O. 8802, the ship had already sailed. The NLRB fought discrimination in unions by refusing to certify representation elections from which minorities had been excluded. The War Labor Board promoted equal pay by prohibiting separate wage scales based on race.[28]

The FEPC particularly needed the cooperation of the USES that worked with the WMC to refer millions of workers to defense plants. In the early stages of the war, before US entry, the USES was doing a very poor job of placing blacks in skilled manufacturing jobs. In early 1941 it placed 8,769 workers in key aircraft production jobs, but only a paltry thirteen of them were black. Local employment service offices in the Gulf Coast region excluded blacks from shipyard employment. One cause of this discrimination was that employment offices in the state-federal system had grown accustomed to accommodating discriminatory hiring in the Jim Crow South. They feared that if they enforced fair hiring practices, employers would simply bypass the USES and hire directly, or through, private employment agencies.[29]

In 1942 the USES established a Minority Groups Consultant position to promote fair treatment and ordered its placement officers to inform employers that federal policy prohibited discriminatory job specifications. At the same time, unfortunately, the 1942 USES operating manual allowed employment offices to accept biased job orders (except in states that banned discrimination by law). However, the office first had to attempt to persuade the employer to drop any racialized requirements. When the WMC assumed control of hiring in areas of labor shortage in 1943, affected employers could only hire through the USES, which gave the government potential leverage in enforcing fair employment practices. When the USES persisted in accepting discriminatory job orders, the WMC attempted to stop the practice once and for all. On September 3, 1943, the WMC directed the USES to refuse to accept such requests. It also ruled that USES staff would be subject to disciplinary action if they disobeyed. In 1944 the WMC took the further step of issuing a revised internal USES training handbook titled *The USES and the Negro Applicant*. (This appears be the first federal training material on fair treatment of black job applicants.) Over the course of the war, the USES, at the national level, improved its effort to promote equal employment. It was another story in the local offices, many of which continued to honor whites-only job orders. This problem remained a continuing sore point for civil rights groups for years and was never corrected until the 1960s (see chapter 9).[30]

In addition to enforcing fair treatment in hiring and on the job, the FEPC was also authorized to require fairness in government-sponsored vocational and training programs for defense work. Training was largely funded by the National Defense Training Act and was supervised by the Office of Education (USOE). Beginning with the hearings it held in Los Angeles in October 1941, the committee discovered that many blacks were denied training opportunities, particularly in the South. While espousing an official policy of equal opportunity, the USOE did not enforce this policy when local training programs excluded African Americans. When the FEPC found considerable discrimination in these programs in Alabama, Georgia, and Tennessee in 1942, it charged that the USOE was not complying with E.O. 8802. The FEPC thereupon issued a series of directives to the USOE, requiring it to stop approving defense training plans if they did not prohibit discrimination; withhold funds, if necessary, from the noncompliant programs discovered in defense plants in Alabama, Georgia, and Tennessee; and reinspect those defense plants to make sure that they did not resume discriminatory training programs. The USOE improved its fair treatment performance and made significant progress in the South. The total number of black trainees in twelve southern states swelled from 3,768 in June 1942 to 4,702 in November, a 25 percent increase in just five months. While defense industry training remained segregated in the South, the USOE was able to see that the proportion of training courses open to blacks grew from only 4 percent in early 1942 to 18 percent by the end of the year.[31]

The agency with the primary responsibility for promoting equal treatment in federal employment was the Civil Service Commission (CSC). Guided by equalitarian racial policies stemming from the New Deal, the commission had banned racial discrimination in federal hiring even before the creation of the FEPC in 1941. In addition, as ordered under the Ramspeck Act of 1940, the CSC had ceased to attach photos of job seekers to their applications. At the committee's request, the CSC resolved most discrimination complaints internally, while keeping the FEPC informed about the disposition of cases. The committee reserved the right to advise the CSC on particular cases and to take over unresolved ones. As a result of the joint effort, black employment in government underwent a remarkable transformation. For example, in 1938 blacks constituted only 8.4 percent of all federal employees in Washington, DC, but by March 1944 that proportion had swelled to 19.2 percent. In addition, the proportion of black federal employees who held noncustodial jobs grew from 10 percent to 60 percent in the same period.[32]

While the FEPC encountered resistance from many federal agencies to fully enforcing E.O.s 8802 and 9346, it also operated in the face of growing criticism and opposition in the Congress. In the eyes of many in Congress, it had a couple of strikes against it. First of all, the FEPC was seen as a bureaucratic "orphan" laid at the doorsteps of a Congress expected to nurture and support it. Worse, Southern Democrats saw the reorganized "Second FEPC" as a particularly serious threat to the discriminatory racial practices they supported. Beginning in December 1943, Representative Howard Smith (Democrat–Virginia) held a series of investigative hearings on the FEPC. Its opponents charged that it was illegal and communist-influenced.[33]

With the testimony from the Smith hearings as a basis, southern members of Congress and their allies plotted in early 1944 to eliminate the committee. In order to do that, Congress first had to gain control of the FEPC's budget, which at that time was provided through the White House. When Congress passed a multiagency funding law in June 1944, Senator Richard Russell (Democrat–Georgia) inserted an amendment prohibiting the executive branch from funding any federal agency for more than twelve months without a specific appropriation from Congress. Designed to eliminate the FEPC forever, the Russell Amendment was permanent legislation that constricted federal fair employment efforts for decades. Supporters of the committee thwarted the intent of the Russell Amendment for the time being by passing an appropriations bill in 1944 enabling the FEPC to maintain its normal level of activity until July 1, 1945. Encouraged by this success, the pro–FEPC forces sought unsuccessfully to make the agency permanent. The battle over fair employment and the FEPC continued into the Truman administration (see chapter 4).[34]

Over the course of World War II, the FEPC received some fourteen thousand complaints, 80 percent of them filed by blacks. Two-thirds of the claims filed were dismissed as invalid, but almost all of the valid ones—about five thousand—were successfully resolved. During the period of peak activity, from July 1943 to December 1944, the committee resolved an average of one hundred cases and dismissed one hundred fifty each month. A few controversial cases involving uncooperative employers received wide publicity, but the preponderance of claims were resolved quietly.[35]

According to the FEPC, the black portion of the defense workforce grew from 2.5 percent in March 1942 to 8.3 percent in November 1944. Laboring and service jobs accounted for the bulk of the increase. However, the number of blacks in skilled, semiskilled, or foreman jobs doubled from half a million to one million.[36]

Mounting labor shortages increased the pressure on employers to hire black workers at all levels of defense-related work. The FEPC took advantage of that pressure to maximize minority opportunities. In cities with labor shortages, such as Detroit and Cleveland, the FEPC brought about satisfactory settlements in almost 40 percent of all complaints. In cities where labor supply and demand were in relative balance, such as New York and Detroit, the results were less satisfactory.[37] Despite the best efforts of the FEPC and other federal manpower agencies, racial tensions had reached the boiling point in those cities by the summer of 1943. In Detroit, thirty-four died and six hundred were injured in a race riot, and in Harlem a riot was barely averted.[38]

While the FEPC revealed and eliminated many violations of the obvious type—racially marked job applications, relegation of minorities to unskilled jobs, and discriminatory want ads—its educational and public relations efforts also had a significant impact. In an example of successful public relations, Dwight R. G. Palmer, president of General Cable, ordered an end to discrimination by his company. He asserted that it was wrong to fight for democracy abroad while slighting it at home.[39]

The results of all efforts, public and private, to employ black workers in war industries and treat them fairly were mixed. According to the official US Army history of industrial employment in World War II, the black proportion of all those employed in defense work doubled during the war. It grew from 4.2 percent in 1942 to 8.6 by 1945.[40] Yet the same study concluded that:

> Practically every industry in the North or South that made an effort to solve its manpower problem by hiring greater numbers of Negro workers encountered new problems that were in many instances as great a threat to production as the manpower shortage.[41]

The impact of the FEPC on this ambiguous picture is impossible to measure. It seems clear, however, that the committee—while carrying a heavy baggage of opposition and controversy—played a significant role in the enormous growth in black employment cited above. It also helped moderate racial tensions during a stressful period. Historian John Hope Franklin concluded that, because the FEPC encouraged employers and unions to voluntarily adopt fair employment practices, its "existence had a salutary effect."[42]

CHAPTER 4

Truman Administration, 1945-1952

As African American veterans and defense workers demobilized after World War II ended in August 1945, they took great pride in their role in the defeat of fascism. Black veterans hoped for fair treatment and better opportunities at home, and black defense workers hoped to retain their wartime economic and occupational advances. President Harry Truman, who as vice president succeeded President Roosevelt upon his death in April 1945, was sympathetic to the postwar hopes of African Americans.

One of Truman's very first domestic priorities was a law to make the FEPC permanent. However, continuing congressional opposition to the FEPC doomed the effort. The committee managed to survive into the fiscal year beginning July 1, 1945, but its appropriations were drastically cut. Worse still, the appropriations bill included an amendment specifying that funds were to be used only for the purpose of terminating the committee's functions by June 30, 1946.[1]

On December 18, 1945, Truman issued E.O. 9664 to focus the lame-duck FEPC on demobilization issues. The order forbade government agencies—which were busy cutting their staffs and retooling for peacetime roles—from discriminating on the basis of race or creed as they laid workers off, transferred employees, or rehired veterans. It also directed the committee to focus on investigating discrimination, both in industries that were producing military supplies and in munitions industries that were reverting to peacetime production. While giving the FEPC important new fair employment goals, Truman did not provide any new enforcement teeth. To the dismay of its proponents, the committee, in effect, was largely relegated to a fact-finding role in its last days.[2]

Just before it went out of existence in June 1946, the committee issued a final report in which it made three main recommendations. First, it warned that black wartime employment gains were threatened by the industries, in which those gains were strongest, were exactly those targeted for the most severe postwar contraction. Second, it emphasized that discrimination should be resolved through negotiation rather than enforcement. Finally, it called for permanent fair employment legislation. While failing to enact such legislation during the Truman administration, Congress relented enough to slightly loosen the strictures of the Russell Amendment. This moderate concession made it possible for the executive branch to provide modest, but regular funding, to interdepartmental committees for the next twenty years without specific authorization from Congress.[3]

Federal fair employment legislation remained stalled, but state governments were free to move ahead. In 1941 the same year the FEPC was born, New York State established a similar committee. In 1945 it passed the Ives-Quinn Act that banned employment discrimination and created a Commission on Human Rights. Like the FEPC, the state commission was not allowed to initiate investigations, and it depended on workers to file complaints. Unlike the FEPC, however, the commission was allowed to issue mandatory cease and desist orders, enforceable in the courts, when it proved the existence of discrimination. A number of states followed the lead of New York, and by the time Truman left office in January 1953, eight had laws against employment discrimination on the books. State fair employment laws were not particularly effective in terms of advancing large numbers of black workers into jobs thus far unavailable to them. However, they helped raise hopes in the black community that discrimination on the job could be defeated. Equally important, they raised expectations that the government, at both the state and federal levels, was a committed ally in the struggle for fair employment.[4]

While stymied in his efforts to enact a fair employment law, Truman promoted national programs and policies that, while not targeted at blacks, had the potential to benefit them. In his January 1946 State of the Union message, he called for a number of general social welfare measures, including raising the minimum wage, increasing unemployment insurance benefits, and promoting a national program of full employment. Congress ignored most of Truman's proposals but, with unemployment a national concern at that time, readily took up the full employment proposal that had considerable public support. The result was the Employment Act of 1946. The concept of literally "full" employment levels, with the implication of potentially massive government programs, was removed from the final bill. Retained, however, was the inclusive goal of seeing that everyone "able, willing, and seeking to work" would find it—provided that free enterprise and the general welfare were not compromised. The law committed the federal government, for the first time, to maintain a high level of employment for all. Black leaders hailed the law as an important step in helping African Americans climb up the economic ladder.[5]

Measures such as the Employment Act of 1946 and the establishment of state fair employment practices commissions, while useful to African American workers, did little to reduce racial tensions that had begun building during the war. As had happened after World War I, racial violence broke out in many parts of the country, as rising black aspirations collided with resistance from a large segment of the white population. Race riots occurred in most southern states, hate organizations spread racial propaganda throughout the country, and individual racial attacks drew national attention. In February 1946 Isaak Woodward, a black war veteran, was attacked and blinded by the chief of police of Batesburgh, South Carolina. That same month in Columbia, Tennessee, the Ku Klux Klan terrorized the black population and killed two. In July 1946 a mob near Monroe, Georgia, shot and killed two black couples because one of the men, a veteran, had stabbed a white man whom he accused of making advances on his wife.[6]

In response to the violence, news media attention, and protests by civil rights groups, Truman revived a wartime proposal for a federal race relations committee. On December 5, 1946, he issued E.O. 9808 establishing the President's Committee on Civil Rights (PCCR). Its mission was to investigate the situation and recommend law-enforcement and governmental mechanisms that would serve "to safeguard the civil rights of the people."[7]

After conducting a thorough investigation into the state of relations between the races, the PCCR submitted its report titled *To Secure These Rights* on October 29, 1947. Truman urged all Americans to read what he termed *an American charter of human freedom in our time*. The committee's recommendations dealt with personal safety, voting rights, and equality of opportunity. The report called specifically for:

> The enactment of a Federal Fair Employment Practice Act prohibiting all forms of discrimination in private employment based on race, color, creed, or national origin. The enactment by the states of similar laws, the issuance by the president of a mandate against discrimination in government employment, and the creation of adequate machinery to enforce this mandate.

The Truman administration delayed acting on these ideas for a time. However, by mid-1948 two factors combined to drive the administration to take decisive executive action. The first was the growing Cold War that had broken out with the Soviet Union, the former World War II ally. This struggle was, to a large extent, a propaganda battle pitting the ideologies of Communism and Western democracy against each other. Each side sought to convince the undecided nations of the world that they alone offered the best road to a just and prosperous future. The struggles and maltreatment of African Americans received wide publicity around the world and condemnation from the Soviet bloc. Truman saw himself as the leader of the noncommunist world and realized that the United States' civil rights problems detracted from its credibility as a moral leader.

The second factor was the election of 1948. Truman was engaged in a difficult struggle for reelection. Many Southern Democrats had deserted their party at the Democratic convention in July 1948 to protest Truman's stand on civil rights. To offset that loss, Truman badly needed to secure strong support from the black community.[8]

In response to these pressures and to the Civil Rights Committee, on July 26, 1948, Truman issued a historic, dual set of executive orders: E.O. 9980, banning discrimination in the federal government; and E.O. 9981, ordering the desegregation of the armed services. Combined, their scope was broader than E.O. 8802 and the FEPC in one way, and narrower in another. Government contractors were not subject to antidiscrimination requirements, but the military—for the first time—was required to eliminate all discrimination. While the full implementation of E.O. 9981 took several years, by the early 1950s the military was almost completely integrated. It became a model of equal opportunity for both government and the private sector.

E.O. 9980 established an official policy of fair employment throughout the federal government without regard to race, religion, or country of origin. The order required every department to set up an equal treatment program for its own employees, run by a Fair Employment Officer (FEO). To review cases from the departments and provide periodic reports to the president, the order set up a Fair Employment Board housed by the Civil Service Commission. By the end of 1948, eighteen departments and agencies had established fair employment programs.[9]

Promulgated with equal parts of moral principle and political expediency, the twin executive orders were warmly welcomed by the black community. This support translated into black votes for Truman in the presidential election of 1948. Locked in a race he was not expected to win against Republican Thomas Dewey, Truman eked out a close victory. Contributing greatly to the upset win, black voters gave Truman 69 percent of their vote.

In gratitude, Truman initiated a number of new civil rights steps right after the election. He immediately met with civil rights advocates and groups. Among them was the National Committee on Segregation in the Nation's Capital, which complained about the pervasive discrimination that existed in Washington at that time. One example the committee cited was a segregated restaurant at the federally controlled Washington National Airport. Truman immediately ended all discrimination at the airport, effective December 27, 1948. At his inauguration on January 20, 1949, Truman broke precedent and integrated all inaugural events. As a result, there were four blacks in the audience at the Truman-Barkley Club dinner on January 18, when Truman gave his first speech of Inauguration Week. While the army's marching platoons at the inaugural parade were not individually integrated, they included both black and white units. The army tank crews and coast guard units were thoroughly mixed. Black dignitaries sat in the reviewing stand and attended the inaugural ball. A number of nominally segregated Washington hotels and restaurants accepted black guests and patrons. The *Chicago Defender* noted hopefully that "it was obvious to everyone that the lily-white era of Washington's official social life had come to an abrupt end."[10]

Fair Employment and the Bureaucracy under Truman

Well before the Truman White House issued E.O. 9980 and E.O. 9981, the Department of Labor and other federal agencies were developing their own internal and external programs for fair employment. There had been a change of leadership at the department at the beginning of the Truman administration. Frances Perkins resigned in June 1945 after twelve years as secretary of labor.[11] She was replaced by former Senator Lewis Schwellenbach, an ardent New Dealer and a strong supporter of rights for African Americans. Despite the new leadership, many local employment offices of the USES continued to accept and honor discriminatory job orders, in violation of official policy. In a poignant letter to the secretary of labor in July 1945, an anonymous writer noted a dearth of black workers in shipyards in Portland, Oregon, and accused the USES of consciously denying blacks employment in this industry. The writer posed the question: "Is slavery returning to the United States of America?"[12]

This lone citizen was joined by the United Automobile Workers (UAW) union in calling for fairer treatment of blacks by the USES. In the fall of 1945 the UAW's Fair Practices Committee accused the USES of practicing discrimination. Director Robert Goodwin strongly denied this accusation but agreed to reevaluate USES policies and practices.[13]

In late 1946 Congress permitted state governments to take over administration of USES activities within their borders effective

January 1, 1947. African Americans feared that this devolution would make it more difficult to eliminate discriminatory job orders. Addressing the National Council of Negro Women in November 1946, Secretary of Labor Schwellenbach tried to allay their fears. He argued that when the USES devolved its local operations to the states, it would be "promoting employment opportunity for all applicants" and working hard to see that employers' "hiring specifications be based exclusively on job performance factors." The USES sought to ease concerns by creating a special office devoted to the problems of minority groups. In addition, the District of Columbia Employment Service, which continued to be operated by the federal government, discontinued racial segregation in its offices.[14]

The USES, among several other federal labor and veterans' agencies, came under strong pressure in 1946 from the American Council on Race Relations (ACRR) to improve assistance to black veterans. A group of eminent civil rights leaders had formed the ACRR in 1944 to promote the equal participation of minorities in all aspects of American society. Its leadership included Charles Houston, Will Alexander, Mary McLeod Bethune, and Lloyd K. Garrison. Concerned about neglect of minority veterans' rights under the GI Bill, the council convened an "Emergency National Conference" (ENC) on April 5, 1946, in Chicago, with Houston presiding. At the ENC it was charged that the USES and other agencies not only provided inadequate service to black veterans but also engaged in discrimination and segregation. The ENC resolved that the ACRR should meet with the heads of the relevant federal agencies. It also joined other civil rights voices pleading for a fair employment practices bill and urged unions to provide full membership rights to all qualifying veterans without regard to race. The conference agreed to convene again in a few months to tally gains and plan further activities.[15]

Although the ENC focused on the Veterans Administration, it also addressed three Department of Labor agencies: the USES; the Bureau of Apprenticeship and Training (BAT)[16]; and the Retraining and Reemployment Administration (RRA), a temporary agency for placing returning veterans and displaced defense workers. The conference also contacted the sub-Cabinet Department of Education and the National Housing Agency. Representatives of the ACRR met with the head of each agency and presented them with specific charges of discrimination, along with proposed remedies.

The USES was the agency of greatest concern to the ACRR, partly because of its planned transfer to the states. The council called for a variety of measures such as placing black advisers and consultants in local USES offices and establishing advisory committees on race relations around the country. They also called for the collection of detailed statistics on placements by race so that the Minority Placement Division in the USES Washington office would have a clearer picture of the agency's performance in relation to blacks. Further, the committee stressed that Secretary of Labor Schwellenbach should implement effective antidiscrimination procedures before the USES's devolution. In a friendly follow-up letter to USES Director Robert Goodwin, in which he used the salutation "Dear Bob," A. A. Liveright of the ACRR expressed appreciation for "your interest and your desire to deal with" all the problems discussed.[17]

ACRR representatives met with BAT Director William F. Patterson and called for the appointment of a black field worker to advise BAT staff and employers on equal opportunity issues. They also called for the collection of statistics on the degree of inclusion of blacks in apprenticeship programs. The committee sought to obtain a "positive, aggressive policy statement" from the Federal Committee on Apprenticeship that would promote inclusion of all groups. The ACRR considered apprenticeship a key element in integrating minorities into the skilled craft occupations. To further that goal, the ACRR recommended that the BAT deny federal approval to apprenticeship programs that were known to practice discrimination (see chapter 9).[18]

At the meeting with the ACRR committee, Patterson expressed strong interest in the problem of discrimination in apprenticeship. He promised to meet as many of the ACRR's requests as possible. The BAT had begun studying the potential contribution of a minority adviser and whether this contribution would justify the salary involved. While Patterson noted that the government could not force employers to indicate the race of participants in their apprenticeship programs, the BAT was looking into ways of obtaining that kind of data through other means. He assured the ACRR that he would bring up their call for a strong policy against discrimination at the next meeting of the Federal Committee on Apprenticeship. He promised to "take proper steps" to deal with federally approved apprenticeship programs that practiced discrimination. But at the same time, he undercut that promise by stressing that both employers and unions have the right to include or exclude whomever they wish.[19]

When the ACRR met with General Graves Erskine, head of the RRA, the representatives were both encouraged about the program and impressed with Erskine's support of fair employment. They noted that the RRA's information centers in the South treated whites and blacks equally, in contrast to the often segregated USES offices. The ACRR representatives suggested that the RRA's policy be publicized in the region and recommended that blacks be involved in the operation of the RRA's various programs, both in Washington and in the field. The representatives particularly sought to assure full inclusion of minority veterans in the RRA's job placement program; they told

Erskine that they expected him to report the RRA's positive steps to reduce discrimination at the follow-up to the April conference.[20]

After meeting with agency heads, the ACRR reported the results to local civil rights and veterans agencies in an effort to establish a benchmark for the performance of local government offices. The ACRR's Information Service provided articles on minority veterans' problems to the black press. The ACRR also followed through with its promise to hold a second conference with federal agencies. On July 12, 1946, representatives of the USES, the BAT, and the RRA, along with the other federal agencies, met in New York City and reported to the ACRR on their progress.[21]

As a result of pressure from the ACRR, in September 1946 the USES, among other agencies, adopted a new antidiscrimination policy. Disappointingly for the ACRR, the policy did not totally ban discriminatory job orders. Rather, it merely required USES staff to encourage employers to remove "nonperformance" (discriminatory) criteria from their orders. Edward Cushman, an aide to Schwellenbach, admitted that the policy was "not a thoroughly satisfactory one." Indicating that the proposal had been reviewed by the NAACP and the NUL, he stressed that it should serve as a middle-of-the-road precedent, and he defended the policy as "the most practical one in the light of existing conditions."[22]

In the arena of federal employment, the Department of Labor exhibited a progressive racial approach well before the issuance of E.O. 9980. The USES had created the position of Minority Groups Consultant (MGC) during World War II to assure equal opportunity to job applicants. Schwellenbach maintained the position, appointing Thomasina Johnson as MGC. Johnson, an African American and a former social worker and teacher, had become active in the Democratic Party in Massachusetts and as a lobbyist in Washington, DC, in order to pursue racial justice.[23]

This activist African American woman sparked an effort to extend equal employment principles to the department's internal personnel policies. In 1947 she urged Schwellenbach to issue a general order requiring that all personnel actions be based "strictly on qualifications and ability." This order, she argued, would both allay criticism from those who charged that the department lacked a strong policy against discrimination and also leave no doubt about the matter in the minds of departmental managers and personnel officers. While she won Robert Goodwin's support, other officials were less interested. Ultimately, Schwellenbach rejected the idea, insisting that Johnson's proposal merely restated orders and procedures already in effect. Schwellenbach's resistance may have resulted, at least in part, from his awareness that Truman planned to issue an antidiscrimination policy "sometime in the near future."[24]

Later in 1947 at the request of Under Secretary David Morse, Johnson investigated and reported to him on equal opportunity efforts at the department. She examined and evaluated not only internal personnel practices but also the external services the department provided to the public. Johnson relied heavily on the report of the Committee on Civil Rights, and she quoted extensively from both the CCR report and the United Nations Charter on Human Rights. Noting that the American race relations picture was "not a pretty one," she stressed that it was time for the department to reevaluate its performance and see "what it can do 'To Secure These Rights.'"

Johnson noted that a number of other government agencies had poor civil rights records, but she also found the Department of Labor to be far from perfect. Relying largely on comments from civil rights leaders, the press, organized labor, ordinary citizens, and employers, Johnson uncovered problems in each Department of Labor agency that dealt with minorities. These included the USES, the Wage and Hour and Public Contracts Division, the BAT, the Division of Labor

Standards, and the Veterans' Employment Service. Only the Veterans Reemployment Rights Division received high marks, largely because of its success in helping returning black veterans receive adequate training for high-skill jobs. She, like most investigators, found that disproportionate numbers of minorities held low-paying, menial jobs, and far too few were in professional positions. She did not make any specific recommendations, calling instead for a detailed comparison of each agency's services, both to whites and to nonwhites. She believed this comparison could then serve as a basis for better and more racially equitable services. [25]

Around the same time, Local 10 of the United Public Workers of America (representing employees of the Department of Labor) complained to Schwellenbach about alleged violations of the department's antidiscrimination policies. Local 10 Chairman Roy Patterson charged in a December 16, 1947, letter to Schwellenbach that "to an alarming degree black employees and prospective employees are subjected to discriminatory and hostile acts." Patterson presented several discrimination grievances and called first for a full "recognition by the secretary of labor and the department that racial discrimination does exist." To deal with this problem, he called on Schwellenbach to follow three recommendations: (1) immediately discipline supervisors guilty of discrimination; (2) guarantee fairness in promotions throughout the department; and (3) issue a department-wide memorandum that strongly reaffirmed a policy of nondiscrimination.[26]

Schwellenbach responded immediately and met with Patterson. He promised "very friendly consideration" of Local 10's requests. Charles Beckett of the Washington Urban League thanked the secretary for responding to the union's concerns and urged him to "continue to lead the way" in fair employment policies. Speaking for Schwellenbach at a Department of Labor staff conference on January 6, 1948, Under Secretary David Morse "made it clear that any evidence of discrimination would . . . not be countenanced and that investigation would be made of alleged instances of discrimination."[27]

Shortly after Truman issued E.O. 9980 in July 1948, the Department of Labor began implementation. On August 12 Acting Secretary of Labor John Gibson[28] issued General Order (G.O.) 40 that stated the department's fair employment goals and created the position of departmental Fair Employment Officer, as required by the order. The first Labor Department FEO was Thacher Winslow, a white who had worked in the NYA and the Wage and Hour and Public Contracts Division. At the time, Winslow was serving as an assistant to David Morse. Winslow's main duties as FEO were to resolve cases of discrimination within the department and assure fairness in personnel policies. Cases that were not resolved were to be appealed to the Fair Employment Board (FEB) created by E.O. 9980. Gibson explained at a press conference that Winslow's duties went beyond internal personnel matters to include the department's services to the public. This broader approach is exactly what Thomasina Johnson had urged in 1947. William Oliver, the UAW's Fair Employment Practices Officer, endorsed G.O. 40 and the idea of an FEO. The day G.O. 40 was issued, Ms. Ruth Steele, a private citizen from Asheville, North Carolina, wrote to John Gibson and praised his action as "a grand example of democracy."[29]

After Truman was reelected president in 1948, fair employment legislation was again blocked in Congress by Southern Democrats, whose party had retaken control of both houses. Secretary Schwellenbach had died in office in June 1948, but fortunately his successor—former Massachusetts governor Maurice Tobin—was also a powerful public advocate for civil rights. Tobin addressed the 1949 convention of the National Council of Negro Women shortly before its founder, Mary McLeod Bethune, retired from her leadership post. He praised her as "one of the great women of America" and "a gallant soldier in the war for human advancement." He noted that students at the all-white Washington University in St. Louis, in "another sign of increasing social consciousness" among young people, had voted by a two-to-one margin to support admitting blacks as undergraduates. He expressed great satisfaction that twelve blacks had recently broken the color barrier as graduate students at the University of Kentucky. Addressing the twenty-fifth anniversary conference of the Brotherhood of Sleeping Car Porters in 1950, Tobin congratulated them for being the first black union to win affiliation with the AFL.[30]

Shortly after Truman's inauguration in January 1949, Tobin had an important opportunity to assist the NAACP. They were organizing a National Emergency Civil Rights Mobilization to meet in Washington to promote equal rights legislation. After the organizers ran into difficulties in obtaining a large meeting hall for the racially mixed group, Roy Wilkins telegraphed Tobin for help. Tobin immediately made available to them the departmental auditorium next to the Department of Labor headquarters. On January 15, 1950, as a result, 4,218 NAACP members and representatives from church groups, labor organizations, civic associations, and other bodies convened at the auditorium for a two-day mobilization and lobbying campaign. The attendance far exceeded the one thousand persons that had been expected.[31]

To strengthen the department's antidiscrimination efforts, Tobin appointed William L. Batt as a special assistant. Batt had played a key role in Truman's 1948 reelection campaign by helping to win black votes. Under Tobin's and Batt's leadership, the department took a number of steps to advance opportunities for blacks and other minorities. In 1950 the Bureau of Labor Standards held a conference of administrators of state fair employment laws to promote better implementation and enforcement. One result of that meeting was the development of enforcement guidelines that could be applied in any state. The USES, which returned permanently to the department in 1949 after a brief postwar relocation to the Federal Security Agency, developed a Minority Group Program, building on the role of the Minority Groups Consultant. Under the supervision of MGC Thomasina Norford (formerly Thomasina Johnson), the program worked to meet the special needs of blacks and other minorities. The USES stubbornly continued its ambivalent policy of accepting discriminatory work requests while refusing to honor them. At the same time, it helped employers, unions, and other bodies deal with discrimination in the workplace. The department also conducted a study of the effects of unemployment on minority groups.[32]

The Department of Labor continued to implement fair employment and E.O. 9980. In December 1949 Clarence Mitchell, NAACP labor secretary, asked Tobin to appoint a special committee to seek qualified black applicants to fill openings that had come up in the Wage and Hour and Public Contracts Division and in the Bureau of Labor Statistics. Mitchell stressed, however, that in the process, the Department must not, under any circumstances, "unjustly deprive qualified white persons of chances for employment." Mitchell believed that the government needed to go beyond E.O. 9980's reliance on specific complaints to fight discrimination and "meet the increasing need for positive action." Tobin, however, defended the department's efforts to implement E.O. 9980 and declined to establish a "positive action" committee.[33]

Thomasina Norford was not satisfied with that response. She immediately launched an informal investigation of minority hiring in the Wage and Hour and Public Contracts Division and the Bureau of Labor Statistics. The disappointing finding that she reported to John Gibson was that less than 1 percent of their staffs were black and that many of these black workers complained of discrimination.[34]

Thacher Winslow, who had to spend much of his time on other duties, resigned as FEO in February 1950 to work for the International Labor Organization. Before departing he sent Tobin several suggestions for improving the fair employment program. Echoing Walter White's call for "positive action," Winslow suggested that the department require supervisors to report all hiring decisions to the FEO. They would have to list the candidates considered and provide their reasons for selecting the one hired. Winslow also called for public posting of vacancies to assure that all departmental employees would have an opportunity to apply. He noted that in the past the department "took a very firm stand against this," but he pointed out that it had worked well for the NYA during the New Deal. He argued that "No one can ever complain that they were not given notice and were not considered for the job openings under such a system." None of these suggestions were adopted at the time, however.[35]

Filling the FEO post vacated by Winslow was difficult. Tobin wanted to appoint Charles Donohue, a white attorney in the Solicitor's Office. John Gibson objected to moving the function outside the secretary's office. Gibson also feared that "the Negroes will regard this as a slough off." He pointed out that when Frances Perkins was secretary of labor, she had had a black employee, Lawrence Oxley, on her staff to handle race issues (see chapter 2). Thomasina Norford also objected to Donohue as FEO. Nevertheless, the appointment went forward, but Tobin specified that whenever Donohue acted in his capacity as FEO, he "shall be directly responsible to the Secretary of Labor."[36]

Government-wide, primary enforcement of E.O. 9980 fell to the individual departments and agencies, with the Fair Employment Board (FEB) serving as the final court of appeals.[37] In some cases, the simple fact of the existence of the order served as a spur to fight discrimination. In July 1949 the Government Printing Office voluntarily abolished the last segregated federal employee dining rooms. This move eliminated an indignity that had been instituted under Woodrow Wilson.

Wielding the stick of E.O. 9980, civil rights groups achieved notable fair employment success at the State Department. For years, they had sought the advancement of blacks into professional positions there, especially Foreign Service posts. The onset of the Cold War, which made it incumbent upon the United States to present a positive face to the noncommunist world, placed additional pressure on the State Department to open opportunities to minorities. By the early 1950s, sixty African Americans were serving in the Foreign Service, seventeen of them in posts previously held by whites.

A number of federal bodies still resisted fair employment practices, however. The District of Columbia, under congressionally appointed supervisors and the oversight of the FEB, virtually ignored E.O. 9980. The Department of Agriculture did not make much of an effort to reverse its past record of discrimination. The Department of the Interior, which pioneered in the fight against discrimination during the New Deal, backslid a bit by allowing field offices in Alaska to deny jobs to blacks unless there were no other candidates available.

The Bureau of Engraving and Printing in the Treasury Department had long resisted hiring blacks for skilled jobs. It came under great pressure from the civil rights community, the FEB, and the White House to open up opportunities to minorities. The bureau was about to provide in-service training for minorities when Congress proposed legislation that would have effectively preserved the white monopoly on skilled engraving and printing work. This change froze the bureau into inaction.

After the legislation failed, the White House ordered the bureau to hire black candidates who performed well in the bureau's competitive examination. As a result, fourteen were placed in the apprenticeship program in January 1951. Unfortunately, a few years later the bureau eliminated the program entirely before any of the fourteen could finish it.[38]

In addition to resistance from a number of agencies, the FEB faced other problems in enforcing E.O. 9980. It lacked adequate data on discrimination in federal employment. The order did not cover segregation in the workplace, so the board was powerless to deal with this abuse. The FEB's limited budget, which was carved out of the Civil Service Commission's (CSC) appropriation, limited the time it could spend on the cases that came before it. In addition, the CSC continued to apply the long-standing "rule-of-three" in civil service hiring. Typically, the CSC certified three applicants at a time for a particular opening, and the hiring agency would interview those three. If none of these applicants were acceptable, the CSC would certify another batch of three. The potential employer did not have to give any reasons for rejecting any candidate. This policy gave employers the effective power to reject minority candidates. Despite the best efforts of the FEB to see that blacks were included on certification lists, it was virtually powerless against prejudiced supervisors.

A serious obstacle to E.O. 9980 was presented by another executive order—E.O. 9835 of March 1947—which instituted an employee loyalty program. Born of the postwar anticommunist hysteria, this measure required the CSC to certify the loyalty of employees of the federal government and investigate any employees with possible communist ties. E.O. 9835 inhibited blacks from raising discrimination complaints for fear of appearing disloyal. Black leaders feared that civil rights would suffer when discriminatory supervisors invoked spurious charges of communist affiliation against minorities. In one prominent case, several federal employees who simply possessed recordings by Paul Robeson, an inspirational black singer and actor with known communist sympathies, were charged by their employers with being of questionable loyalty.

Despite the loyalty program, the FEB made a significant contribution. By 1950 the number of black federal employees had tripled over the 1940 level and accounted for 8 percent of the federal workforce. As of 1952 one-third of all federal agencies had broken the color barrier and appointed at least one black person to either a supervisory or professional position. By December 1951 a total of 488 complaints in 27 agencies had been filed with the FEB. Most of these complaints were found to be without merit or else were resolved by the agencies. The board heard sixty-two appeals, finding in thirteen of them that discrimination had occurred. The board continued operations well into the Eisenhower administration, which eventually put a new system into place (see chapter 5).[39]

Korean War Period

In June 1950 troops from Communist North Korea suddenly poured across the border into US ally South Korea, almost driving US and United Nations forces into the Sea of Japan. As the mostly American forces rallied to defend South Korea, Truman quickly took steps to gear up defense production and mobilize labor to deal with another protracted military conflict. Civil rights advocates once again pressed for strong antidiscrimination efforts in the defense industry. Clarence Mitchell urged Tobin to order the BAT, which was working feverishly to increase the supply of skilled labor, to also assure that blacks would be allowed full participation in apprenticeship programs across the country. Tobin directed BAT Director Patterson to follow through on this decision.[40]

At the request of Walter White, Tobin appointed several blacks to advisory committees on defense labor mobilization. White reiterated the black community's long-standing request that the USES cease designating race on workers' application cards and stop accepting discriminatory work orders from employers, whether they were defense contractors or not. For reasons that are not clear, Tobin failed to respond directly to this request and told White only that the matter was under review.[41]

Randolph, White, and others were now pressing the administration for new executive actions on discrimination. In August 1950 they proposed a revival of the FEPC and urged Secretary Tobin and White House adviser Stuart Symington to develop an executive order based on such a committee. The Labor Department endorsed the idea and developed a draft order, which was shown to a group of black leaders in November. This group criticized the failure to provide either effective enforcement or a mechanism for central administration. The department corrected these flaws and in December 1950 sent Truman a new draft with beefed-up enforcement powers. Like the FEPC, the new committee would require that all government contracts include a clause in which the contractor promised not to discriminate. Aggrieved individuals would have the right to file a civil suit if the committee could not obtain compliance. In presenting the draft to the White House, Tobin cited both moral and practical reasons for making full use of minorities in defense work. He argued that it would be *unthinkable* if the federal government did not enforce strong antidiscrimination standards.[42]

While not rejecting the proposed order, Truman decided to take a different approach at this time, in light of the Korean emergency. Like previous wartime presidents, he needed support for the war effort from those in Congress who opposed antidiscrimination efforts. As part of the National Manpower Mobilization Policy, in January 1951 he included a program to help private industry maximize its use of minorities and other groups. He followed the establishment of this program with a series of executive orders that eventually applied to ten federal agencies. Contracts under their control were required to include nondiscrimination clauses. Unlike the fair employment program of World War II, however, Truman's policy did not provide for enforcement, or establish a committee to oversee the effort. Truman, however, confided privately in May 1951 that he planned to take more substantial action as soon as practicable.[43]

Finally, on December 3 Truman issued E.O. 10308. The order required the head of each contracting department, or agency, to stipulate that contractors comply with the standard nondiscrimination clause already in effect. At that point the Korean War was going well for the UN forces, and Congress was not in session—having adjourned for the year. The order set standards for evaluating contractors' fair employment efforts. It also established the President's Committee on Government Contract Compliance (PCGCC) to oversee and assist the agencies and advise them on enforcement. Truman had deliberately chosen a name that would not remind anti-FEPC members of Congress of that controversial agency. The committee had the power to hold hearings and publicize cases of discrimination through press releases, but it was even weaker than its World War II counterpart.[44] Truman's approach succeeded in insulating the PCGCC from the kind of vicious attacks that opponents had unleashed on the FEPC.

Truman appointed Dwight R. G. Palmer, the racially progressive chairman of the board of General Cable Corporation (see chapter 3), as chair. Under Palmer, the PCGCC provided central guidance and promoted uniformity in equal opportunity programs throughout the government. However, the responsibility for enforcement still resided with the individual agencies and was heavily dependent upon the degree of commitment each administrator held to fighting discrimination. The committee lacked the power to subpoena witnesses to hearings or issue legal orders against violators. Like the FEPC, it had to rely heavily on voluntary compliance. Unlike the FEPC that ultimately boasted a staff of over one hundred, the PCGCC had to make do with only ten employees on its payroll.

The committee started very slowly and held its first meeting more than two months after issuance of E.O. 10308. Palmer was not an aggressive leader. As he stated at one meeting: "Our directive from the President had [sic] no teeth attached to it. It is probably better that it has not." He agreed with the decentralized approach of the order and argued that "the best work can be done by the people who are in the front-line trenches."[45] It was late 1952 when the committee finally adopted procedures for contracting agencies to follow in enforcing the nondiscrimination clause in contracts.

The committee relied heavily on publicity and educational campaigns by the agencies. The PCGCC guidelines for inspectors at work sites stressed the nonpunitive and educational nature of their role. The inspectors were to record known instances of discrimination. However, rather than immediately issue orders for amelioration, they were to discuss the situations with the employer and seek voluntary remedies. If the employer did not cooperate, then the agency could send the inspector back and conduct a more thorough investigation as a basis for possible sanctions or penalties.[46]

Although relatively toothless, the PCGCC did succeed in exposing the laxity in fair employment efforts that prevailed in most contracting agencies. Three agencies had not even bothered to include nondiscrimination clauses in contracts they issued. Fortunately, this glaring lapse was soon remedied. The committee studied conditions nationwide, heard over three hundred complaints, and unearthed widespread discrimination by government contractors. As with similar bodies in the past, the mere presence of the PCGCC exerted significant pressure on firms, and it regularly exercised its powers of moral suasion.

African Americans did make significant gains in employment and promotions during the tenure of the PCGCC. However, the committee deserved only partial credit for these advances. Broader economic conditions led to increased hiring and, therefore, low unemployment levels. Perhaps the greatest contribution of Truman's PCGCC was to establish, once and for all, fair employment policy as a permanent and continuous effort of the federal government.[47]

In March 1952 Truman announced he would not seek another term as president. America's black community was dismayed. He had contributed greatly toward a climate in which African Americans had a better chance to improve their employment and living standards. He had actively applied the prestige and moral force of the White House to that end and had spoken out in support of civil rights more strongly than any previous president. He had also taken more decisive actions against discrimination and appointed more blacks to executive positions in the government than any previous president. Through executive action, Truman virtually eliminated segregation in the armed forces and significantly reduced racial discrimination in federally funded employment.

CHAPTER 5

Eisenhower Administration, 1953-1960

In November 1952 Republican Dwight D. Eisenhower, retired commander of the victorious allied forces in Europe in World War II and a national hero, was elected president in a landslide election. Eisenhower strongly supported equal rights in principle, and he followed in Truman's footsteps by dealing with employment discrimination primarily through executive orders establishing special bodies to deal with federally funded employment. However, Eisenhower's belief in limited government was equally strong. As a result, he was not as outspoken nor ardent an activist as Truman. Furthermore, having won only 27 percent of the black vote, he had little political incentive to emphasize civil rights.[1]

However, Eisenhower (like FDR) made key appointments that guaranteed civil rights would continue to be an important element of government policy. In September 1953 his first secretary of labor, Martin Durkin, resigned in a policy dispute. Eisenhower named James P. Mitchell, a former retailing executive from New York City, as Durkin's replacement. Mitchell was an assistant secretary of the army, where he had promoted the elimination of segregation on all army bases and built a reputation as a progressive on racial issues. In his second key appointment, Eisenhower filled the vacant position of chief justice of the Supreme Court in 1953, naming the moderate Republican governor of California, Earl Warren. Under Warren's leadership, the court unexpectedly overturned the Jim Crow principle of "separate but equal" treatment of blacks in the historic *Brown vs. Board of Education* decision of May 17, 1954, outlawing segregation in public schools. James Mitchell hailed the *Brown* decision and became the most enthusiastic supporter of civil rights of any member of Eisenhower's cabinet. Mitchell served until January 1961 and was dubbed the *social conscience* of the Eisenhower administration.[2]

Important changes in the 1950s exerted strong pressures on the administration to protect the rights of black citizens. An increasingly vigorous civil rights movement was marked by direct action and mass demonstrations. The movement first achieved national prominence with a boycott of the Montgomery, Alabama, bus system that resulted in the elimination of segregated seating. The boycott was led by a young black minister named Martin Luther King Jr. and kicked off on December 1, 1955, with the arrest of NAACP official Rosa Parks who refused to sit in the "Blacks Only" section of a bus. In 1957 the third anniversary of the *Brown* decision was marked by a "Pilgrimage of Prayer," led by King and A. Philip Randolph. A crowd estimated at thirty thousand gathered at the Lincoln Memorial to air their grievances. In the fall of 1958, Randolph organized a march of a thousand students from New York City to Washington in a "Youth March for Integrated Schools." He repeated the march in 1959, and King addressed the rally in Washington in support of voting rights for blacks.[3]

The black migration accelerated in the 1950s as 1.5 million more African Americans left their homes in the South and crowded into northern ghettoes. At the same time, large numbers of the industrial jobs they sought were shifting out of the cities into the suburbs as factories expanded onto cheaper land. Many of the nation's labor unions opened their doors wider to blacks. Randolph and Willard Townsend, black president of the United Transportation

Service Workers, were elected vice presidents of the AFL-CIO in 1955.[4] However, discrimination within unions remained a problem, prompting Randolph to protest so vehemently at the 1959 AFL-CIO convention that president George Meany shouted, "Who the hell appointed you the guardian of all the Negroes in America?"

In addition to resistance among segments of organized labor, there was also a strong reaction in parts of the white community against equal rights for blacks in voting, housing, and employment. Nonviolent White Citizens Councils and the terrorist Ku Klux Klan in the South actively resisted school integration and the civil rights movement in general.[5]

The Eisenhower administration's civil rights effort concentrated on public persuasion and the elimination of legal sanctions allowing discrimination. Eisenhower relied on his appointees, especially Mitchell, to speak for the administration on civil rights. The Eisenhower administration continued Truman's policy of supporting equal rights as part of a worldwide competition with the Communist bloc, and this support intensified with the Soviet Union's launching of the Sputnik satellite in 1957. Mitchell asserted in October 1954, "Human equality in America is a weapon against Communism."[6]

The White House made a strong effort to include blacks in policy positions. Just after Eisenhower took office, he followed up on a campaign promise and had Chief of Staff Sherman Adams develop a list of qualified black candidates for appointive positions. By August 1956 he had appointed over three hundred, compared to only ninety-four during the entire Truman administration. The most prominent appointees were Special Assistant to the President E. Frederick Morrow and Assistant Secretary of Labor for International Affairs J. Ernest Wilkins (brother of NAACP president Roy Wilkins). Ernest Wilkins was the first African American ever to attend a cabinet meeting and only the second to serve at the assistant secretary level.

While Morrow held a high position, he was (unfortunately) largely ignored by the administration. The principal White House adviser on racial matters was Maxwell Rabb, a white man.[7]

In his first State of the Union address, Eisenhower boldly promised, despite his usual public reticence on civil rights, to end all segregation in Washington, DC. While he did not quite accomplish this goal, by the end of 1953 the White House had succeeded in pressuring the District of Columbia government into integrating its hotels, restaurants, and theaters. Integration of the public schools after the *Brown* decision—to which the DC Board of Education was a party—came more slowly but was largely complete by 1960. The administration supported enactment of the Civil Rights Act of 1957, the first civil rights law in eighty-two years. It was a limited measure primarily protecting the right to vote. It also created the President's Commission on Civil Rights and elevated the Justice Department's Civil Rights Section, created in 1939, to the Division level. In June 1958 Eisenhower hosted Martin Luther King Jr. and other civil rights leaders in a historic meeting at which the president endorsed further legislation on voting rights. In 1960 Congress strengthened franchise rights and outlawed the defacing of black churches and other houses of worship.[8]

Court decisions and executive branch policy resulted in a number of gains for blacks in the 1950s. By 1956 all branches of the military were desegregated. However, implementation of the *Brown* decision met substantial resistance in some areas, and in 1957 Eisenhower had to send troops to enforce admission of black students at Central High School in Little Rock, Arkansas. Building on a 1950 Supreme Court decision banning segregation on railroad dining cars, in 1955 the Interstate Commerce Commission ordered an end to all segregation on interstate rail and bus travel. That same year, to improve housing opportunities for blacks, the Federal Housing and Home

Finance Agency urged lenders to provide more home mortgage loans for qualified minority members.[9]

To promote equal opportunity in the workplace, the administration relied on executive orders—the patient spadework of the permanent federal agencies—and moral suasion, as provided by Labor Secretary Mitchell and other spokespersons. While endorsing the administration's policy of limited government, Mitchell spoke more frequently on civil rights than any previous labor secretary. In speeches and appearances from 1953 to 1960, he regularly presented his views on the problem of discrimination in society and the workplace, the efforts of the federal government to deal with it, and the responsibilities of business, organized labor, and the nation at large. In a characteristic speech in 1954, the year of the *Brown* decision, Mitchell addressed the New England Governor's Conference:

> We all know that despite our professed beliefs in the equality of man, certain groups among us are discriminated against because of their race, color, religion or national origin. When this discrimination affects a person's opportunities for employment, it is particularly pernicious. The freedom to earn a living without being discriminated against is as important to the individual as the better known civil rights and freedoms guaranteed by the Constitution. Freedom of speech, assembly, and religious worship may seem to be empty phrases to a person who is deprived of his chance to make a living because of the color of his skin, or the way he worships God, or because his ancestors were members of a particular national group. [10]

The President's Committee on Government Contracts

An important preexisting program for equality on the job was the President's Committee on Government Contract Compliance (PCGCC), created late in the Truman administration by E.O. 10308. The committee had gotten off to a slow start, and by the time it was fully staffed, Truman's term in office was over. The members appointed originally began resigning as the Eisenhower administration was getting organized, and the PCGCC was largely ignored. In the meantime, committee staff kept busy, producing a detailed study of the history of fair employment clauses in federal contracts since World War II.[11]

The press, however, did not forget about the committee, and reporters began asking administration officials about it at press conferences. Clarence Mitchell of the NAACP met with Attorney-General Herbert Brownell and called for the establishment of a new government contract compliance committee to replace the PCGCC. As a result of this interest, Sherman Adams, Maxwell Rabb, and other White House staff began to address the issue. The Bureau of the Budget recommended the extreme position of disbanding the PCGCC and abandoning its mission. Adams and others agreed that the old body should be eliminated, but they supported Clarence Mitchell's call for a replacement. Eisenhower agreed, and Rabb was given the task of developing a new program for fair employment in government contracts.[12]

Jacob Seidenberg, staff director of the PCGCC, came to Rabb's aid and drafted a proposal. The White House adapted it to serve as the basis of a new executive order. On August 13, 1953, Eisenhower issued E.O. 10479. The "Whereas" clauses defined the rationale and nature of the order: (1) it is in the national interest to "promote the fullest utilization of all available manpower"; (2) promotion of equal employment opportunity has been established policy on government contract work; (3) government agencies are responsible for ensuring equal treatment by employers with whom they hold contracts; (4) such contracts are required to contain a clause forbidding discrimination in employment; and, most importantly, (5) "review and analysis" demonstrates that the existing system of compliance with federal policy "must be revised and strengthened to eliminate discrimination in all aspects of employment."

To reform the system, E.O. 10479 established a "Government Contract Committee," which quickly became known as the President's Committee on Government Contracts (PCGC). The word *Compliance* was dropped from the Truman committee's name to emphasize the more voluntaristic approach of the new body. The PCGC consisted of fourteen members, one each from six designated federal agencies and eight appointed by the president, including the chair and vice chair. Lacking strong legal tools and relying largely on persuasion, the PCGC was given a three-part mission: (1) to develop stronger antidiscrimination clauses for government contracts; (2) to accept complaints directly from contract workers alleging discrimination and refer these to the contracting agencies; and, (3) to encourage employer, labor, civic, and other groups to develop educational programs to eliminate "the basic causes and costs of discrimination in employment." The last clause expanded the potential scope of the order, at least in terms of educational programs, from contractors to the national economy as a whole. While not drawing much comment or making any significant public relations impact when issued, E.O. 10479 helped set a precedent for broader national action against discrimination in the workplace.

It authorized the PCGC to develop "cooperative relationships" with local governmental and nongovernmental organizations and to set up its own procedures. It was also to report annually to the president. But in compliance with the Russell amendment, the

PCGC received no direct appropriation, instead receiving funds and support from the six agencies represented in its membership. The Department of Labor provided office space and logistical support, and the Justice Department supplied legal services, but the executive branch was barred from providing direct funding.

E.O. 10479 defined the working relationships between the PCGC and the contracting agencies. The head of each agency was assigned primary responsibility for requiring that contractors comply with nondiscrimination clauses. He or she was authorized to take "appropriate measures" to ensure compliance. These measures included the possibility of disbarment and other legal action. The agencies were to cooperate fully with the committee and provide information as needed. They were also to report any actions taken on complaints of discrimination, whether referred by the PCGC or received directly from contract employees. Based on these reports, the committee maintained oversight of the agencies, but it did not have the authority to serve as a court of appeals to resolve complaints or review agency decisions.

The organizational core of the PCGC consisted of the representatives of the six federal agencies: the Atomic Energy Commission; the Departments of Commerce, Defense, Justice, and Labor; and the General Services Administration. However, the other eight appointees brought visibility and power to the body. They included such prominent figures as Walter Reuther, president of the United Auto Workers union; George Meany, president of the AFL and later of the AFL-CIO; Congressman James Roosevelt, the son of FDR; and Fred Lazarus, a leading retailing executive. Jacob Seidenberg was appointed executive director.

Recognizing that a program based mainly on persuasion required a highly visible leader, Eisenhower appointed Vice President Richard Nixon as chair. Nixon took an active interest in the PCGC, and the press soon began to refer to it as the *Nixon Committee*. J. Ernest Wilkins, representing the Labor Department, was initially named vice chair. When James Mitchell was appointed secretary of labor, he supplanted Wilkins. Working with Nixon, Secretary Mitchell played an active role in the committee. In fact, the PCGC occupied offices in the Labor Department for its entire existence.[13]

Most of the committee's positions were filled quickly, and the first meeting was held within days after issuance of E.O. 10479. In a letter to Nixon on that occasion, Eisenhower laid out the basis for the committee's mission in terms of both the Cold War and human rights:

> [T]here are those in the world who doubt our fidelity to the ideal of human brotherhood. Both as answer to that doubt, and proof of our own faith, we are called to practice the principles of equality that we preach . . . On no level of our national existence can inequality be justified. Within the Federal Government itself, however, tolerance of inequality would be odious. What we cherish as an ideal for our nation as a whole must today be honestly exemplified by the Federal establishment.[14]

It was clear that the PCGC's mission had important implications on both the national and international stages. However, when Eisenhower met with the committee shortly after its creation, he stressed the need for substantive accomplishments without a great deal of publicity. This approach was carried out so rigorously that, in the view of some White House staff, the administration lost a number of opportunities to take deserved credit for civil rights accomplishments. However, the low-key approach served to reassure the business community and the South, both of which were concerned that the PCGC would become a new version of the FEPC. Also reassuring to those favoring a voluntaristic approach was the fact that the word *compliance* did not appear in the name of the committee.[15]

Vice Chair Mitchell consistently emphasized the PCGC's voluntary approach to compliance. He told a business audience at a 1955 PCGC conference that, "As you all know, the [PCGC] is an educational and promotional outfit. It has no enforcement power." Rather, Mitchell interpreted E.O. 10479 to mean that the PCGC had "an obligation to work with interested and responsible groups to develop and use the processes of education and persuasion" in dealing with discrimination in employment. The PCGC fostered the idea that its main function was to serve as an educational forum on equal opportunity and to show federal support for fair employment. The organizational structure further reinforced this notion by including special subcommittees on liaison with outside groups, education, and public relations.[16]

Contract compliance, however, remained an important part of the mission. The agencies were responsible for the bulk of the compliance work, contract by contract. The PCGC staff, never numbering more than twenty-five, paled beside the resources the contracting agencies brought to bear. Approximately five thousand contract officers were available to investigate complaints, review compliance by contractors, and develop educational programs mandated by the committee. Generally, the agencies avoided the tools of litigation and disbarment, seeking instead to engage contractors informally in voluntary compliance.

In 1955 contracting agencies began inspecting selected contractors for compliance, conducting two thousand inspections in the first year. At Nixon's request, the agencies provided regular compliance reports to the committee. To assist the agencies in detecting the existence of discrimination, the PCGC prepared a guidance manual for inspectors. Agency inspectors were advised not to accept the existence of token or limited employment of minorities as de facto proof of compliance and nondiscrimination. However, the manual did not specify a minimum acceptable percentage or quota of minority employment. The compliance determination was left to the discretion of the individual investigators.[17]

The committee assisted the agencies in numerous ways. It helped them to develop more efficient systems for processing complaints and improve their compliance methods. One of the committee's first accomplishments was to persuade the government of the District of Columbia, a federal body, to include an antidiscrimination clause in its contracts for goods and services. Mitchell persuaded the Defense Department, the leading contracting agency, to strengthen contracting regulations. The committee provided guidance to the agencies' contracting representatives on checking contractors for compliance and investigating complaints. The committee also set up mechanisms within the contracting agencies to make sure employers were aware of their antidiscrimination responsibilities.[18]

E.O. 10479 also required the committee to recommend improvements in contractual nondiscrimination clauses. Up to that time, there was no uniform wording. The only existing (and very skimpy) guidance was provided in Truman's E.O. 10210, which was largely devoted to regulating defense contracts under the War Powers Act of 1941. Buried in it was a brief requirement banning discrimination by contractors and ordering that all contracts contain a provision (not specified) against discrimination.

To remedy this leniency, the PGCG—in consultation with contracting agencies—called for a standard antidiscrimination provision to be used in all government contracts. It turned to Deputy Attorney General William P. Rogers, one of the administration's leading advocates for civil rights, to develop a proposal. Rogers drafted a nondiscrimination clause, the PCGC accepted it; and on September 3, 1954, Eisenhower promulgated it as E.O. 10557.[19]

The order stipulated that the contracting employer "agrees not to discriminate . . . because of race, religion color, or national origin." The new clause elaborated on the vague wording in E.O. 10479, which referenced the rights of "persons employed or seeking employment" with government contractors to "fair and equitable treatment in all aspects of employment." E.O. 10557 provided a comprehensive statement that covered all aspects of employment, requiring that a contractor's equal employment effort

> shall include, but not be limited to, the following: employment, upgrading, demotion or transfer; recruitment or recruitment advertising; layoff or termination; rates of pay or other forms of compensation; and selection for training, including apprenticeship.

The contractor was required to post a summary of the clause conspicuously in the workplace, and the committee provided a poster-sized notice. Under the title "Equal Economic Opportunity," in very large letters, the poster stated the basic provisions of the clause and displayed the seal of the PCGC next to its address. The committee also trained agency officials on how to enforce the clause. While E.O. 10557 applied to almost all contracts executed ninety days after its issuance, there were exceptions for contracts that did not involve recruitment of workers within the United States. The PCGC was also empowered to exempt contracts in special or emergency situations.[20]

While compliance work occupied a great deal of its time and resources, the PCGC consistently placed its primary reliance on education, persuasion, and conciliation. The members felt their main purpose was to serve as an educational forum on equal opportunity and to demonstrate federal support for fair employment. The educational program consisted of promoting cooperation among involved groups and convincing the public of the need for national action. To develop public support, the PCGC relied on a wide range of publications, films, television spots, and public appearances by its members. One of its most useful products was the 1954 pamphlet *Equal Job Opportunity Is Good Business* which it sent to all major government contractors.[21]

The committee worked most extensively with the business community, frequently appealing to employers for voluntary action. Addressing the 1955 PCGC Conference for business leaders, Mitchell sought to cajole and flatter them into greater efforts against discrimination, noting that, "undoubtedly there is in this room sufficient imagination and experience, determination and expertness, to develop a workable solution to any businessman's problem." The committee made frequent contacts with the business community in order to bring the administration's equal opportunity program to their attention. It sought to convince employers that, as Mitchell put it, "the program is not only morally right but economically sound."[22]

In his January 1956 speech to a meeting of the Cleveland Urban League, Mitchell laid out the committee's philosophy on industry's role in solving the problem of discrimination. He explained that the PCGC did not wish to depend entirely on resolving discrimination complaints to achieve the goals of E.O. 10479: "This would be like trying to dip up the ocean with a teaspoon." He did not consider legislation a solution either, noting that "even where there are excellent state programs based on legislation, principal reliance has had to be on education and persuasion." He asserted that the committee's main task was "to get industry to do several things that only industry can do." These things included instituting thorough, company-wide antidiscrimination policies, making sure that each company maintained open recruitment and training channels for all groups, and assuring minorities equal chances for advancement within the firm. He pointed out that "it is no triumph for equality to obtain jobs for blacks as janitors . . . It is a goal of the committee to open some of the doors that go upward in industry through the normal promotion channels."[23]

Such meetings played an important role in promoting voluntary compliance. The PCGC met frequently with business, labor, civil rights, and religious groups, beginning with a November 1953 meeting with the NAACP, the Urban League, and several social service groups. In December 1954 it met with several trade associations, in March 1955 with top union officials, and in October 1955 with a group of business leaders. At the October 1955 conference, Mitchell addressed sixty-five chief executive officers and board chairs on ways to

> pool our knowledge and experience in this area with a view to determining how we can best achieve throughout the Nation the equality of employment opportunity in which all of us here believe . . . We meet here as friends, in private session, in order that we may be as frank and helpful to each other as possible.[24]

The PCGC's Youth Training Incentives Conference of 1957 resulted in the establishment of programs promoting youth employment in six cities. After religious leaders met with the committee in 1959, they established a Religious Advisory Council to work with local communities to open up job opportunities for minorities.[25]

During the course of its history, the committee's funding and staffing tripled, albeit starting from a relatively low level. With an initial staff of nine and annual funding of $125,000, it was impossible for the committee to be fully functional. As civil rights issues became more prominent after 1956, the staff grew and an executive vice chairman was added to relieve the administrative burdens on Mitchell and Seidenberg. The PCGC established four regional offices and conducted a general survey of industry compliance. By January

1961, the end of the Eisenhower administration, funding had tripled to $375,000 and the staff had grown to twenty-five.[26]

As with the FEPC before it, the PCGC's contribution to opening up new opportunities for blacks is difficult to determine. Within the strictures of limited resources and the limited mandate of E.O. 10479, it made a significant effort. As time passed, the committee became more aggressive in response to civil rights events of the period and pressure from civil rights groups. While its compliance manual was silent on acceptable minority hiring levels, in practice, the PCGC edged toward a goal of proportional hiring. For example, in 1960 it encouraged government contractors in Washington, DC, to engage in limited preferential hiring of African Americans in cases where white and black applicants were equally qualified. Partly due to the committee's evolving support of preferences and racial proportionality, the civil rights community became more accepting of the Eisenhower administration's equal employment efforts.[27]

Over the course of its existence, the PCGC and the enforcing agencies mitigated discriminatory hiring patterns in a number of industries, including meatpacking, electronics, chemicals, and utilities, although progress was limited in others. The committee played a role in the elimination of discrimination by the Capital Transit System in Washington, DC, and also required over one hundred thousand contractors nationwide to display equal opportunity posters. When discrimination complaints began to pour in (largely instigated by the NAACP) the PCGC arranged favorable settlements for a number of employees. Racially separate lines of promotion at Atlantic Steel were eliminated. The tobacco industry partially relaxed its segregation policies. At the Lockheed aircraft plant in Marietta, Georgia, segregated black and white locals of the International Association of Machinists (IAM) were required to merge.[28]

However, except for the case of the IAM, the committee did not stress action against discrimination by unions. For one thing, its ability to intervene was limited by the fact that unions were not parties to procurement contracts between the government and employers. Basically, the PCGC depended on the NLRB to bring about progress in this area by enforcing the Wagner Act's requirement that unions provide "fair representation" to all members. The NLRB, however, took little action on this requirement. While the PCGC did not generally investigate complaints against unions, committee members from the labor movement did look into problems in specific unions when requested. In 1958 the committee's compliance guide called for federal agencies reporting violations to identify whether discriminatory union practices were involved.[29]

The business community was always the central focus of the PCGC's compliance effort. However, as with unions, the committee's ability to intervene in cases of discrimination by employers was limited. Contract revocation and other legal sanctions for overt discrimination were solely at the discretion of the contracting agencies and beyond the committee's control. To detect failure to deal with "institutional discrimination"—employment policies that limited the chances of minority members to be considered for employment—PCGC inspectors could consider the extent to which minorities were present in a given workplace. But the committee did not specify minimum acceptable percentages that would indicate de facto compliance, nor did it require employers who were found not in compliance to take compensatory actions. Instead, it emphasized voluntary action. In its final report, "Pattern for Progress," the committee implied that employers should make a special effort to deal with institutional discrimination:

> Overt discrimination, in the sense that an employer actually refuses to hire solely because of race, religion,

color, or national origin, is not as prevalent as is generally believed. To a greater degree, the indifference of employers to establishing a positive policy of nondiscrimination hinders qualified applicants and employees from being hired and promoted on the basis of equality.[30] [emphasis added]

Federal Agencies: Employment and Policies

Truman's Fair Employment Board (FEB) continued its task of promoting equal employment opportunity for federal workers into the Eisenhower administration. In 1954 the FEB was looking into a complaint against the Bureau of Engraving and Printing that had earlier resisted efforts to eliminate discriminatory practices (see chapter 4). Treasury Secretary George Humphrey, to whom the bureau reported, opposed the investigation. Then, perhaps influenced by the recent *Brown* decision, the press started asking questions about the investigation at presidential press conferences. To avert an embarrassing crisis, Maxwell Rabb recommended in September 1954 that the FEB be abolished and replaced with a new body with the same portfolio. Eisenhower agreed and issued E.O. 10590 on January 18, 1955, establishing the President's Committee on Government Employment Policy (PCGEP). The NAACP, which had been critical of the FEB, supported the new committee.[31]

The PCGEP's mission was to advise the president on ways to improve opportunities for minorities in federal employment and to evaluate government performance. Unlike the FEB, the PCGEP reported to the president and, therefore, had greater stature within the government. It served largely in an advisory capacity to departments and agencies. Each agency head was made responsible for ensuring equal treatment within their jurisdiction, as well as for hearing and ruling on complaints filed by their employees. Complainants had the right to request an advisory opinion from the committee, although this opinion was not binding on the agency head. The agencies were required to file enforcement regulations with the committee and report on the disposition of each complaint. Every federal agency was to appoint an Employment Policy Officer (EPO). (This position replaced the Truman–era position of Fair Employment Officer.) The EPO was responsible for processing complaints, recommending remedies, and assuring that personnel offices implemented E.O. 10590 properly.

To avoid any conflicts of interest with the agencies, EPOs in each agency were independent of the personnel office. There were seven members on the PCGEP. They included J. Ernest Wilkins, Civil Service Commissioner W. Arthur McCoy, two Defense Department representatives, and two public members. Archibald Carey, a black minister and attorney from Chicago, was chair. President Eisenhower did not make a public statement when he issued E.O. 10590. However, he asserted later that the PCGEP exemplified the administration's policy "that equal opportunity be afforded all qualified persons" seeking employment within the federal government.

By issuing guidelines for government supervisors, pamphlets for federal workers, and checklists on equal rights procedures for human resources officers, the PCGEP educated bureaucrats on the administration's antidiscrimination policies and helped make the federal work culture more tolerant. However, its own procedures ultimately limited its effectiveness. Complaints were handled within the accused agencies, and this proximity gave agency supervisors an opportunity to dismiss, or resolve, disputes in the agencies' favor. The committee was also hampered because, unlike the FEB, it could not utilize the Civil Service Commission to investigate complaints, relying instead on its own miniscule staff. The committee's efforts to discover and evaluate discrimination were hampered for some time because the government stopped collecting data on the race of its employees.

Nevertheless, the Eisenhower administration praised the PCGEP's performance. Vice President Nixon asserted in 1958, "Americans are now assured that Government service . . . is open to one and all, on the basis of ability . . . [T]he Government not only sets an example for other employers but directly protects the rights of more than two million workers to equal opportunity." The PCGEP's 1958 annual report assured that segregation within federal government had been eliminated and noted that, of over one thousand complaints received, only thirty-three required corrective action. The committee collected data on race in federal employment in Washington, DC, and four other cities.

The report analyzed black employment in career, nonpolitical positions in all of the Civil Service System's General Schedule (GS) levels. These levels ranged from GS-1, for the lowest paid, non-skilled workers, to GS-18, for the most senior career officials. The report found that from 1956 to 1960, black employment in GS grades 5 to 15 had grown from 3.7 percent of all employees to 5.9 percent. However, independent studies in major southern cities revealed a pattern of poor employment opportunities for blacks and a tendency to relegate them to janitorial or other low-skill jobs. One bright spot for black employment in the South was the US Post Office Department, which placed large numbers of blacks in skilled, well-paying jobs. But, despite the government's best efforts, by 1961 blacks still made up only 1 percent of all federal employees at the GS-12 level or above.[32]

During the Eisenhower administration, the Department of Labor continued to wrestle with the ongoing problems of discriminatory job orders and other unfair treatment in the local offices of the USES. To help deal with these problems, Mitchell revived the Truman–era Minority Groups Program (MGP). It was located within the new

Bureau of Employment Security (BES) that now supervised the USES. Mitchell intended the MGP to be the means through which the department "promotes the principle of hiring workers on the basis of merit." The MGP was of such prominence in the administration that Mitchell, speaking at Fisk University in 1955, cited it as one of the two principal federal equal opportunity programs (the PCGC was the other). Mitchell also revived the position of Minority Groups Counselor (MGC) to oversee the MGP. To fill it, he appointed Roberta Church, an African American human relations worker from Memphis, Tennessee, and a Republican Party operative.[33]

The Minority Groups Program, according to Robert Goodwin, now BES director, dealt with "problems involved in promoting employment of workers belonging to minority groups." Roberta Church, the sole human relations professional in the program, had as one of her main goals the elimination of segregation in all offices of the USES. While some progress was made, many offices in the South resisted integration. Church worked with the National Urban League and other welfare organizations to promote job opportunities in local communities. She focused particularly on persuading employers to drop discriminatory requirements from job orders. Church also persuaded the state branches of the USES to appoint Minority Groups Representatives (MGRs) to serve as her counterparts.[34]

Impressed with Church's activism, Secretary Mitchell appointed her as an adviser to the assistant secretary for Manpower and Employment. Now her portfolio included not only the USES and BES, but other departmental programs, such as the BAT and the independent PCGC. Many officials now looked to her for advice on fair employment matters. In 1957, at her request, Mitchell made official her broadening role and designated her as departmental Minority Groups Consultant.[35] Church saw her expanded role as providing all DOL agencies with a departmental source of current information about minority groups, the activities of organizations established to work with minority groups, legislation affecting these groups, and other pertinent data.[36]

To assist the growing federal-state minority groups effort, in 1955 and 1956 the department called together conferences on the national Minority Groups Program. The 1955 MGP Conference afforded the sharing of news on fair employment efforts in the labor market and the opportunity to review the MGP at all levels. The focus of the larger 1956 MGP Conference was the preparation of minority youths to enter the labor market and the growing need for skilled labor in the US economy. At the 1956 conference, Church spoke optimistically of social and economic changes for blacks in American society. She noted that, due to recent events, "it appears we can view the future with some degree of optimism, although there is much to be done."[37]

In order for the BES and USES to be effective and credible advocates of equal treatment, they had to put their own house in order. Mitchell fully shared Church's goal of the elimination of segregation in the USES in every state. Arkansas, which would soon be a battle ground in the civil rights movement, was a case in point.[38] In March 1956 Robert Goodwin met with Arkansas Governor Orval Faubus to discuss segregation in the state's USES branch. Faubus was surprisingly conciliatory and promised Goodwin that he and Arkansas USES head, James Bland, would take care of the problem. Goodwin thus reported to Rocco Siciliano, the White House's liaison with the Labor Department:

> They are not giving publicity to the decision, and they have developed their program in such a way as to avoid conflict to the maximum extent possible. For instance,

> although separate offices and separate entrances will be eliminated in connection with moves to new quarters, there will for a time be scheduling of white and colored unemployment insurance claimants at different hours of the day. It is planned to drop the separate scheduling after it is clear that there will be no difficulty from the other changes.[39]

In April 1956 Bland reported to Goodwin that separate entrances for whites and blacks had been eliminated at the Little Rock ES office. He attached newspaper clippings and went on:

> This problem was approached with some caution, and there have been no serious repercussions. However, elements who are opposed to the plan of paying unemployment insurance benefits in any form, and perhaps antagonistic toward Governor Faubus, have been successful in obtaining publication of critical articles . . . I am not alarmed . . . I hope you will find opportunity to inform Secretary Mitchell of this development. It was not an easy job.[40]

Mitchell wanted to send a note to Bland, commending his efforts, but first there was a skirmish among aides over its wording. Deputy Under Secretary Millard Cass wanted Mitchell to tell Bland:

> Your actions have demonstrated how progress can be made when people of goodwill try to solve their problems with imagination, courage, and patience.

Under Secretary John J. Gilhooley scribbled a caution on Cass's note: "No, goes to [sic] far." Cass's phrase was dropped, and the letter was sent.[41] Despite this example of progress in Arkansas, as of 1959 segregation persisted in USES offices in 110 southern cities. In seventy of those cities, the offices had racially separate service areas; in an additional twenty-five cities, the offices had one entrance for whites and another for blacks; and in fifteen cities the local ES went to the extreme of maintaining completely separate offices for the races.[42]

One of the important elements of the Cold War, as it developed during the Eisenhower administration, was the competition with the Soviet bloc in technological advancement. The administration was concerned that the American workforce did not have the necessary skills and professional expertise, and it sought to improve the nation's educational and training resources. Secretary Mitchell spoke often about the increasing need for skilled workers and the lack of adequate skills in the workforce, particularly among African Americans. He pointed out that black workers were often barred from training programs and apprenticeships. He considered equality of training opportunities to be an important element in fighting job discrimination. E.O. 10557 required that equal opportunity clauses in government contracts encompass training and apprenticeships. In 1956 the department developed a "Skills of the Work Force" program to promote the training of the skilled workers needed for both economic growth and national defense. While this program did not specifically target blacks, one of its main goals—according to E. R. Chapell, who coordinated the program—was "the full utilization of all our people without regard to race, creed, age, sex or physical handicap."[43]

One of Roberta Church's main goals was to use the regulatory authority of the BAT to open up more apprenticeship opportunities for black youths. This bureau, because it provided certification of apprenticeship programs, had some potential for influence in this area. However, it depended largely on voluntary help from the private sector to maintain and upgrade the quality of apprenticeship programs. It lacked statutory authority to directly enforce equal treatment in apprentice programs. The only "stick" the BAT had was the power to exclude violators from its registry of federally certified programs. Unfortunately, it never used that sanction during the Eisenhower administration (but it did so later—see chapter 6); however, the BAT did require that programs associated with government contractors have the imprimatur of registration with the BAT. In conjunction with this requirement and with E.O. 10557, the bureau also sought "to stimulate those [contractors] responsible for such training to provide equal opportunities for all qualified individuals to acquire skills without regard to race, creed, sex, age or physical handicaps."[44]

In 1960 the NAACP released a report titled "The Black Wage Earner and Apprenticeship Training Programs," in which it charged that blacks were excluded from most apprenticeship programs. In the NAACP's view, the BAT bore part of the responsibility for this state of affairs. In order to provide the maximum apprenticeship opportunities to blacks, the NAACP called on all parties involved, especially the BAT, both to eliminate racial barriers and to significantly increase apprenticeship programs. Reflecting its close ties to the providers of apprentice programs, the BAT leadership thought the report was useful but off the mark. In a memo to Under Secretary O'Connell, Newell Brown, assistant secretary of labor for the Wage-Hour Administration, praised the "well written and cleverly handled" booklet. He had asked BAT for their comments on it and found that

> They are of the opinion that so long as their effectiveness depends heavily upon the goodwill of employers and workers, they cannot attempt to assert pressure for integration to any noticeable extent. They do agree that perhaps they could do a little more "soft selling."
>
> I am inclined to agree with their comments. Where the report in its recommendations goes beyond proposals

for expanding and improving Apprenticeship generally, it calls for Federal action which we would have to oppose if we are to retain employer and employee goodwill.[45]

By the end of the Eisenhower administration in January 1961, the federal government had, for two decades, issued executive orders and operated highly visible presidential committees intended to alleviate discrimination in federally funded jobs. These bodies, supplemented by the Department of Labor and other executive branch agencies, applied limited resources to the difficult task of turning around long-established practices and prejudices that limited opportunities for black workers.

The results of this twenty-year effort were modest and incomplete. Black wages and employment opportunities did improve, but African Americans still lagged well behind the rest of the workforce. In 1960, 45 percent of minority men, mostly black, held laborer jobs. Only 13 percent of white men were relegated to such work. The black unemployment rate was twice the white rate, and the average black family earned 55 percent of the average earnings of white families.[46] The hopeful side of this picture was that twenty years of executive branch efforts had succeeded in institutionalizing the concept, if not the reality, of equal employment opportunity. Thus was provided a policy base for further federal efforts to attain this elusive goal.

Part III
Culmination of Executive Action, 1960–1964

With the election of John Kennedy as president in 1960, action by the executive branch, driven by the exploding civil rights movement, reached a new, more intense level. In 1961 Executive Order 10925 established the President's Committee on Equal Employment Opportunity (PCEEO). As discussed in chapter 6 ("Birth of the President's Committee on Equal Employment Opportunity"), chapter 7 ("The Committee Gets Underway"), and chapter 8 ("The Kheel Report and Beyond"), the PCEEO administered a unified program that focused on equal opportunity compliance both in federal contract work and also in federal employment. Added to the dual mission of the PCEEO was "Plans for Progress," a controversial voluntary effort which included the nonfederally funded private sector. With broad-based support for the committee, Congress increased funding significantly over the levels for previous equal employment opportunity programs. Chapter 9, "The Department of Labor in the Kennedy–Johnson Era," covers the continued process of instilling equal opportunity policies in the US Employment Service and details the issuance of a historic affirmative action regulation governing apprenticeship programs. The chronology concludes at the enactment of the Civil Rights Act of 1964, which largely superceded existing executive action and moved equal employment opportunity enforcement into the new realm of legislated, mandatory enforcement.

CHAPTER 6

Birth of the President's Committee on Equal Employment Opportunity

On February 1, 1960, four black student activists from the North Carolina Agricultural and Technical College entered a Woolworth's department store in Greensboro, North Carolina. They made a few purchases and then sat down at the whites-only lunch counter. The students were never served, but they remained quietly on their stools until the store closed. They came back on each of the following six days, attracting ever-larger crowds and extensive television news coverage. This historic "sit-in" sparked similar actions throughout the South, spreading to fifty-four cities in nine states within three months.[1]

The immediate effect was to boost the Civil Rights Movement to a higher level and give African Americans unprecedented political influence. As a result, candidates seeking the presidential nominations of both major political parties worked harder than ever to gain black support. Vice President Richard Nixon, virtually unopposed for the Republican nomination, worked to reverse the long-term erosion in black support for his party. Senator John F. Kennedy (JFK), the leading contender for the Democratic nomination, met with Martin Luther King Jr. in June and endorsed the sit-in movement before the party convention took place. Kennedy won the nomination on the first ballot. He persuaded his chief rival, Senate Majority Leader Lyndon Baines Johnson (LBJ), to be his running mate as vice president. The convention adopted a strong civil rights plank that called for federal action to end discrimination in housing and education, and for enactment of a fair employment practices law. The Republican convention—which, as expected, chose Nixon as its nominee—adopted the strongest civil rights plank in the party's history, urging the total eradication of racial discrimination.[2]

In the fall, Kennedy campaigned vigorously for the votes of African Americans. Kennedy promised to establish, through an executive order, equality in federally funded housing with the stroke of a pen. Shortly before the election, he telephoned Coretta Scott King—her husband, Martin Luther King Jr. had been sentenced to four months hard labor by a Georgia judge in retribution for civil rights activities there. Pressure from JFK, and his brother and close adviser Robert F. Kennedy, quickly led to an order releasing King from jail. This episode contributed to an election-day shift of black support to the Democratic camp. In one of the closer elections in American history, Kennedy carried 70 percent of the black vote. He won the election by a total of 115,000 popular votes nationwide and by 84 votes in the electoral college, 303 to 219.

The Kennedy administration came into office with an ambitious domestic agenda. Black hopes for significant civil rights actions in Washington were high. However, as had been the case under past Democratic presidents like Woodrow Wilson and Franklin Delano Roosevelt, power in Congress continued to rest largely with segregationist Southern Democrats. Kennedy needed their support in order to achieve his highest domestic priority: recovery from the stubborn grip of a recession that began in 1959. To this end, the administration decided early on to avoid conflict with Congress over civil rights and to rely instead on executive action.

Inauguration Day, January 20, 1961, marked the initiation of what was soon labeled the New Frontier. Black participation in JFK's inaugural festivities was more extensive than it had ever been before.[3] Many black dignitaries were invited, and President Kennedy made a point of dancing with their wives at the balls. Kennedy's inaugural address, however, dealt largely with the Cold War. His only allusion to civil rights was when he spoke of "those human rights ... to which we are committed today at home and around the world."[4] Civil rights leaders were encouraged both by the fact that the president chose to mention civil rights, and also by the tone of governmental activism that he projected.

Despite giving minimal attention to black concerns in the speech, the Kennedy administration soon focused on a number of civil rights issues. Kennedy himself said relatively little in public on the subject. However, his brother Robert, whom he appointed Attorney General; Vice President Johnson; Secretary of Labor Arthur Goldberg and successor W. Willard Wirtz; and others spoke eloquently and regularly on equal rights. The administration tied this issue closely to the Cold War and competition with the Soviet Union, as had the Truman and Eisenhower administrations. Kennedy made himself more accessible to civil rights leaders than any previous president. He met with Martin Luther King Jr., A. Philip Randolph, and Roy Wilkins, among others.

After assuming office, Kennedy appointed African Americans to high political posts at a rapid pace, giving them more power and responsibility than in previous administrations. His most prominent appointment was that of Robert C. Weaver, who had served in FDR's Black Cabinet, to head the Housing and Home Finance Agency.[5] In his first two months in office, JFK appointed forty blacks to high positions in a wide range of policy areas. However, he appointed Harris Wofford, a white—albeit also a racial liberal—as the senior White House civil rights adviser and liaison. Nevertheless, Kennedy put great pressure on agency heads to appoint blacks to high advisory positions. In September 1961 he appointed Thurgood Marshall, the principal attorney in the 1954 *Brown v. Board of Education* decision, to the US Court of Appeals in Washington, DC, making him the first black jurist ever to serve at that level.[6] While neither of Kennedy's appointees for secretary of labor was black, both Arthur Goldberg, a labor lawyer and an architect of the merger of the AFL and the CIO in 1955, and Willard Wirtz, a law professor with extensive experience in government, were strong supporters of civil rights. Earlier, Wirtz had advised Democratic presidential candidate Adlai Stevenson on civil rights issues during his 1956 campaign.[7]

The administration quickly began implementing an equal opportunity agenda through executive action. Executive orders were issued to promote fair housing, desegregate public transportation, and promote equality in the workplace. Despite the fact that the executive branch was acting more vigorously than ever before to promote equal employment opportunity, African Americans were critical of the administration's slow pace and limited scope in civil rights activities.

In the early 1960s, the Civil Rights Movement rapidly became a civil rights crisis. Activists mounted Freedom Rides, at considerable risk to themselves, in an attempt to desegregate southern public transportation. Large numbers of blacks began to exercise their right to register and vote. Perhaps most crucially, the Reverend Martin Luther King Jr., leader of the 1955 Montgomery Bus Boycott, emerged as a powerful and charismatic leader. In May 1963 King led a series of marches and demonstrations in Birmingham, Alabama. The marchers were assaulted by Police Commissioner Bull Connor's police dogs and water cannons in full view of a national television audience.

In June 1963 in response to the mounting crisis, Kennedy stopped stalling and called for a strong civil rights law. Congress soon took up bills on the issue. Adding pressure for enactment was the historic "March on Washington for Jobs and Freedom," staged on August 28, 1963, and led by A. Philip Randolph, father of the 1941 March on Washington Movement. At the march, where King gave his immortal "I have a dream" speech, a quarter of a million people demonstrated peacefully in support of a new civil rights act. A further, if tragic, impetus came in November 1963 when President Kennedy was assassinated in Dallas. When Vice President Johnson succeeded Kennedy, LBJ took advantage of the national period of mourning to call for enactment of the Civil Rights Act in Kennedy's memory.

Segregationists stoutly resisted the legislation. President Johnson then shifted gears and mounted a separate initiative, dubbed the Great Society, to improve the social and physical quality of life in the United States, including race relations. An allied LBJ program, the War on Poverty, focused on reducing severe economic disparities, regardless of race. Institutionalization of both programs began with the Economic Opportunity Act of 1964.

After a tremendous battle in Congress, LBJ won passage of the Civil Rights Act and signed it into law on July 2, 1964. Title VII specifically banned discrimination based on race, religion, or gender in the workplace, created an Equal Employment Opportunity Commission to investigate and assist in enforcement, and required affirmative action to eliminate discrimination. The following year, Johnson issued E.O. 11246, establishing a permanent Office of Federal Contract Compliance to enforce equal employment opportunity in government contracts.

Enactment of the Civil Rights Act and the initiation of the Great Society and War on Poverty ushered in an era of legislative remedies for discrimination and its economic and social effects. The Civil Rights Act marked an end to the period of reliance on executive action to provide equal employment opportunity. The law developed while action by the executive branch was at its apogee. This effort helped lay the groundwork for the transition to legislative remedies.

Issuance of Executive Order 10925

During the 1960 presidential campaign, Kennedy had charged that the President's Committee on Government Contracts (PCGC), established by President Eisenhower, was ineffective. Calling for large-scale executive action to promote civil rights, Kennedy promised to reorganize and strengthen the committee. After the election he designated LBJ, who had championed the 1957 Civil Rights Act, to organize the drafting of a presidential order to establish a new committee.

Beginning before the inauguration, Johnson led a collective effort involving the Justice Department, Secretary of Labor-designate Goldberg, LBJ adviser and journalist Bill Moyers, and Abe Fortas and Hobart Taylor, two lawyers and longtime Johnson associates. Johnson also consulted widely outside government. The drafters used the PCGC and the legacy of twenty years of executive orders as a starting point.

On March 6, 1961, JFK issued E.O. 10925 abolishing both the PCGC and Eisenhower's PCGEP on federal employment (see chapter 5). In their place, E.O. 10925 created the President's Committee on Equal Employment Opportunity (PCEEO), which covered both contract and federal employment, thus eliminating the traditional bureaucratic separation of these areas. The order incorporated a number of features intended to make the PCEEO more effective than its predecessors. The secretary of labor was designated vice chair, reporting to the vice president, who served as chair. The secretary was responsible for seeing that the committee fulfilled its duties. The order also included a beefed-up antidiscrimination clause for government contracts, allowed contract debarment as a sanction, and required detailed surveys of minority employment in federal agencies. Kennedy announced E.O. 10925 and the PCEEO with great fanfare at a press conference on March 7, 1961, and promised vigorous administration and enforcement.

E.O. 10925 was longer, more detailed, and more sweeping than any previous order of its kind. The Whereas clauses at the beginning laid out the basis for the order in law, policy, national interest, and administrative functioning. As a matter of law, discrimination was found to be clearly against the Constitution, and it was the duty of the federal government to promote equal employment opportunity for all in the workplaces of both the government and federal contractors. It was also found that efficient use of the entire labor force was necessary for a sound economy and for national security. The concluding clause asserted that existing government orders and procedures were not adequate to the task of eliminating workplace discrimination and that the government's efforts to meet its antidiscrimination responsibilities should be coordinated in a single agency.

The heart of federal contracts enforcement was a new, far-reaching, and mandatory nondiscrimination clause which was to be included in most government contracts. Contractors were to post the clause conspicuously in the workplace, include a promise of equal employment opportunity in any job announcements, and inform unions about employers' duties under the order. In addition, subcontracts also were to include a nondiscrimination clause. The contractor was primarily responsible for enforcement, under the direction of the agency. The committee could, at its discretion, allow agencies to omit the clause from specific contracts, and to exempt small contracts or contracts for work not involving US residents.

The most innovative feature of E.O. 10925 was the inclusion of the phrase "affirmative action." Section 301, specifying the wording of the antidiscrimination clause for government contracts, required that contractors take

> affirmative action to ensure that applicants are employed, and that employees are treated during employment, without regard to their race, creed, color, or national origin.

The order also called on the PCEEO, in Section 201, to suggest "affirmative steps" for agencies to take for promoting nondiscrimination for their own employees.

Affirmative Action was not defined, but it was a recognizable phrase with a history. It had first been used by the federal government in the National Labor Relations Act of 1935. In that context, it referred, not to racial discrimination, but to providing redress to employees victimized by unfair labor practices. A few years later, during discussions among policy makers leading to the formation of the Second FEPC, the concept was discussed in reference to equal employment. Budget Bureau head Harold Smith objected to a proposal (not adopted) to allow the FEPC to require, as a remedy for discrimination, "affirmative action such as employment, reinstatement, and payment of back pay." State FEPCs, however, often had the authority to order affirmative action by employers. In the 1950s the PCGC applied the notion in settling several discrimination complaints. By 1960 "affirmative," "affirmative action," and similar phrases were in common use by those, including President Kennedy, calling for more aggressive governmental efforts to deal with a number of issues. As Willard Wirtz later noted, in 1961 affirmative action had little specific meaning beyond that of expressing a need for "taking an initiative instead of just sitting back and waiting for things to happen." It was a kind of shibboleth expressing the activist spirit of the new administration.[8]

BIRTH OF THE PRESIDENT'S COMMITTEE ON EQUAL EMPLOYMENT OPPORTUNITY

Under E.O. 10925, contractors were to provide the PCEEO with periodic compliance reports on their practices and policies, along with fair employment statistics. Contractors were also to open their records to the contracting agencies to allow independent evaluation of their efforts. The order also specified that contract bidders, who had previously come under its purview, would have to submit a past compliance report.

E.O. 10925 broke new ground by applying its requirements to organized labor, which had been excluded from past executive orders. Because the Civil Rights Movement in the late 1950s had publicized long-standing discrimination within unions, the Kennedy administration, while strongly supportive of organized labor, felt obliged to take this step.

All contracting employers' compliance reports were to describe, to the extent known, any practices and policies of the relevant unions related to fair employment. Any firm seeking government contracts would have to obtain a statement from unions representing their employees, certifying that the unions were free of discrimination and would comply with the order. Furthermore, the committee was charged to use its best efforts to seek compliance and cooperation from the relevant unions.

The committee was also empowered to hold hearings on any labor organization's fair employment practices and to report their findings to the White House. When it encountered discriminatory practices or lack of cooperation by a particular union, the committee could recommend, though not require, remedial action and notify the government agencies involved.

E.O. 10925 designated the contracting federal agencies as the primary enforcers of its provisions. The agencies were to comply with the order and the committee's rules and provide any assistance or information the committee might ask. Each agency was to designate one of their employees as the compliance officer. These officers were to avoid confrontation and conflict and seek compliance through, as the order put it, "conference, conciliation, mediation, or persuasion" whenever possible.

The committee was responsible for a wide range of contract compliance functions. To ease the burdens on its limited resources, it was authorized to delegate functions to the agencies. For example, the committee was free to investigate any contractor's employment practices for possible violations, or it could ask that the contracting agency or the Labor Department do so. Employees could file discrimination complaints with the committee, which would initiate an investigation resulting in recommendations for remedial action. The committee had a broad mandate to hold hearings around the country on any facet of employment discrimination. The committee also had a mandate to support educational efforts by employers, unions, and other concerned groups to eliminate discrimination in employment. In theory, E.O. 10925 included educational work in all workplaces, not only federally funded ones. While this mandate had little practical effect, nevertheless, it did constitute a widening of the federal role. As such, it foreshadowed the sweeping changes instituted in Title VII of the Civil Rights Act.

The sanctions and penalties available to the PCEEO under E.O. 10925 were stronger than those available to any previous federal fair employment body. Before taking any formal action, the committee and contracting agencies were allowed to publish the names of contractors and unions who were not in compliance with the order. For employers whose policies and practices met the requirements of E.O. 10925, the committee could publish their names and award an official Certificate of Merit.

If the public "dishonor roll" of violators failed to bring about compliance, stronger measures were available. When any person or organization, whether an employer or a union, was found to be in actual or potential violation of the mandatory antidiscrimination clause, the committee could ask the Department of Justice to bring legal action against them. This action could even include criminal proceedings if the violator had furnished false information. When the committee ruled that a contractor had violated the clause, it could either terminate their contract forthwith or allow continuation, provided the contractor developed a satisfactory program to bring about compliance. Agencies could also debar noncomplying contractors from further government work until they had remedied all violations.

In reality, legal action, cancellation, and debarment were rarely invoked. Before pursuing such remedies, the PCEEO and the contracting agencies were required, under the order, to follow the long-established principle of voluntary compliance by instituting conferences, conciliation, and other voluntary measures. However, Vice Chair Goldberg stressed in a television interview that while the compliance policy of the PCEEO would be at heart voluntaristic, the committee would seek to apply it as rigorously as possible:

> We will use reason, we will use persuasion, we will use common sense. We will, however, use firmness. There is no justification . . . for anyone to be denied fair opportunities for government employment . . . [or] employment opportunities on government contracts.[9]

E.O. 10925, unlike its predecessors, combined the portfolio of the federal workforce with contract work. The order adopted the abolished PCGEP's goal of prohibiting discrimination against federal employees or job applicants based on race, color, religion, or national origin. There were no formal penalties for violations of government employees' rights. Sanctions were not really necessary since all federal agencies are directly accountable to the president. As with federal contractors, the order made federal agencies, rather than the committee, directly responsible for meeting nondiscrimination standards. E.O. 10925 required that the committee immediately study employment practices in all agencies of the federal government and recommend steps to promote equal employment opportunities. To assist the committee, agencies were instructed to survey their internal employment conduct and policies in detail and, as soon as possible, send the committee a full report, including recommendations for improvement. The committee would then report the results of the federal survey and the recommendations to the president. Shortly after issuing E.O. 10925, Kennedy broadened its scope to include recreational associations that federal agencies provided for their employees. These associations were barred from using federal facilities, or even the name of the agency with which they were associated, if they practiced discrimination.[10]

Regarding both federal employment and contractors, the committee was authorized to adopt procedures to implement the order and consider reports from government agencies on progress made. The chair could appoint subcommittees as needed to conduct studies on specific issues, and members could bring up specific concerns for consideration. The committee was to report to the president at least annually on the antidiscrimination performance of each federal agency.[11]

Start-up of the PCEEO

Shortly after President Kennedy announced the creation of the PCEEO on March 7, 1961, his staff began selecting and appointing the members of the new committee. Prescribed for membership under the order by reason of their positions were the vice president (Lyndon Johnson), chair; the secretary of labor (Arthur Goldberg), vice chair; the secretary of defense (Robert McNamara) and the heads of the four military branches; the secretary of commerce (Luther Hodges); the attorney general (Robert Kennedy); the Atomic Energy Commission chair (Glenn T. Seborg); the National Aeronautics and Space Administration director (James Webb); the Civil Service Commission chair (John W. Macy); and the General Services Administration director (John L. Moore). The order also gave the president a free hand to make additional appointments. Kennedy used the opportunity to bring in a wide-ranging group of luminaries. These additions included Abraham Ribicoff, secretary of Health, Education and Welfare; retailing mogul Fred Lazarus; philanthropist Mary Lasker; black businessman John H. Wheeler; and three prominent religious leaders: Monsignor George Higgins, Washington National Cathedral Dean Francis Sayre, and Rabbi Jacob Weinstein. Because of the importance of organized labor to the success of the order, Kennedy named AFL-CIO President George Meany and Vice President Walter Reuther as members.[12] In addition to Lazarus, Kennedy appointed six more business representatives, three from the South and three from the North. In total, he appointed twenty-eight members, fourteen each from government and the private sector. Assistant Secretary of Labor (and Johnson friend) Jerry Holleman was appointed executive vice chair, an ex officio position with wide-ranging responsibilities for carrying out the functions of the committee. Holleman was only available part-time, however, as he continued to serve in his Labor Department post.

The committee leadership began work well before the official kick-off meeting scheduled for April 11. Members for the committee were still being selected, but Johnson was anxious for the committee to get off to the fastest possible start. He asked each agency head to immediately designate a compliance officer to serve as a contact with the committee on all matters and, using a form to be supplied by the committee, conduct a quick survey of employment of minorities by contractors and by the agency. The agencies were then to report to the committee on their compliance plans. Agency heads notified personnel directors that they were to fully implement E.O. 10925.

As of April 3 the committee had failed to develop a survey form for the agencies. To help assure that the survey would meet Johnson's reporting deadline of May 5, Goldberg provided the agencies with a form the Labor Department had already devised for its own use.[13] The Labor Department and its agencies facilitated the PCEEO's start-up in other ways. The Bureau of Apprenticeship (BAT) and the Wage and Hour and Public Contracts Divisions (WHD) were especially useful. Vice President Johnson wanted to include the controversial issue of equal opportunity in the nation's apprenticeship programs on the agenda of the committee's first meeting. To facilitate this presentation, Secretary Goldberg ordered a background study on the extent of the problem, which the BAT quickly provided.

The WHD became a key component in administering the order. A joint body created in the 1930s to enforce the Fair Labor Standards and Public Contracts Acts, the WHD maintained a staff of 650 inspectors in all fifty states. It was often called upon to enforce regulations related to other labor laws. WHD Administrator Clarence Lundquist reported that, while a small amount of additional funding would be necessary, the divisions were "ready, willing, and able" to enforce E.O. 10925. Their expertise made an invaluable contribution to the work of the PCEEO.[14]

Like other federal employers, the Department of Labor was required to put its own house in order under E.O. 10925. Goldberg was determined to see that the department was a leader and role model among federal employers. On March 7, 1961, the day President Kennedy announced the order, Goldberg sent out an all-employee departmental memo on the White House initiative, which he termed "a vigorous, positive program to ensure that all Americans . . . will have equal access to employment opportunities."[15] Goldberg highlighted Kennedy's requirement that all government agencies were to "take immediate action" to open more opportunities for minorities. Reinforcing that theme, Goldberg issued a call for affirmative action in federal employment:

> IT IS MY INTENTION THAT THERE SHALL BE NO RACIAL OR RELIGIOUS BARRIERS TO EMPLOYMENT AT ANY LEVEL IN THIS DEPARTMENT . . . WE ARE TAKING AFFIRMATIVE STEPS TO ACQUAINT MEMBERS OF MINORITY GROUPS WITH THE OPPORTUNITIES FOR EMPLOYMENT THAT EXIST IN THIS DEPARTMENT AND IN THE GOVERNMENT GENERALLY.[16] [original emphasis]

In the same memo, Goldberg announced that letters had gone out to the presidents of every black college in the country, informing them of job opportunities for their graduates at the Department of Labor. To follow up, Goldberg sent his personnel director, Edward McVeigh, on a four-week recruiting trip to seventeen black colleges. Goldberg was careful, at the same time, to make sure that affirmative action would not deprive qualified white students of job opportunities:

> We will expect, of course, that members of minority groups meet the same qualification standards, follow the same staffing procedures, and qualify in the same examinations or evaluations as others seeking employment or promotion. *To do otherwise would in itself be a form of discrimination.*[17] [emphasis added]

By March 9, 1961, Goldberg had named three blacks to high positions in the department. George L. P. Weaver was named assistant secretary for International Affairs and US Representative to the

International Labor Organization (ILO). He and Robert C. Weaver (no relation) were the two highest-ranking African Americans in the administration. While Goldberg sought (as a matter of principle) to appoint African Americans to high positions, George Weaver was seen as a particularly appropriate choice, by virtue of his color, to speak for the United States in the racially diverse ILO. Goldberg appointed Arthur Chapin, a labor, civil rights, and Democratic Party activist from New Jersey, as Minority Groups consultant in the Bureau of Employment Security, and Dolly Robinson, an African American, as a special assistant to Women's Bureau director Mary Dublin Keyserling. Goldberg ordered a careful study of the department's personnel practices to determine the extent to which discrimination was, or had been, present. He rushed a hand-carried memo on these activities to the vice president. Johnson immediately thanked Goldberg: "I'm glad you acted with your characteristic speed and dispatch."[18]

Edward McVeigh's recruiting trip was revealing. He discovered firsthand that few black students at the campuses he visited had taken the civil service examinations required for eligibility for federal white-collar jobs. McVeigh reported that they either did not know about the tests or did not believe they had a real chance for a federal job. By the time he reported to the secretary, the Civil Service Commission (CSC) had completed its regular schedule of examinations for the year. Goldberg asked CSC head Macy, a member of the PCEEO, to provide an additional examination day. Macy consented, and the CSC held a special exam session on May 13, 1961.[19]

With the help of the Labor Department and other agencies, the committee was able to be ready for its inaugural meeting on April 11, 1961, as scheduled. At this high-profile event, held in the Cabinet Room at the White House, Johnson swore in the members. President Kennedy spoke, stressing that E.O. 10925 was "both an

BIRTH OF THE PRESIDENT'S COMMITTEE ON EQUAL EMPLOYMENT OPPORTUNITY

announcement of our determination to end job discrimination once and for all, and an effective instrument to realize that objective. . . . I don't think there's any more important domestic effort in which we can be engaged." In a reference to the continuing international and Cold War significance of US race relations, Kennedy also noted that Johnson had just returned from a trip to Senegal that reflected "the importance of our establishing our image in accordance with our Constitutional promise." Kennedy pointed out that the committee was not an honorary body but had important enforcement powers that he expected to be firmly applied. At the same time, he sought to calm fears that the committee would be heavy-handed and intrusive in the nation's workplaces. He stressed that its responsibilities were to be discharged "with fairness, with understanding, with an open mind, and a generous spirit of cooperation." He noted, "There is no intention to make this a harsh or unreasonable mandate for those sincerely and honestly seeking compliance." He concluded his remarks by saying that "this is the best way I know how to do it . . . [W]hen [the committee's] powers and responsibilities are put together, it will be moving along a very important, useful, and national road."[20]

Echoing Kennedy's sentiments, Johnson expressed strong determination to eliminate discrimination in the workplace. Using a phrase that became an unofficial motto of the committee, he asserted, "we mean business."[21] To facilitate the PCEEO's work, he organized it into subcommittees on: skill improvement, training and apprenticeship, vocational education, promotion and upgrading, franchise industries, and religious cooperation.

Johnson described the PCEEO's role as national in scope. Its mandate was to bring about "voluntary compliance throughout the government, throughout industry and throughout the labor movement." While recognizing that eliminating discrimination from government-funded employment areas could not be accomplished quickly,

173

he emphasized that "it is long overdue; and it must be accomplished with all reasonable speed." He noted that the new committee differed from its predecessors in that it was to be devoted largely to matters of policy, with members "carrying the gospel of the Executive Order to every corner of this land." Freeing up the PCEEO's members to pursue this purpose, the vice chair, executive vice chair, and forty full-time staff members were to carry out the day-to-day operations. Johnson concluded:

> The President's Executive Order is framed not merely in the negative terms of avoiding discrimination, but in the positive direction of taking steps to make sure that all persons . . . have a full opportunity to participate in [government-funded] employment . . . It is your obligation . . . to see that this positive and affirmative program is fulfilled, in spirit as well as in letter.[22]

After Johnson's remarks, the committee members who represented government agencies initialed a prepared statement committing their agencies to the elimination of discrimination in federally funded employment. Specifically, they pledged to complete the surveys already begun and initiate any follow-up actions that were needed. Johnson announced that the committee would meet soon in Washington with the major government contractors, followed by a separate meeting with union leaders. After that meeting, committee members would travel around the country to convene with more contractors and unions. He emphasized that "the ultimate solution to this problem must be found among the people themselves . . . [Equality] must be translated into specific action and that transition will take place best when people sit around the table and discuss the specific problems."[23]

Shortly after the April 11 kick-off meeting, Holleman directed each agency head to immediately appoint an Employment Policy

Officer (EPO) to carry out the requirements of the order regarding federal employment. The EPOs were to be under the immediate supervision of the agency head and were not supposed to be connected with the agency's personnel division. The agencies designated high-ranking officials, usually assistant secretaries, to serve as EPOs. The larger agencies assigned full-time staff to work with the EPOs.[24]

The committee began with a staff of forty full-time workers left over from the PCGC and PCGEP. There were thirty-one positions in Washington, DC, and nine in offices in Chicago and Los Angeles.[25] Funding for the first year came from the unspent budgets of the two old committees. After that, as specified under E.O. 10925 and in compliance with the Russell Amendment (see chapters 3 and 4), the PCEEO received all funding from the contracting departments and agencies. No single agency could provide more than 50 percent of the committee's total budget, which was set at $500,000 per year. However, the agencies were permitted to contribute staff and other nonbudgetary assistance. The Department of Labor provided office space and facilities.[26]

By June 1961 the committee had filled most of its top staff positions. To serve as executive director, Johnson appointed John Feild, a white with roots in the labor movement and civil rights experience, including service as a staff member with the Michigan Fair Employment Practices Commission.[27] Other staff appointments included John D. McCully Sr. as director of Information; Percy Williams as assistant executive director for Contract Compliance; John Hope II as assistant executive director for Federal Employment; Ward McCreedy as director of Complaint Investigations; Raymond Shelkofsky as administrative officer; and Hobart Taylor Jr. as head of the Office of Special Counsel (OSC).[28]

In the position of Special Counsel, Taylor had the difficult and sensitive jobs of interpreting E.O. 10925, developing rules and regulations for the committee, and reviewing discrimination complaints before final action by the committee. A successful black lawyer and the son of a Houston businessman who had a long-standing political and business relationship with Johnson, Taylor was the principal drafter of the order. He later claimed responsibility for including in it the phrase "affirmative action." Taylor took a methodical and nonconfrontational approach that Wirtz, Robert Kennedy, and others interpreted as a lack of enthusiasm for the committee. Wirtz later stated that Taylor's was "not a firecracker approach." Johnson appears not to have shared that view. While still vice president, he showed enough confidence in Taylor's capabilities to make him his special assistant in the White House.[29]

Under Taylor, the OSC was designated to be a watchdog on the federal agencies as they administered E.O. 10925. The OSC reviewed and coordinated agency rules and worked to assure the establishment of uniform procedures throughout the federal government. Although many agencies did not want to set specific deadlines for processing complaints, the Special Counsel required them to adopt a thirty-day time limit for most complaints. Agencies were also required to file a copy of each complaint they received with the committee. The Special Counsel worked to assure that all discrimination complaints would be reported to the committee so that it could review them. When an agency conducted a hearing on a complaint, the Special Counsel made sure that the officer investigating the complaint did not also serve as the hearing officer. The Special Counsel also saw that complainants' legal rights under the order were fully protected. The OSC stressed that the job of the EPO "was not to protect agency personnel, but to find and establish the truth." The OSC also emphasized that employees did not have to go through the supervisory chain of command to file complaints and could approach the EPO directly instead.[30]

Taylor's main initial task was to draft the permanent rules and regulations defining the PCEEO's procedures. The committee had earlier approved a preliminary set of operating rules and regulations that served as a basis for Taylor's work. After consulting with the committee and with interested outside parties, Taylor submitted a draft of the rules to the committee in June 1961. The committee published them in the *Federal Register* for public comment and held hearings.[31]

After considering the numerous comments received, the PCEEO made a few revisions, developed separate sets of rules governing contractors and federal employment, and published the whole package of proposed rules in the *Federal Register* on July 22, 1961. The rules, filling an eighteen-page booklet, spelled out the nuts and bolts of administering the order. The principal provision was a set of requirements to protect the rights of contract firms accused of violations. The proposal also contained wording that somewhat mitigated the language of the order setting forth sanctions and penalties.[32] Regarding the spirit of the rules, Taylor later wrote that "the underlying philosophy which guided their formulation was a belief that greater cooperation could be secured . . . through the development of procedures which would eliminate unnecessary paperwork, which would be simple to handle, and which would at the same time afford an opportunity for a fair and reasonable hearing to all who complain of discrimination."[33]

Despite Taylor's efforts to reduce any burdensome impact due to the rules or the executive order, Senator Lister Hill, Democrat from Alabama, sent a blistering letter to the committee protesting both the proposed rules and the very existence of the committee itself. Senator Hill charged that the PCEEO "represented both an unauthorized and unwise extension of Federal interference with and control of the Nation's private businesses in the name of so-called equal employment opportunity." Furthermore, he charged, E.O. 10925 and the rules were "an unconstitutional usurpation of the legislative powers of the Congress." He expressed special concern regarding the potential burden on business and the interference in what he viewed as the fundamental rights of persons to set up companies and conduct them as they see fit: "This personal freedom of contract is the basis of our free-enterprise system and the whole American concept of individual freedom. . . . The full power of inquiry and investigation authorized will vex and harass those doing business with the government to the point where orderly plant management and efficient production could well be impossible. . . . I strongly urge that . . . the Committee reject and defeat the proposed rules and regulations."[34]

Hill's blast seems to have had the opposite effect on the committee and the rules from what he intended. The PCEEO not only adopted their rules proposal virtually verbatim, but the committee actually strengthened them. Their most important change was to broaden enforcement to include the previously excluded category of contracts for standard commercial supplies worth at least $100,000. The PCEEO also decided to grant or withdraw exemptions for whole categories of contracts, instead of having to deal with each contract individually.[35]

Senator Hill's implicitly racist tirade washed over the PCEEO like water off the back of a duck. The question was whether his response was a precursor to virulent attacks of the kind that crippled and ultimately destroyed the FEPC. The PCEEO was even more far-reaching and had the power to have a much greater impact on discrimination in employment. This realization led to a second question: If the PCEEO was not crippled, to what extent would this carefully

BIRTH OF THE PRESIDENT'S COMMITTEE ON EQUAL EMPLOYMENT OPPORTUNITY

constructed and seemingly well-oiled machine live up to its potential? These questions must have been on the minds of everyone who wished it well as it prepared to enter the fray of race relations in the nation's workplaces.

CHAPTER 7

The Committee Gets Underway

As one of its initial tasks, the committee began the jobs of offsetting its critics and of motivating federal agencies and the nation on E.O. 10925. PCEEO staff—from Holleman and Feild on down—spoke frequently before labor, business, civil rights, social service, and student groups.[1] To indoctrinate agency personnel, the PCEEO held workshops and conferences both in Washington and around the country, and conducted training sessions with the cooperation of the Brookings Institution and other bodies. Holleman and Feild met with federal staff who dealt with contract compliance and, separately, with those who dealt with federal employment to discuss implementation of the order.[2]

The PCEEO held the first of several conferences with contract compliance officers on April 21, 1961. While the focus of public attention was on Washington, DC, with its heavy concentration of federally funded jobs, the PCEEO recognized that substantial federal employment also existed outside the Washington area. Accordingly, the PCEEO, with the aid of the Civil Service Commission, held a series of meetings with agency leaders in each of the fourteen federal regions, beginning in July 1961, to explain the goals of E.O. 10925 and to discuss how they could be realized.[3]

In May 1961, even before the PCEEO's operating rules were complete, it plunged into the meat of its mandate: compliance work.

Johnson and Goldberg initiated liaison efforts with the private sector, holding a group meeting on May 2 with heads of the fifty largest defense contractors. The next day they held a similar meeting with national labor leaders. President Kennedy addressed both meetings and won a pledge from each group to cooperate with the PCEEO. At the contractors' meeting Goldberg reassured them that "this Committee was not set up as a 'policing' agency. It will not have the staff or the facilities—even if we were so inclined—to handle such a task."[4]

The PCEEO worked with government contractors and the contracting agencies along two tracks: mandatory efforts specified in the order, such as filing and processing complaints and providing compliance reports, and voluntary efforts that operated outside the legal requirements of E.O. 10925. The complaint process was set in motion as soon as the order was issued. By the time the PCEEO held its first meeting, there was already a backlog of employee complaints that it worked hard to reduce. Over the course of the next year, it developed a policy of treating legitimate complaints as indications of the need for a company or union to change a policy or practice. A main goal of complaint investigations, whether by the agency or the PCEEO, was to evaluate—not just the specifics of the case—but the underlying circumstances in the workplace to find patterns of discrimination.

Resolution of these complaints led to placing blacks in numerous production and other well-paying jobs in oil refineries, metal fabrication plants, aircraft manufacturing plants, and numerous other industrial facilities.[5] By June 30, 1962, after just 15 months of operations, the PCEEO had received 819 complaints from contractor employees, equivalent to an annual rate almost 5 times that of the old PCGC, which received 1,042 complaints over its 7.5 year history. The PCEEO dismissed 105 complaints as being outside its jurisdiction and completed investigations of 291 of the remaining 714. That left action pending in 423 cases as of July 1, 1962. In 108 of the 291 completed cases, the PCEEO dismissed them as being without cause. Corrective action, such as promotions, reinstatements, or hiring of minorities, followed in 183 cases, resulting in a correction rate of 63 percent. By comparison, Eisenhower's PCGC achieved a correction rate of only 20 percent.[6]

Compliance reports were required of any employer with a government contract for $50,000 or more and with at least fifty workers. This requirement covered thirty-eight thousand employers with 15.5 million employees nationwide. The agencies that received the reports shared them with the PCEEO. These reports, in addition to indicating the extent of the discrimination problem in the individual firms, provided the PCEEO with detailed patterns of minority employment by areas and by industries. The reports also provided a measure of past equal opportunity efforts by the contractors and an indicator of where further effort was needed. The reporting system also gave employers a tool both to evaluate the effect of their personnel policies on minorities and also "to afford an opportunity for an affirmative approach" by all parties to identify and eliminate discriminatory practices.[7]

The PCEEO was determined to make sure that compliance reporting would not place an excessive burden on contractors. It consulted with representatives of business and organized labor in devising a filing process. The reporting rules, approved on December 1, 1961, specified that since many contractors held multiple contracts, each contractor could file one consolidated report for each operating location, regardless of the number of contracts involved. In the case of firms working under contracts at multiple sites, a separate report would have to be filed for each location. In the case of firms dealing with more than one federal agency, the agency holding the largest dollar volume of contracts with the contractor would be designated the Predominant Interest Agency (PIA). The PIA would be responsible for enforcing equal opportunity for all government work done by that contractor. This designation eliminated the possibility that one firm might have multiple agencies enforcing the order.[8]

In developing the reporting rules, the PCEEO tried to be "very mindful of the impact of the reporting system . . . [and] made every effort to minimize the reporting burden on Government contractors." Contractors were allowed to use a familiar, previously used reporting plan developed by the Social Security Administration. To make things easier for both the contractors and the agencies, the reports could be filed with the PCEEO, which would then process them and distribute them to the agencies.[9]

As an aid to contractors, the PCEEO produced a number of posters and other graphic materials. These included an "Equal Employment Opportunity" poster which contractors were required to display, a leaflet reprinting E.O. 10925, and several short films. In July 1961 the PCEEO developed an "Equal Employment Opportunity" emblem (oval shaped with the words *for all qualified applicants* inside) for employers to use in recruitment advertising to demonstrate that they supported the order.[10]

In early 1962 the PCEEO took important steps to enforce and expand the reporting system. For the first time, Executive Vice Chair Jerry Holleman ordered the withholding of federal contracts, penalizing two firms until they could provide compliance reports, as required under PCEEO rules. This decision came after complaints had been filed and the committee had found reasonable doubt that the firms were in compliance with the order. In addition, in consultation with the Associated General Contractors and the AFL-CIO's Building Trades Department, the PCEEO began developing a compliance reporting system for the construction industry, which it had initially exempted from filing reports.[11]

To ease the compliance burden on federal agencies, the PCEEO encouraged them to hold discussions with contractors on developing voluntary affirmative action programs. At the same time, an unexpected phenomenon began to appear. The PCEEO began to receive evidence of antidiscriminatory actions taken voluntarily by a number of companies around the country. Elimination of racial barriers at one plant sometimes spontaneously spread to other plants and then to companies within and even beyond the local area. The PCEEO's newsletter reported regularly on this "snowballing effect."[12]

Soon the PCEEO had collected and published anecdatal evidence of a "quiet change" taking place in employment policies. At many locations around the country, blacks were being hired in occupations and industries where they had been seriously under-represented, or even completely locked out. Examples of these jobs included production work in South Carolina textile plants, tobacco production in North Carolina, technical and clerical jobs in oil production facilities in the St. Louis area, and skilled electronics jobs in Dallas.[13]

"Plans for Progress" and other PCEEO Programs

A surprising early development involving voluntary compliance greatly expanded the scope of the PCEEO. It began on April 6, 1961, when Herbert Hill of the NAACP filed complaints with the PCEEO against Lockheed Corporation's Marietta, Georgia, aircraft plant on behalf of thirty-two employees. The manufacture of the air force's new C-141 jet transport had just begun there. At the time it was the largest military procurement ever conducted. The Marietta plant was highly segregated, and the small number of black employees was concentrated in low-level jobs. Skilled white workers were largely organized under an International Association of Machinists (IAM) local union. The white local union operated a separate, dual local for blacks only, in violation of the national IAM's equal treatment policy. The white local effectively barred blacks from most skilled jobs. The NAACP had complained to the PCGC about the Marietta plant, but got little response.[14]

When the NAACP filed its complaints, the PCEEO launched an investigation. John Feild flew to Lockheed headquarters in California to meet with company president Courtlandt Gross to try to obtain a compliance agreement. At the same time, the national IAM forced the two Marietta locals to integrate. Defense Secretary Robert McNamara backed Feild and the PCEEO.[15] Lockheed quickly removed "White" and "Colored" signs from rest rooms, drinking fountains, and cafeterias. On May 25, 1961, Gross and Vice President Johnson met ceremonially and formally agreed to what they called a "Plan for Progress" to eliminate discrimination in hiring and promotions. President Kennedy joined the ceremony. The plan was not a contract but a voluntary statement of Lockheed's intentions. Kennedy hailed it as a milestone in civil rights, asserting that it set a pattern for voluntary action in achieving equal employment opportunity.[16]

Kennedy proved to be prophetic. The seed sown by the Lockheed agreement landed on fertile ground. The May 1961 White House meetings with business and labor leaders helped make the climate more favorable to voluntary cooperation with the government. At the same time, committee members realized the potential of voluntary compliance efforts, like the Lockheed program, to allow the use of scarce PCEEO resources in other areas and free agencies to concentrate on compliance under the order.[17]

The PCEEO immediately institutionalized Plans for Progress (PFP) and soon won the participation of the bulk of the defense contracting sector. PFP was the most innovative effort of the PCEEO and became one of its principal means of implementing affirmative action, as it was understood in this period. PFP agreements were tailored to each specific firm, but all included the following elements:

a statement of the firm's policy in support of equal employment opportunity; a list of specific steps the firm planned to take to implement it; and specific types of assistance the PCEEO would provide.

PFP was never meant to be a compliance program. While it encouraged voluntary measures to eliminate segregation and discrimination, it did not attempt to identify specific discriminatory actions or measure progress by the degree that they were eliminated. Rather, progress was measured in terms of employment results. The question to be answered was: To what extent did the employer increase the numbers of minorities it employed and raise the income and skill levels of those already employed? While no racial goals or quotas were adopted, employers were expected to exercise affirmative action and go out of their way to recruit and promote blacks and other minorities (see related discussion of apprenticeship rule in chapter 9).[18]

The real sparkplug of PFP was prominent white Atlanta attorney Robert Troutman, who had been appointed to the PCEEO to add regional balance. Troutman was an ambitious entrepreneur, a southern racial progressive, and something of a self-promoter who cultivated ties with JFK. He saw the nascent program up close and immediately became its most enthusiastic supporter. He may have seen PFP as a way to gain prominence in the administration while doing good for the nation. He persuaded the PCEEO to set up a special committee to administer PFP and got himself appointed chair.[19] To help the program get started, he set up its offices next to his law firm in Atlanta and paid the startup expenses himself.[20]

With Troutman at the helm, PFP grew almost explosively. On July 12, 1961, the CEOs of eight major contractors signed PFP agreements at the White House, with Kennedy presiding. In the fall of 1961, Holleman, Feild, and Troutman met with representatives of dozens of major contractors to enlist their participation in PFP. On

November 30 twelve more CEOs signed on in a White House ceremony. This addition brought the total to twenty-one.[21]

Troutman soon began to seek the participation of companies that did not hold federal contracts and to enlist the voluntary participation of business leaders who were legally beyond the reach of E.O. 10925. On January 17, 1962, the PCEEO and a group of existing PFP participants held a seminar for officials from 150 large corporations from the nondefense sector to share ideas on equal employment opportunity and to talk about PFP.[22]

The roll of participants continued to grow. Before the summer of 1962, fifty-two agreements had been signed.[23] On June 22, 1962, the program reached its apogee. In a White House ceremony, the CEOs of thirty-three major corporations signed up, bringing the total to eighty-five. The June enrollment culminated the effort to expand beyond the defense industry. A large number of these firms were purely civilian and doing private sector work, such as communications, metal production, chemicals, and manufacturing. At the signing ceremony, President Kennedy reminded the assembled CEOs that just signing up was not the end, but the beginning of the process. "There is no use in . . . putting out an order," he told them, "and assuming that that is enough. There is no use in all of you doing it voluntarily, even though that is important symbolically, then letting it go at that."[24]

One of the PCEEO's major goals was to seek the cooperation of labor unions and other employee organizations in opening up opportunities for blacks and other disadvantaged groups. Union segregation and discrimination had helped perpetuate a situation whereby in the South, for example, 45 percent of nonwhite males were in laboring jobs, as opposed to only 13 percent of white males. Most national labor leaders actually did support E.O. 10925. George Meany wrote to Johnson and Goldberg the day after the issuance of the order, endorsing it as a way to "make good on the promise of equal opportunity for all Americans enshrined in our Constitution." Meany expressed particular pleasure with the enforcement sanctions and penalties provided by the order, and he promised full cooperation. He enclosed a statement on civil rights which the AFL-CIO had recently adopted. It termed the denial of equal rights "one of the nation's most grievous problems and certainly its No. 1 moral problem." The statement spelled out steps for organized labor to take in eliminating discrimination. It stressed that labor could make a major contribution by eliminating segregated locals and all other discrimination within its ranks, provided it received cooperation in turn from the federal government and also from employers.[25]

Among the national unions most supportive of the PCEEO was the United Steelworkers of America (USWA). Francis Shane, a member of its Committee on Civil Rights, reported to Goldberg in August 1961 that USWA president David J. McDonald had sent a directive on equal rights to all national and local officers. McDonald urged them to fully implement the union's statement of principles and observe the requirements of the order. He attached copies of both documents to the directive and required that they be posted publicly and read aloud to members and employees of the union. He also directed officers to investigate discrimination complaints and settle them at the local level, while providing copies of the case files to the national USWA office.[26]

In order to promote cooperation from organized labor, the PCEEO established a Trade Union Liaison Section in August 1961. This body worked both with local unions in connection with individual complaints and with national unions on elimination of discrimination within their ranks. It turned out that a large portion of the formal complaints under E.O. 10925 involved local or international unions, rather than employers. The PCEEO reported in 1962 that in every such instance the union in question cooperated fully in seeking a resolution.[27]

The PCEEO worked jointly with the Labor Department and national unions to open up equal opportunity in apprenticeship programs (see chapter 9 for more on apprenticeship). The Bricklayers Union joined with the Mason Contractors and the Associated General Contractors to voluntarily include an equal opportunity clause in both national and local apprenticeship standards. The International Brotherhood of Electrical Workers worked with the National Electrical Contractors Association to include similar clauses in their apprenticeship standards.[28]

The PCEEO developed an Educational and Community Relations (ECR) program to mobilize community organizations and leaders and supplement formal compliance efforts. As part of the ECR, the PCEEO met and worked with a wide range of groups, including civil rights organizations, civic organizations, trade associations, and religious and educational groups. It sought both to educate organizations and community leaders on the PCEEO mission and to help them, in turn, provide information on the program to their membership. As of May 1962 representatives of the PCEEO had made over 180 appearances before community groups.[29]

The PCEEO held several special conferences with social service organizations in 1962. Among the major events it convened was the Community Leaders Conference on Equal Employment Opportunity held in Washington, DC, with over six hundred representatives of government bodies, social service agencies, and civil rights groups. The PCEEO also met with members of the Conference of Commissions Against Discrimination (CCAD), an organization of state and local commissions enforcing antidiscrimination laws, to promote better cooperation between the federal and local EEO efforts. The CCAD reported that the PCEEO's program had produced "increased acceptance by employers and employees of the equal employment opportunity concept."[30]

The ECR program included several initiatives devoted to educating and training minority youths. The PCEEO's major effort in this area was a pilot project in Southern California designed to provide skilled workers to meet local defense industry needs. The project included training for anyone who had difficulty finding employment and was not specifically targeted toward blacks. It was conducted under a grant through the Manpower Development and Training Act of 1962 and administered by the Department of Labor. PCEEO staff studied the local employment and training situation and mobilized private organizations and government agencies. The bodies involved included public school systems, the Los Angeles Urban League, the Council of Mexican-American Affairs, religious groups, and twelve aircraft manufacturers in the area (all of them PFP participants).[31]

The PCEEO's tools for implementing E.O. 10925 within the federal government were analogous to those available in the contracting sector. Complaints were a major mechanism for initiating compliance review. The PCEEO rules defined the complaint system, streamlined processing, and gave the PCEEO the power to review and, if necessary, reverse complaints received by the agencies.[32]

To inform federal employees about the order and their rights under it, in July 1961 the PCEEO distributed a poster to be prominently displayed in all agencies. Titled "Your Right to Employment Opportunity," it focused on the right of employees or applicants to file complaints. The poster promised fair investigation and remediation and provided assurance that "there shall be no fear of reprisal on the part of the complainant."[33]

Months before the poster was distributed, discrimination complaints from federal employees and job applicants started pouring in. The Post Office Department and the military services generated the greatest number. By June 30, 1962, the PCEEO and the agencies had received 1,413 complaints. Investigations were completed in 908 of the cases and actions taken on 665 of those. Corrective actions followed in 231 cases, or 35 percent of the 665 cases. This statistic compared with only a 16 percent corrective rate under the PCGEP.[34]

By June 1962 the PCEEO had developed what Feild described as "a comprehensive affirmative action program" for federal employees. It included a series of conferences and training programs, meetings with a new subcabinet working group on civil rights, and regional meetings at which the PCEEO introduced its program to 1,300 federal staff at facilities employing half a million federal workers. In cooperation with the CSC, the PCEEO developed a series of training programs for those federal employees who were assigned to work full time on equal employment programs.[35]

Like government contractors, federal agencies were required to survey the racial make-up and structure of their workforces. No broad federal survey of this nature had ever been conducted before. The first survey provided a benchmark for future progress as measured by subsequent annual surveys. The PCEEO oversaw completion of the survey, which was largely accomplished by June 1961, and it identified areas where equal opportunity was problematic. The survey showed that 12.6 percent of all federal employees were African Americans—a very good participation rate. However, these workers were overwhelmingly concentrated in the lower-paying job series. There were only two blacks in the highest civil service grades of GS-17 and GS-18.[36]

In response to the survey, the CSC and several agencies immediately launched recruitment programs to hire minority workers at the skilled and professional levels, as the Labor Department had begun doing earlier. At Johnson's instigation, the PCEEO instructed agencies to determine whether any of their minority employees had been denied advancement because of race or other personal characteristics. The agencies were then to remedy the situation whenever possible. Due to such efforts, during fiscal year 1962 blacks constituted 18 percent of new federal hires, a proportion significantly above the 10 percent proportion of blacks in the general population. However, most were still hired in subprofessional positions. The low overall proportion of black federal employees improved only slightly in 1961.[37]

On April 3, 1962, Johnson—accompanied by Goldberg and Holleman—formally presented to President Kennedy the PCEEO's report on "The First Nine Months," covering the period through January 1962. Later that day, Johnson and Goldberg held a joint press conference to discuss the report and highlight the committee's progress. In a press release, Johnson asserted that the PCEEO had made substantial progress in equal employment opportunity and had laid the groundwork for future advances. He cited that it had received almost as many discrimination complaints in its first year as the two Eisenhower committees had received together in six years. Goldberg argued that the PCEEO had "cut a big hole" in the problem and described the first year as one of "tooling up." The PCEEO, he asserted, "has scored . . . tremendous victories against bigotry and discrimination."[38]

Criticism and Response

Despite the rosy image of progress that Johnson and Goldberg portrayed, the PCEEO was drawing a lot of criticism. Unlike the case with the FEPC, a program hated by race conservatives, the PCEEO's toughest critics were its friends in the black community. They were disappointed that the PCEEO had not made more progress. C. Sumner Stone, editor of the *Washington Afro-American*, wrote a polite but highly critical letter to Johnson. "Plans for Progress" received the brunt of Stone's criticism, but other aspects of the PCEEO were not unscathed. In his March 9, 1962, letter he wrote:

> Because of this newspaper's deep affection and respect for you, we are taking the liberty of raising a problem which has been disturbing America's black community . . . These are some of the shortcomings of the Committee as we view it:
>
> No effective steps have yet been devised or even contemplated which would seek to have labor put its racial house in order. The Plans for Progress effort has been more of a publicity sham than an accomplishment deserving of further continuation. Under Robert Troutman, the emphasis has been on voluntary compliance with a total absence of compulsion. Voluntary efforts should be explored, but not to the exclusion of the enforcement's salutary effect. . . . Affirmative action is needed, not paper-made programs tailored to the whims of one man. The hard core of racial segregation and ongoing discrimination in the Federal government has not been attacked. We fail to understand how the President's Committee can expect private industry to move faster than the Federal government in wiping out racial discrimination against employees. There has been a criminal lack of executive leadership in the President's Committee. To put it more bluntly, there is no leadership. There is no direction. There is no imaginative approaches [sic] in attempting to solve the problems. In short, the . . . executive leadership has a lousy corporate image. In the black community, it doesn't even exist. . . . It infuriates us that competent and outstanding personnel on the Committee become bogged down in the administrative mediocrity and colorless inefficiency of the Committee's major executive [i.e., Jerry Holleman].

> To restore public confidence in the Committee, we submit that changes in its executive personnel are necessary . . . While the President's appointments and your own personal actions and convictions have decidedly altered the pace at which this country was proceeding . . . we still have not kept pace, we believe, with the tempo and the demands of the 'New Frontier'. . . . I do hope you will not regard me as importunate in writing to you, but it is only this newspaper's genuine respect and my personal affection for you which has permitted this temarious gesture.[39]

About a month later, Herbert Hill of the NAACP sent Goldberg an even harsher evaluation. Hill conceded that E.O. 10925 was "a vast improvement in policy," but he argued that:

> Policy is not practice. How seriously the provisions of the Executive Order will be applied is not yet apparent. What *is* apparent is the presence of dangerously nullifying tendencies in the Administration's performance to date. . . . These tendencies relate to one question: whether fear of conservative Southern forces in Congress will be allowed to strangle the antidiscrimination employment program in its infancy.

Hill gave the PCEEO credit for important accomplishments—using limited resources—in processing complaints, establishing a reporting system, and reducing discrimination in federal employment. In his opinion, "The present Administration has made much of the broad mandate and strengthened powers of its committee. Yet it has provided not a single additional man nor a single additional dollar with which to do the job."

Hill saved his strongest words for Robert Troutman and the Plans for Progress program that Troutman headed. Hill charged that PFP "yield[s] high returns in press notices and only superficial and token results in new job opportunities. . . . Instead, [PFP] divert[s] attention and energy from the systematic, across-the-board job which it is Government's responsibility to carry out." He charged that participants treat PFP like a grant of immunity from compliance. Hill argued that Kennedy and the administration "must decide, quite simply, whether the Executive Order on equal employment means what it says. And if it does, they must decide to stand up firmly against . . . those who are opposed to fair employment practices." Roy Wilkins felt Hill went too far, but Martin Luther King Jr. supported Hill.[40]

Hill and Stone had allies within the PCEEO who were also critical of PFP and Robert Troutman. Compliance-oriented equal rights professionals like John Feild felt that Troutman overemphasized voluntarism and did not recognize the importance of enforcement. Johnson had been following the internal debates and external critique. After a December 1961 meeting of the PCEEO, Johnson appointed a special subcommittee consisting of himself, Goldberg, and Robert Kennedy to monitor PFP. In February 1962 the PCEEO leadership met with Wilkins and Hill to hear their views on PFP firsthand. Johnson's group also hoped to win their backing for the PCEEO's other programs. Wilkins professed support, but Hill refused to ease up on his opposition.

Johnson responded in April by commissioning an independent study of the PCEEO as a whole, including recommendations for change. To head the effort, he selected Theodore Kheel, a prominent labor mediator and one of the advisers in the drafting of E.O. 10925. The report was due July 1, 1962.[41]

By June the controversy had received prominent attention in the press. In an attempt to defuse the publicity until Kheel's report was ready, Johnson wrote a letter to the *New York Times* that it published on June 20, 1962.[42] In the letter, he emphasized without specifically mentioning PFP, that compliance and voluntarism were complementary (not competing) aspects of the PCEEO. Downplaying the disagreements, he argued that "controversy, like beauty, is in the eye of the beholder." He claimed that the voluntary program enabled the PCEEO to economically expand the scope of its actions. He stressed that voluntary compliance did not in any way relieve employers of the duty to comply with E.O. 10925.

Robert Troutman now recognized that he had become a serious public relations liability for the PCEEO and that significant restrictions on PFP were likely to come. Accordingly, he announced his resignation from the PCEEO on June 30, 1962, just before what became known as the *Kheel Report* was due out. Troutman's resignation was effective at the end of August. His announcement, however, was preceded on May 11 by Jerry Holleman's abrupt resignation from his positions at both the PCEEO and the Labor Department. Holleman had come under fire from civil rights leaders, but he was actually forced to leave the government because of his involvement in a Washington corruption scandal involving Billie Sol Estes, a Texas businessman and Johnson associate.[43]

Ironically, on the day of his resignation, Holleman initiated a first step toward reform of PFP. In a new guidance memo to all federal agency heads dated May 11, 1962, he stressed that PFP was trying only to supplement, not supplant, compliance with E.O. 10925. PFP was designed, he wrote, "primarily for those companies that wish to develop a program which will be perhaps even more positive than that required by the Order."[44] Holleman's memo continued the policy of exempting contractors from filing compliance reports with the PCEEO. However, they were now to file a compliance report with their contracting agency. The memo also required all agencies to directly monitor their contractors who participated in PFP. This memo, plus the resignations of Troutman and Holleman, helped set the stage for the *Kheel Report* and for reforms, not only in PFP, but in the PCEEO itself.

CHAPTER 8

The *Kheel Report* and Beyond

———◆———

In July 1962 Ted Kheel submitted his special report on the PCEEO. In preparing the report, Kheel had consulted not only with the committee but also with representatives from labor, industry, and the civil rights movement. After initially examining the performance of the PCEEO as a whole, he decided to limit the scope of his investigation and report to federal contractors only. In his judgment, the government was making progress in the arena of federal employment, and he saw no major problems that required attention. While he devoted a substantial portion of the report to the historical background of the PCEEO, his main purpose was to identify problems and recommend improvements in the area of federal contract work.[1]

First of all, Kheel praised the mission of the PCEEO, asserting that "the potential of significant accomplishment is almost without limits." He believed that E.O. 10925 depended primarily on voluntary compliance to achieve that potential. He credited employers with providing significant cooperation so far, but a higher level of commitment was necessary. In order to provide an incentive for cooperation, he argued, the PCEEO needed to make it clear to employers that it was fully prepared to use the sanctions of E.O. 10925. This is exactly what critics within and outside of the committee had been calling for. Accordingly he urged the PCEEO to use "all procedures and approaches available to it."

Turning his attention to Plans for Progress (PFP), the preeminent voluntaristic effort under E.O. 10925, Kheel was sympathetic to the embattled program. "Under the imaginative and energetic leadership of Robert Troutman," he wrote, "this type of activity has been placed on a more systematic basis." Kheel approved of the policy requiring all PFP participants to also comply fully with E.O. 10925. He praised Troutman for extending the program to employers who did not hold government contracts and so were under no legal obligation to comply with the order. Kheel went so far as to argue that the PFP "has proved in some ways to be [the PCEEO's] most notable" program.

However, improvements were badly needed, both to make the PFP more effective, and also to assure that it would be more acceptable to the civil rights community. To those ends, Troutman himself had recommended that the program be separated from the PCEEO and operated as an independent, private effort. Kheel, however, rejected that approach: "All of the branches of the Committee must be unified so that the limited resources of the Committee can best be utilized." He found that the performance of PFP participants often varied greatly from one division of a firm to another. This inconsistency was partially the result of a lack of adequate follow-through by PFP staff with new participants. Another problem was that the PCEEO failed to provide promised assistance, such as helping to locate qualified minority job applicants or working with the contracting agency to help a firm carry out its plan. He warned that unless companies received periodic follow-up visits from the PCEEO, "the initial impetus supplied by the Plan is bound to diminish and then disappear."

Looking at the PCEEO as a whole, Kheel had a number of thoughts and suggestions. Somewhat surprisingly, he did not call for any increase in funding over the existing level. Accepting budgetary realities, he recommended that the PCEEO maximize its available resources by concentrating on the elimination of patterns of discrimination that affected large numbers of employees, rather than resolving each individual complaint as it came along. He pointed to the fact that PCEEO staff were dispersed around several locations in Washington and suggested that PCEEO members meet more often. To compensate for the lack of paid staff, he suggested that appointed members take on more speaking engagements for the PCEEO and assist the staff more actively. Another shortcoming he found was the PCEEO's lack of a strong public relations program. He suggested that it implement the hitherto neglected "certificates of merit" program, broadcast the names of major civil rights offenders, and hold well-publicized public hearings.

Kheel disapproved of the fact that the executive vice chairman, the position with specific responsibility for overall administration of the PCEEO, was not a full-time position and lacked the authority to do the job effectively. The first incumbent, Jerry Holleman, had retained his demanding position as an assistant secretary of labor. Kheel called for the position to be reclassified as full time, and he also suggested that it include direct supervision of the PFP.

Shortly after Kheel submitted his report, Robert Troutman (before leaving his post) provided a report of his own on the goals and accomplishments of PFP to President Kennedy and Vice President Johnson.[2] Troutman's initial goal, he wrote, was to invite 150 major contract employers to participate in the voluntary program and then obtain PFP agreements from 100 of them. Though 150 employers were invited, only 85 had actually signed on to the program. Troutman argued that, since another 25 were working on plans and were expected to sign them shortly, the goal of 100 was met and exceeded. He believed that the number of enrollees would have been higher, but several firms expressed reluctance to become involved because of criticisms of the program and worries that participation would offend the black community.

Troutman documented, as best he could, the costs and benefits of the program. He measured hiring using statistics from 38 PFP participants. First he calculated the estimated number of African Americans that they would have hired, which came to 1,200 positions. He then looked at actual hires and found that 4,900 African Americans had been hired, more than four times the expected number. According to Troutman, the salaries of the additional 3,700 African American hires amounted to $20 million.

On the cost side, Troutman kept complete records of the federal budget for the program. The total expenditures were $75,000, of which he had personally advanced $50,000 from his own funds. The $20 million additional income blacks earned in the 38 firms looked very impressive against a public expenditure of only $25,000, a total that covered the entire PFP. However, much of the cost of hiring outreach was borne by the employers, who, Troutman pointedly noted, had received little assistance from the black community in locating qualified black applicants. The cost was undoubtedly significant, but it was impossible to calculate.

Troutman was convinced that full employment was the key to the problems of the black population and that PFP was a valid way to accomplish this goal. He won a measure of vindication in his waning days with the PCEEO: in a meeting, Roger Wilkins indicated that he was impressed with gains in black employment among plan participants.[3] Concluding his report, Troutman mused:

> The situation of our black population, once the life and concern of but one section, now involves the nation. The difficulties are far beyond the knowledge or understanding of almost everyone. Varied and deeply rooted, these problems have no single, simple or quick answer . . . [T]here must be unity of . . . those who seek solutions. Neither lasting answers nor lasting progress can come

from divided thought. The problem is now one; the nation's desire in meeting it should also be.[4]

Troutman's report and resignation, combined with the *Kheel Report*, defused much of the critical pressure on both the PCEEO and PFP. It also provided useful evaluations and benchmarks of accomplishments and helped move the PCEEO in a less controversial direction. The *Kheel Report* had received so much publicity that Prentice-Hall published the full text.[5]

Vice President Johnson immediately implemented Kheel's recommendation to make the executive vice chairman job a full-time position. In September 1962 he promoted Hobart Taylor Jr. to the post. Congressman Adam Clayton Powell (Democrat–New York) and Roy Wilkins endorsed the move. The position of director of PFP was downgraded, reflecting both a subordination of the program to the PCEEO's control and a stronger emphasis on enforcement. PFP, however, still retained strong support from President Kennedy, who termed its results *impressive* and dismissed much of the criticism. He expressed concern that participating companies might drop out and embarrass the administration if the program was deemphasized or weakened.[6]

Kennedy's support, the *Kheel Report*, and the departure of Robert Troutman could not, however, inoculate PFP or the PCEEO from further criticism. Troutman's final report provoked a stinging "Special report" from the Southern Regional Council (SRC), a civil rights organization of black and progressive white Southerners. It was released very shortly after nineteen more firms signed PFP agreements in the White House on January 17, 1963.[7] Dubious of PFP's voluntaristic approach and Troutman's claims of significant employment gains for blacks, the SRC prepared its own evaluation.

Noting that Troutman's numbers were aggregated with no regional breakdowns, the SRC focused on the extent of job gains in the South, where discrimination was still generally legal. The SRC researchers undertook a survey of PFP participants in the Atlanta area, focusing on twenty-four firms with a total of twenty-six thousand employees. The SRC's findings were based mainly on interviews with executives from the twenty-four companies. Three firms—Lockheed, General Motors, and Ford—together employed twenty-three thousand workers, many of them in manufacturing. The remaining three thousand workers were mostly employed by service, sales, and distribution companies.

The SRC study found that the hiring results were "unimpressive." It charged that, "except for a handful of the companies, the Plans for Progress were, for the regional office in Atlanta, largely meaningless." Of the twenty-four firms, only seven "produced evidence of affirmative compliance with their pledges," and only three of these showed "a vigorous desire to create job opportunities." The attitude of the other seventeen firms toward their own PFP programs ranged "from ignorance to indifference." One of the key SRC findings was that blacks were generally not considered suitable for customer-contact jobs such as sales and service, largely because the companies feared that white customers would not accept them. Some firms hired blacks as token affirmative action gestures and placed them in janitorial jobs.

The SRC report drew considerable news media attention. An article in *Newsweek* titled "Progress or Publicity?" included numerous quotations casting a poor light on the PCEEO and on PFP efforts in the Atlanta area.[8] Both the report and the article caused great concern in the White House. Kennedy ordered reports from the National Aeronautics and Space Administration, the Defense Department, and the General Services Administration on their experience with companies surveyed in the SRC report.[9]

Kennedy also asked the PCEEO to analyze the SRC report.[10] Hobart Taylor put John Feild in charge of the effort and sent PCEEO staff to Atlanta to gather data. Taylor believed firmly that the PCEEO had, if anything, enforced the order more stringently with PFP participants than with nonparticipating contractors. However, when the investigation was completed, Feild reported that it "confirms the findings" of the SRC. The investigators found that the PCEEO had received complaints against nineteen of the twenty-four firms studied by the SRC, although only three complaints involved operations in that region. Furthermore, one-third of all the complaints the PCEEO received involved PFP firms.

Feild made several recommendations to deal with the problems highlighted in the SRC report. First, he urged that PFP discontinue use of its own reporting form and suggested that participants instead use the standard form completed by all other federal contractors. Second, he urged discontinuation of further efforts to sign up new companies with PFP until the performance of all current participants had been adequately evaluated. Third, he called for the abolition of the separate PFP staff in Atlanta (set up and funded personally by Troutman) and the consolidation of all PFP operations in Washington. Feild wrote: "I am confident that if these recommendations are followed, the Plans for Progress program can make a significant contribution."

After seeing Feild's report, Johnson convened a "Vice President's Study Group" consisting of the leadership of the PCEEO and other top federal officials concerned with civil rights. The group endorsed Feild's approach and directed that "the Plans for Progress program should be brought along rather slowly, and that our recent gains [should] be consolidated before new companies are taken in . . . It was also decided to take in any companies with whom we are currently carrying on negotiations."[11] After the ceremonial induction of nineteen more firms into PFP at the White House in January 1963, over the next six months only three more entities signed agreements: American Motors, Atlantic and Pacific Tea Co., and Wayne State University (the first university to participate). Furthermore, there were no more signing ceremonies in the White House until after President Kennedy's death in November 1963. Despite efforts to assuage PFP's critics, the administration had temporarily withdrawn one of its most publicized civil rights programs from view.[12]

To develop further ideas for reform, Taylor set up a special advisory committee of industrialists headed by G. William Miller, president of Textron Corp. The Miller committee proposed the establishment of a permanent Advisory Council on Plans for Progress, suggested a list of members, and developed a set of goals for the new body. The PCEEO endorsed the idea and established the Advisory Council in August, appointing nineteen prominent industrialists, with Miller serving as chair. The president, the secretary of labor, and the executive director of the PCEEO served ex officio.[13]

The Advisory Council promoted and oversaw the expansion of the redirected PFP, gave it greater credibility with critics, and restored a measure of public support. Membership in PFP doubled by May 1964, from about one hundred to over two hundred companies employing seven million workers. The council held several meetings with PFP companies and President Johnson at the White House. Formal induction ceremonies for new PFP signers were resumed. At a January 16, 1964, White House meeting, President Johnson claimed strong job gains by PFP companies. As a contrast to the fact that 14.7 percent of new hires at participating firms were nonwhites, he borrowed a page from Troutman and compared that percentage to an "expectable" rate of only 5 percent in nonwhite hires.[14]

At a meeting of the PCEEO in May 1964, Secretary of Labor Wirtz praised the Advisory Council and PFP, asserting that there was "more being done on this front than almost any other." In later years, Wirtz emphasized the more intangible results of PFP. He remarked in an oral history interview that "I think there was an attitudinal change during that period which probably had a significant effect" and helped lay the foundations for the Civil Rights Act of 1964.[15] PFP had redeemed itself in Wirtz's eyes. In 1977 historian Carl Brauer concluded that:

> The Plans for Progress were worthwhile. They did . . . establish a valuable yardstick. They resulted in greater numbers of blacks being hired. In addition, unnoted in 1962, they also softened the attitude of big business toward giving the federal government a statutory role in the area of hiring. In 1964 large government contractors readily acceded to equal employment legislation, but if they had not had the Plans experience, they might well have constituted a powerful opposition to this concept.[16]

A Union Counterpart

Paralleling the business sector's Plans for Progress, but developing more slowly, was the PCEEO's "Union Program for Fair Practices" (UPFP). It had its roots in E.O. 10925's inclusion of unions and in President Kennedy's May 1961 meeting with union leaders at the White House, held the day after his meeting with business leaders. Over the summer and fall of 1961, a group of union leaders and the PCEEO took preliminary steps toward a program of voluntary compliance plans for organized labor that would specify what organized labor should do to ensure equal opportunity in all union activities and how the PCEEO and government agencies could assist.[17]

Unfortunately, the AFL-CIO was still very divided on racial matters. In general, the unions from the former CIO supported equal opportunity and inclusion of blacks as members. Many unions from the old AFL maintained racial restrictions on membership and employment. Because of this division, the PCEEO was forced to delay implementation of the UPFP until it could win broader support from organized labor.

This change took time. At the PCEEO's February 15, 1962, meeting, Jerry Holleman (at that time still serving as executive vice chair) noted that it was still too soon to launch the program. Acknowledging the readiness of individual unions to adopt voluntary plans, he emphasized that "it was important that this be attacked on a broad basis . . . and that it not be a single shot approach."[18]

Several unions had already jumped the gun and started their own plans. The International Brotherhood of Electrical Workers and the United Steel Workers of America instituted fair employment plans; and the United Auto Workers, the International Union of Electrical Workers, and the United Shipbuilding Workers of America had plans in the works. The Civil Rights Department of the AFL-CIO, in cooperation with the PCEEO, assisted individual unions in this effort.

The PCEEO finally won the support of a critical mass of unions, and the UPFP kicked off at a White House ceremony on November 15, 1962. The leadership of the AFL-CIO—115 affiliated national and international unions and 340 affiliated local unions, representing 11 million union members—signed statements promising to cooperate with the PCEEO in implementing E.O. 10925. The agreements provided that the unions would apply equal treatment policies in all employment, not just government contract work; accept into membership and treat equally all applicants without regard to race; work to eliminate segregation in local unions; and attempt to include equal treatment clauses in collective bargaining agreements. The PCEEO promised to assist unions in living up to their agreements.[19]

The labor movement participated extensively at all levels in the UPFP. George Meany appointed a committee to work with the various departments of the AFL-CIO and the local labor councils to develop antidiscrimination strategies. He established biracial committees in more than eight hundred Central Labor Councils. Further, he initiated regular consultations by the Civil Rights Department with the PCEEO and the international unions to identify problems that needed special attention. The Civil Rights Department also regularly informed the PCEEO about voluntary actions unions were taking and, on the PCEEO's behalf, investigated complaints filed by affiliated unions. By March 1963 eighty participating unions had appointed a full-time representative responsible for implementing their UPFP. The PCEEO and the AFL-CIO provided support and guidance for these representatives.[20]

A number of unions and councils in all parts of the country, representing a wide range of industries, continued to voluntarily promote equal opportunity. The USWA eliminated discrimination in Birmingham, Alabama, steel mills, and the UAW corrected inequities in an auto plant in the South where complaints had been lodged with the PCEEO. On the West Coast, the Marine and Shipbuilding Workers worked with the PCEEO to eliminate segregation in its locals.[21]

While not as troubled and controversial as PFP, the UPFP was not without its problems. In 1963 the PCEEO sent questionnaires to all international unions and their locals to complete voluntarily; the questionnaires surveyed the racial makeup of their membership and any progress made under the UPFP. While many unions readily complied, others objected to questions on racial composition as intrusive, or found it onerous to compile data because of their own incomplete records. David Dubinsky, president of the International Ladies' Garment Workers Union and a pioneer in civil rights, told the PCEEO privately that he did not plan to distribute the questionnaires in his union due to objections from the locals. By November 1963 only one-third of all union locals participating in UPFP had completed and submitted the questionnaires, which had been due at the PCEEO by August 31.[22]

Although the PCEEO sought in principle to include as many unions as possible in UPFP, one union was not welcome: the unaffiliated International Brotherhood of Teamsters. Both the union and its president, James R. Hoffa, were under investigation by Attorney General Robert Kennedy and the Justice Department for alleged corruption. In a series of letters to the PCEEO, Johnson, and Kennedy in 1963, Hoffa repeatedly offered to cooperate with the PCEEO and asked to join the UPFP. However, he received only neutral responses, and the teamsters remained excluded.[23]

Despite these glitches, the UPFP mobilized much of organized labor to treat black members equally and improve their job opportunities. It played a key role in launching unions in the papermaking industry, a southern-based sector that employed large numbers of blacks, on a course to eliminate segregated locals.[24] By March 1963 seven more international unions had joined the UPFP, bringing the total to 122. Later that year Kennedy set a broader challenge to labor unions. In a meeting on civil rights with a large group of labor leaders on June 13, 1963, and in the aftermath of antiblack violence in Birmingham, Kennedy called on these leaders to work more actively on the economic front to help reduce the disproportionately high unemployment rates blacks faced.[25]

The UPFP survived and continued to develop after Kennedy's assassination in November 1963. President Johnson established a Labor Advisory Council (LAC) to the PCEEO, composed of sixteen AFL-CIO union presidents. He introduced the LAC to the public at a White House ceremony on March 16, 1964. Its purpose was both to assist union participation in the UPFP and also to facilitate communication between the leadership of organized labor and the PCEEO. Wirtz believed that direct access to top union officials would be a big help.²⁶ Echoing Kennedy's exhortation to labor leaders from the previous June, President Johnson told the sixteen union presidents, "We will never have the kind of fair employment we are talking about until we have full employment. Our goal is not to reach equality in jobs by spreading unemployment, or to replace men who are now working with those who are unemployed."²⁷

Other PCEEO Activities

As it continued its mission before being overshadowed by the Civil Rights Act in July 1964, the PCEEO, in the words of historian Hugh Graham, "moved with an authority and effectiveness that considerably exceeded the record of all its predecessors."²⁸ By April 1964 some 2,444 complaints had been filed against government contractors. Of the 1,676 that were adjudicated, the employers had taken corrective action in 65.5 percent of the cases. The number of complaints filed per month had declined by 1964, and in Hobart Taylor's view, this decline was a positive development. He believed it was a result of increased voluntary compliance, which often averted the need to file a complaint.²⁹

After 1962, as indicated earlier, the PCEEO used the complaint resolution process to seek broader remedies where patterns of discrimination were revealed. The results were summarized in a special study that PCEEO staff conducted of complaints against contractors in seven industry groups: petro-chemicals, textiles, steel, tobacco, aircraft, shipbuilding, and food processing. About two-thirds of all complaints filed under E.O. 10925 in these industries involved promotions and transfers, with initial hiring and discharges accounting for the rest. As part of the resolution of specific complaints in the seven industries, contracting agencies often succeeded in identifying and eliminating, or weakening, discriminatory patterns in the workplace.

Complaints resulted in nationwide corrective actions by several steel manufacturers. For example, blacks mired in low-level jobs in a Texas steel mill also had to endure segregated restrooms and other facilities. As a result of a complaint, several blacks were transferred into a line of seniority (previously for whites only) that made them eligible for higher-level jobs. The company promised to promote, transfer, and upgrade without regard to race, and opened bathrooms and other facilities to all employees. Similar breakthroughs in discriminatory patterns were reported in other industries covered in the special study.[30]

By 1963 E.O. 10925 had resulted in measurable employment gains by African Americans in white-collar contract work. This was an area in which blacks had long been underrepresented because of both racial discrimination and inadequate education. Unlike the stagnant blue-collar labor market, white-collar work was a rapidly growing sector that offered blacks the possibility of significant economic and social gain. Among the 4,000 federal contractors who filed compliance reports in both 1962 and 1963, total white-collar employment increased by 17,270 positions, of which 1,830 (or 10.65 percent) were African Americans. Since they held only 1.14 percent of existing white-collar jobs in 1962, the new black hires equaled almost ten times the expected number. The percentage also approximated the 10 percent black proportion of the general population.[31]

In federal employment, the PCEEO received 2,005 complaints of discrimination by March 1963. Of that total, 1,169 cases were settled, with corrective action taken in 423 (36.1 percent) of the cases. This figure matched the trend for the first year of the PCEEO enforcement in the federal government. The number of complaints per year was significantly higher than the annual number under the PCGEP during the Eisenhower administration. This statistic would seem to indicate much greater interest in eliminating discrimination in this period.

Clearer results can be seen in the employment picture for African Americans in the federal government during the early 1960s. A total of 101,448 new employees were added to federal payrolls from 1961 to 1963. Of those, 19,273 were black, constituting 19 percent of all new hires. This number was considered a credible indicator of significant progress.[32]

In response to Johnson's request to federal agencies in 1961 to identify and upgrade underutilized employees, a number of agencies took steps to make better use of their whole workforces, particularly African Americans. While the populations of employees identified were not large in most cases, the Departments of Defense, Commerce, Labor, and others promoted or provided training for hundreds of low GS-grade employees, a large portion of them blacks.[33] Their efforts were bolstered when the PCEEO directed the Civil Service Commission to see that all federal employees had equal access to job training.[34] Government-wide increases were reported in hiring and promotion of blacks in professional, managerial, and policy-making positions. African Americans were still woefully underrepresented in high level federal jobs, but the problem had become much less one of outright discrimination, and more one of finding applicants who had had the training and education necessary to qualify for the work.

After the 1963 violence in Birmingham, the PCEEO faced new challenges and pressures. At its May 29th meeting, Secretary Wirtz noted that "under the circumstances which obtain in the country today, [this meeting] is an opportunity that we have to do whatever we can to meet what is surely the most serious domestic problem facing us." Attorney General Robert Kennedy, the lead official on civil rights in the administration, was a member of the PCEEO but until then had not been very active in its operations. After the riots in Birmingham, however, he began to play a more active role and demand more action of the committee. At the May 29th meeting, he reproached the leadership for failing to forcefully promote compliance. He pointed out that the government's own statistics on Birmingham, hastily compiled after the riots, showed that most government offices there were segregated. Worse yet, of the two thousand nonmenial federal jobs located in Birmingham, fewer than 1 percent went to blacks, who constituted 37 percent of the local population. Kennedy pointed out that this discrepancy would make it difficult for the government to require private employers to comply with E.O. 10925.[35]

At Robert Kennedy's request, the PCEEO prepared a detailed report on federal contractors in Birmingham, with recommendations for assuring more equal treatment and better compliance with the order. The PCEEO and several federal agencies also reported on black employment by the government in Birmingham. Based on this local effort, the PCEEO developed a nationwide program to assist federal employers and investigate federal employment patterns. As PCEEO member John Macy stated: "We have an obligation to see to it that Federal managers become participants in community action to create an effort for improvement."[36]

The events in Birmingham also prompted a long-contemplated expansion of the PCEEO's jurisdiction. As early as April 1961 the president's subcabinet group on civil rights had agreed that the PCEEO's authority over federal construction should be extended to the considerable work that was funded by federal grants. By the time the Justice Department had drafted a proposed executive order to this effect in December 1961, the White House had decided not to issue it because it was dealing with stiff resistance from Southern Democrats to its broader legislative program of economic recovery.[37] After Birmingham, however, the urgency of civil rights action overcame the White House's deference to Southern Democrats. On

June 22, 1963, Kennedy issued E.O. 11114 to implement the proposal. In an attempt to minimize publicity, and thereby controversy, the White House issued it on a Saturday without a statement or public ceremony.

The inclusion of grant-funded construction under E.O. 11114 allowed a fourfold increase in the coverage of workers and workplaces in the construction industry.[38] In addition, this order contained another significant broadening of coverage. Buried in it were amendments to E.O. 10925 intended "to clarify the authority of the [PCEEO]." Included was wording on its jurisdiction over a contracting firm's facilities that were physically separated from areas where work was done on federal contracts. After stating in Section 202 that the PCEEO had the authority to exempt the separate facilities from compliance, E.O. 11114 required that "in the absence of such an exemption all such facilities shall be covered by the provisions of this order [E.O. 10925]."[39] This statement meant that, theoretically, every federal contractor—unless specifically granted an exemption—was now required to comply with E.O. 10925 in all of their facilities and operations, not just those where contract work was performed. The practical impact of Section 202 was limited, however, because of the permanent limitations placed on the resources of the PCEEO by the Russell amendment, which was still in effect. However, an important precedent had been set for greater breadth in the federal effort to provide equal opportunity on the job.

E.O. 11114 was the last significant expansion in the scope of the PCEEO. After enactment of the Civil Rights Act of 1964 and the issuance of E.O. 11246 in 1965 governing government contractors, the PCEEO was essentially superfluous and was abolished in 1965. Addressing the PCEEO in May 1964 at its last meeting before enactment of the Civil Rights Act, President Johnson said that serving as its chairman was "as important a job as I have ever been associated with." He asserted that in the future "they will point to . . . this committee and say this is when some of the breakthroughs began." Wirtz seemed less sanguine in an assessment of the PCEEO's achievements forty years later, bluntly asserting: "I don't think it amounted to a great deal." He corrected himself, however, adding that he believed it achieved important intangible results. It contributed to "a considerable attitudinal change" on the part of employers and unions and helped prepare the way for the Civil Rights Act.[40]

Like similar presidential committees from the 1940s and 1950s, the PCEEO was severely constrained by its limited powers and resources. Nevertheless, it marked the strongest effort of its kind so far and no doubt accomplished more, both tangibly and intangibly, than its predecessors. Ironically, the African American community, which had become more activist and more demanding of government in the early 1960s, was more dissatisfied with government fair employment efforts than ever. It seemed clear by 1964 that presidential action via executive orders had reached the limits of its effectiveness and its ability to satisfy the needs and aspirations of the African American community.

CHAPTER 9

The Department of Labor in the Kennedy–Johnson Era

While the PCEEO was maximizing the potential of presidential action to promote fair employment via executive order, the Department of Labor was treading a different path toward the same goal. The department was under the leadership of Arthur Goldberg until September 1962, when he resigned to accept an appointment to the US Supreme Court. Willard Wirtz, then under secretary, succeeded Goldberg and served through the end of the Johnson administration.

Early in his term, Goldberg resolved a nettlesome and longstanding issue that had dogged the USES and annoyed the African American community since the 1930s: the practice of accepting and honoring employer requests for white-only job applicants. The USES, as allowed under the Wagner-Peyser Act, had previously adopted standards prohibiting employment offices from accepting discriminatory job orders or from making discriminatory referrals to fill them. For the most part, it had treated the rules as only advisory. However, beginning in 1961 the USES categorically banned all employment offices from accepting any more discriminatory job orders.[1]

In 1962 the very reverse of that issue came up. A number of government contractors, in an effort to comply with the PCEEO, started submitting job orders requesting black-only job candidates.

The USES felt it had no choice but to treat such requests the same as those based on racial prejudice, and it refused to accept them. However, after consultations with the PCEEO, the USES started to work with federal contractors to allow local employment offices to honor requests for minority applicants from selected employers.[2]

The USES initiated a well-meaning but somewhat counterproductive policy in 1961. In an effort to be completely race-neutral, it asked that government employment offices stop recording the race, creed, color, or national origin of job applicants. By early 1962 mention of race in applicant files and forms had been virtually eliminated. In May 1962 the policy was made permanent through publication in the *Federal Register.* The unfortunate result was that much valuable data on race and employment was lost, making compliance very hard to measure.[3]

The USES continued efforts begun in the Eisenhower administration to desegregate employment offices in the South. Employment offices in Oklahoma and Tennessee were quickly integrated. In Atlanta, employment offices began administering typing tests for both black and white applicants in the same room. At the request of the USES, more state employment services provided minority group representatives, modeled on the USES's Minority Groups Representative (MGR) program. In 1962 the department achieved a notable success in this effort in Arkansas with Orval Faubus, the controversial governor who had attempted to block integration of Little Rock's Central High School in 1957. Faubus agreed not only to hire an MGR, but also to make sure that that person was an African American.[4]

The Fight for Fairness in Apprenticeships Begins

While the USES and PCEEO worked to integrate federal employment offices, the status of apprenticeships came under question. By the

1960s apprenticeship in a skilled trade was well recognized as a potential gateway for African Americans to obtain high-paying, secure jobs in the construction industry. The problem was that, historically, relatively few apprenticeship slots went to blacks. The Bureau of Apprenticeship and Training cooperated with and promoted the privately run system of apprenticeship programs. It also registered apprenticeships that sought its recognition, and most did. Under Goldberg and Wirtz, the BAT played a much more active role in expanding apprenticeship opportunities for blacks than ever before.

In the past, the BAT had encouraged apprenticeship plan sponsors to decide to open more training slots for black youths. While not completely abandoning that voluntary approach, Goldberg wanted to take stronger action. In July 1961 he announced that the BAT would begin requiring the inclusion of a statement of nondiscrimination in all current apprenticeship program plans where government contractors were involved. Furthermore, the statement would be required in any new apprenticeship program, whether involving a government contractor or not. Failure to include the statement would disqualify the plan for registration with the BAT. The statement specified that the "selection of persons to be trained through apprenticeship will be made from those qualified without regard to race" or other extraneous factors. Numerous state apprenticeship councils, which registered programs independently of the federal BAT, voluntarily adopted the new requirements. By January 1962 over three hundred apprenticeship programs included the nondiscrimination provision.[5]

In August 1961 George Meany added key support to the Labor Department's efforts. He suggested to Johnson that the BAT hire several full-time training representatives to work on elimination of discrimination in apprenticeships. The suggestion passed through bureaucratic channels, and in November 1961, Ansel Cleary of the BAT informed Meany that the bureau was planning to set up positions of this type in four cities. The BAT asked Roy Wilkins, Whitney Young, and A. Philip Randolph to help locate qualified black candidates. The process developed into a mini-affirmative action effort in its own right.[6]

In November 1961 Labor Department officials and leaders of major civil rights organizations met to discuss the sensitive issue of recruiting for the BAT positions. Addressing the civil rights leaders, Arthur Chapin (who was MGR in the USES) pointed out that "talent is located by a sort of chain conversation—gossip, if you like," and noted that minorities had often been left out of the circle of gossip. Edward McVeigh assured the group that Goldberg was anxious to find minority candidates for the training representative positions. McVeigh invited the civil rights leaders to get the word out to the black community about the available positions and the required civil service test.

McVeigh asked for comments and suggestions at the meeting and got a mixed response. The black leaders agreed to support the recruitment plan, but they were skeptical that the apprenticeship training representatives would be able to accomplish much, given the extent of discrimination that had existed for decades in some regions. They also felt that the BAT's prerequisites for candidates were too rigid and would make it difficult to find black candidates who met the requirements.[7]

The hiring effort finally bore fruit in June 1962. The BAT hired three black applicants to serve as Industrial Training Advisers (ITAs). The newly minted ITAs—Amy Terry of New York City, Cicero Scott of Cleveland, and Charles R. Jaymes of San Francisco—had much experience in apprenticeship, training, and minority issues. Soon after their hire, the BAT hired three more black ITAs, making a total of six. In addition to promoting the acceptance of qualified minorities in apprenticeships and other training for skilled jobs, the ITAs worked with unions and employer groups to promote voluntary nondiscrimination, and with minority groups to encourage minorities to apply for apprenticeships and training courses.[8]

In 1963 the Department of Labor established in Washington, DC, the first of what eventually developed into a nationwide network of Apprenticeship Information Centers (AICs). These resource centers were designed to enhance apprenticeship opportunities for local minorities. The Washington, DC, AIC came about primarily because the federal government wanted to be sure that construction employment by federal contractors in its own backyard—especially involving the skilled trades—made the fullest possible use of the large local black workforce. Completed in June 1963, the Washington, DC, AIC was a joint undertaking of the BAT, the USES, the D.C. Apprenticeship Council, and local schools, employers, and labor unions. It included a library of apprenticeship information and provided counseling and testing services for apprenticeship applicants, information on employment opportunities in skilled crafts, and referrals to apprenticeship providers.[9]

In November 1963 the Labor Department's new Manpower Administration (MA), which now housed the BAT, began establishing similar centers in labor market areas with large numbers of minorities. The AICs were housed in local employment service offices and were administered jointly by the BAT and USES. To support and oversee their operation and assure local input to deal with possible problems, the MA required each center to establish both a coordinating group of federal, state, and local officials; and an advisory committee representing local labor, management, minority, and civic organizations.[10]

To assist the BAT in its growing program of equal treatment of minorities, on February 27, 1963, Wirtz established an Advisory Committee on Equal Opportunity in Apprenticeship and Training. The committee was composed of fifteen members from management, labor, the education community, minority groups, and the general public. Chaired by the Manpower administrator, the committee served two main functions: to help the Department of Labor devise more effective programs for equal access to apprenticeships and skilled occupations; and to recommend specific actions for implementing those policies. At its first meeting in May 1963, it called for a number of changes: research on the actual degree of participation (or lack of same) of minorities in apprenticeship programs; adequate enforcement of existing antidiscrimination provisions in BAT-registered programs; and the establishment of pre-apprenticeship training to help young persons qualify for admission into a program.[11]

The Birmingham violence of May 1963 had galvanized the Kennedy administration into almost feverish activity that spilled over into apprenticeship. This activity now became a key element in the administration's efforts to overcome racial barriers to better jobs. On June 4, 1963, Kennedy ordered Secretary Wirtz to "require that the admission of young workers to apprenticeship programs be on a completely nondiscriminatory basis." Kennedy also called for an immediate investigation into the current status of minorities in apprenticeship programs and into their employment by contractors on federal construction projects.[12]

The next day, Wirtz reported to Robert Kennedy that the department had hastily organized a task force of fifty investigators to conduct on-site surveys of minority participation both in federal construction work and in associated apprenticeship programs in fifty cities nationwide. Investigations began on the following day.

Wirtz also notified thirty state apprenticeship offices about the survey, which was a joint effort by the BAT and the PCEEO. The first phase of this accelerated effort involved collecting information on the supply of employees and apprentices for construction work. The second phase involved reviewing apprenticeship programs in which black participation was extremely limited and then examining union procedures for referring candidates for apprenticeships. A week later Wirtz provided the shocking finding to Kennedy that hardly any black workers were employed in the construction trades in twenty cities that were studied. Outraged, Kennedy met with union leaders and sent cabinet officials to a number of cities to promote greater opportunities for black workers. The upshot of all this research was that on June 22, 1963, Kennedy issued E.O. 11114 banning discrimination in federal construction work (see chapter 8).[13]

A Rule is Born

Kennedy's other June 4 order to Wirtz—to begin opening up minority access to apprenticeships—led to an almost instantaneous and far-reaching result. On June 5 Wirtz issued a departmental rule designed to promote fair access for minorities to apprenticeships. The enforcement stick was that the BAT would refuse to register programs that did not comply. Registration was a seal of approval, in effect, and no program wanted to be without it. The PCEEO had already begun developing an apprenticeship standard, which Wirtz drew on to serve as a basis for the DOL rule.

Wirtz's action was destined to arouse strong opposition from both business and labor leaders. Typically, apprenticeship programs for each skilled trade were operated jointly by the relevant trade unions and the major employers, or employer groups, involved. Unions and employers valued the relative autonomy and freedom with which they administered their programs. The federal government's only formal involvement was registration with the BAT, heretofore a routine process. The program operators liked it that way.

More important than the program operators' preference for autonomy was the fact that the children of journeymen in most trades had traditionally been given first consideration for apprenticeship slots. Many families had been able to pass down the same skilled trade from father to son through the family-tie system, which had become part of the fabric of their lives. Any interference, however noble the goal, was bound to arouse fierce opposition. However, the practice amounted to de facto racial discrimination since almost all journeyman construction workers were white because of many years of exclusion of blacks from construction unions. The family-tie practice guaranteed that almost all apprentices would be white, an intolerable situation for African Americans and for the government agencies that wanted to help them.[14]

Secretary Wirtz announced the rule in identical letters mailed on June 5 to state government apprenticeship offices and divisions. The two standards that made up the rule itself followed an introductory statement:

> The elimination of . . . discrimination depends, where there are apprenticeship programs involved, on taking steps to assure that significant opportunities are provided to qualified minority group applicants to gain admission to these apprenticeship programs.
>
> Such opportunities may be provided:
>
> 1. Where the selections made would not themselves demonstrate equality of opportunity, by the selection of apprentices on the basis of merit alone, in accordance with objective standards which permit review, after full and fair opportunity for application; and

2. By taking whatever steps are necessary, in acting upon application lists developed prior to this time, to offset the effect of previous practices under which discriminatory patterns of employment have resulted.[15]

The rule seems somewhat opaque at first reading, but it was carefully crafted to take into account the process and the social realities of the apprenticeship system. Admission to an apprenticeship program was a two-stage process: first, lists of applicants who were found eligible for apprenticeships were put together jointly by the program administrators; then came the actual selection of apprentices from those lists. Standard 2 of the BAT rule addressed the creation of the lists. When the BAT determined that a list was discriminatory, the program was to offset the effect of past discrimination by any means necessary. The implication was that if the program deliberately added minorities, the list would then be considered to be in compliance with the standard.

As for minority participation in the apprenticeship program itself, it was clear that the presence of a significant number would be considered prima facie proof of compliance, just as with the lists. The implication, again, is that minorities could be deliberately chosen over whites. If, however, the BAT did not deem minority participation to be adequate, the program then had to demonstrate that the apprentices were selected by a provably fair and objective method. Obviously, selection based on family ties would not pass muster. Hence, it would be in the interests of the labor and management groups operating an apprenticeship program to make sure that they placed enough minorities to avoid scrutiny of the father-son system.

While a quota of minorities was not prescribed, the idea of at least approximating proportionality to the general population was implied. However, this implication was not intended to be a club to force equal treatment. Rather, it was designed to make compliance easier for the apprenticeship programs. If they arbitrarily brought in enough blacks, their traditional system would not be examined and could proceed almost as before. Wirtz and the BAT knew that unions and management would fight strenuously against abolition of the traditional system. It remained to be seen whether they would accept the BAT's approach.

Wirtz directed that the standard also apply to government contractors, who were required under E.O. 10925 to take "affirmative action" to eliminate discriminatory employment practices such as limiting apprenticeship opportunities for blacks. He also directed the BAT to apply the standard when it evaluated apprenticeship programs seeking renewal of their registration. He asked that local apprenticeship councils voluntarily apply the rule as well. While Wirtz did not characterize the standard itself as "affirmative action," he did urge state apprenticeship offices to give "affirmative consideration" to their implementation.

Wirtz clarified and slightly revised the rule a few days after the June 5 announcement. It now required:

> 1. The selection of apprentices on the basis of merit alone, in accordance with objective standards which permit review, after full and fair opportunity for application, *unless the selections otherwise made would themselves demonstrate that there is equality of opportunity.* [emphasis added]
>
> 2. The taking of whatever steps are necessary, in acting upon application lists developed prior to this time, to offset the effects of previous practices under which discriminatory patterns of employment have resulted.[16]

Standard number 2 was unchanged from the original rule, but number 1 was rearranged for easier understanding. It was made clear that the phrase "selections otherwise made," that is, through deliberate choice of minority candidates, provided an acceptable alternative to applying objective standards. A few weeks later, Wirtz added a third standard to the rule after being asked whether the department also expected the actual training under apprentice programs be conducted in a fair and objective manner. That had been his intention, and Wirtz now made it explicit, requiring

> nondiscrimination in all phases of apprenticeship and employment during apprenticeship after selections are made.[17]

Wirtz was able to implement the apprenticeship rule almost immediately because it was only a departmental rule, not a formal federal standard. The process of issuing the latter would have required publication of a proposed rule and an invitation for public comments before promulgation. The BAT quickly informed federally-registered Joint Apprenticeship Committees about the rule and started registering only those new apprenticeship programs that were in compliance. The BAT was also to review all currently registered programs and remove from the register ("de-register") any that were not in compliance.

Wirtz asked the BAT to issue a guidance bulletin on the standards for the use of its staff. He wanted the guidance to make it clear that the standards were adopted in response to discrimination against blacks. It should stress that, while other forms of discrimination should be eliminated, "specific attention needs to be directed to racial discrimination." He also provided commentaries on standards 1 and 2. Regarding the objective selection criteria in standard 1, he noted that this did not mean that all programs must have identical criteria for admission. Rather, admission was to be based on whatever objective factors the operators of a particular program deemed appropriate. These factors could include test scores, physical qualifications, impartial interviews, and so on.

Wirtz sought to assure that under standard 2, when application lists were found to be biased, minorities would be given fair consideration for inclusion:

> Necessary action in connection with application lists previously developed means that programs whose past selections have not demonstrated equality of opportunity will not give such preference or priority in selection to those who have previously applied for apprenticeship, as to reduce significantly the opportunity for selection of those who will be encouraged to apply under the new selection procedures.[18]

The BAT issued the guidance in the form of Circular 64-7 on July 17, 1963.[19] The circular included Wirtz's three standards verbatim, incorporated his guidances, and added a few more explanations. The cumulative effect of all the revisions, clarifications, and guidances over the summer of 1963 was to make it abundantly clear that neither Wirtz nor the BAT sought the abolition of the traditional, father-son selection system. They only wanted to see evidence that new apprenticeship opportunities were somehow being opened up for African American youths.

However, it soon became clear that, despite the department's calculated concession to the status quo, the bulk of the apprenticeship community was not going to accept what it saw as unwarranted interference. As soon as the department issued the original rule, it started receiving strong objections from both labor and management. Opposition was significant even within the enforcing agency—the BAT itself.

On the day Circular 64-7 was issued, David Christian (an aide to Wirtz) sent Manpower Administrator John Donovan a background memo on Wirtz's planned participation in a meeting of BAT regional officials in Washington where the new circular was to be presented.

Christian's comments on the culture of the bureau at that time are revealing:

> We will be confronting a skeptical audience, not because they approve of discrimination in these programs. . . . They do, however, tend to have a quasi-religious fervor for the promotion of apprenticeship. In this way of thinking anything which discourages or makes more difficult the maintenance and growth of apprenticeship programs is prima facie bad. In short, at the moment the psychology tends to be that it is more important to develop apprentices and apprenticeship than it is to insist on equal opportunity. This is the system of relative values that we need to change.
>
> In day-to-day operations, the change we must achieve is from the historic position of "hands off the selection process" to one of active concern and intervention in these processes. This will also cause major pains for these people who are not only generally conservative but who are also basically promoters. It tends to be fundamentally distasteful to them to take on an enforcement role and quite legitimately they see the latter role as destructive of the former.

Even as he expressed these reservations, Christian gave the BAT credit for progress in the racial make-up of the field staff. A number of blacks had been hired in the professional grades. He found "no reluctance at all" to hire staff without regard to race.[20]

Responding to the growing opposition to its rule, the department decided to withdraw it and issue in its place a formal federal regulation, which would be published in the *Federal Register*. This was a historic decision. For the first time, the federal government proposed to enforce what amounted to affirmative action in employment through a formal regulation. The department quickly developed the proposal, combining and codifying Wirtz's standards, Circular 64-7, and the BAT guidance materials. In a key clarification, Section I specified that new programs established after the effective date could only obtain BAT certification by creating and applying objective, reviewable standards of selection. They would not have the option of complying purely through showing an acceptable racial composition in their classes of apprentices. With this change, the rule constituted a more direct attack on the father-son system. To be sure, however, the change applied only to new programs. The proposed rule appeared in the *Federal Register* on October 23, 1963. Public comments were invited.[21]

Comments poured in. Most state apprenticeship councils expressed support for the proposed regulation, as they had supported the earlier rule. Labor and industry remained strongly opposed to federal intervention in the apprenticeship system. Reflecting shared goals for the system, their critical comments converged and reinforced each other at many points. Some of the objections went beyond the specifics of the regulation to concerns that government would seek to regulate apprenticeship systems more broadly and worries about excessive government power in general.

A case in point was the fifteen-page statement from R. P. Sornsin, representing the National Association of Plumbing, Heating and Cooling Contractors (PHCC). He opposed the regulation on several levels.[22] While strongly against discrimination and supportive of the federal effort to provide equal opportunity, the PHCC objected to using the sanction of deregistration against registered apprenticeship programs. Sornsin charged that the regulation improperly raised registration to the level of a substantial legal right that brought with it new regulatory powers for the BAT. He also feared that BAT review of apprenticeship programs would "become a tool for the enforcement of fluctuating day-to-day movements of administrative policy and would, in our opinion, range far beyond the question of discrimination." Noting that the BAT had worked collegially with PHCC members in a nonregulatory way for many years, Sornsin argued that if the BAT "tries now to speak with two voices urging and advising today, commanding tomorrow, neither voice is going to be heard." Additionally, apprenticeship committees were not prepared to deal with, as he put it, "the intricacies of federal regulations written in flowing federalese."

The PHCC's principal objections, however, dealt with the substance of the standards. Regarding the "alternative test" under standard 2, the association argued that this would produce a quota system, in effect, "if program managers conclude that they can save themselves a lot of trouble rejecting more qualified majority race applicants and selecting a sufficient number of lesser skilled minority applicants to achieve a favorable 'racial and ethnic composition.'" Sornsin argued that "the government enters forbidden territory when it decrees that the private employers, or committees, must first lay down 'objective standards' from which the ultimate selections will follow by mathematical necessity." Dealing with the preference issue, he posed the case of a contractor whose own son is near the top of the list of eligibles for an apprenticeship. Under the standards, Sornsin posited, "a black boy is 2 points higher than the contractor's son. So the rest of the Committee tells its fellow-member, 'Sorry, you've got to take the black boy.' This is democracy!" Using less colorful language, the Colorado Labor Council made almost the identical point, claiming also that 5 percent or less of all apprentices were admitted because of a father-son relationship.[23]

Sornsin claimed finally that by tying an antidiscrimination program to expanded regulation of apprenticeship training, the Department of Labor raised the issue of excessive government control over the economy:

> Practically every racial fight in the country gets compromised by becoming embroiled in the larger issue of federal control over the states and federal control over free enterprise. We urge the department to avoid this entanglement so far as it possibly can with respect to apprenticeship training.

If the department would only withdraw the proposal, Sornsin wrote, the PHCC would be happy to discuss how to achieve an effective equal opportunity plan.

Ford Motor Vice President M. L. Katke, a member of the BAT's Advisory Committee on Apprenticeship (ACA) did not reject the rule or take an ideological position on it. However, he questioned the need to regulate contractors whose apprenticeship programs were already covered by E.O.s 10925 and 11114. These additional regulations, Katke feared, would place an unnecessary burden on the contractors, and he recommended that the companies be exempted. He was concerned that the regulation implicitly sanctioned numerical goals or quotas. If quotas were indeed to be allowed, Katke wrote, "it is contrary to the published objective of the Equal Employment Opportunity Program." He too defended the need to give at least some weight to familial relationships in selections for apprenticeships.[24]

Commenters from organized labor were as dissatisfied with the regulation as their management counterparts. In November 1963 the AFL-CIO's Building and Construction Trades Department (BCTD), without specifically citing the proposed BAT regulations, went on record with a resolution

> condemning the US Department of Labor for attempting to create a policing agency within the Bureau of Apprenticeship [and Training] and for meddling into the internal affairs of the craft unions in attendance at

this Convention, to satisfy the ill-directed activities of a group of individuals.[25]

The BCTD maintained that apprenticeship programs had been successfully operated independently of the federal government since before the establishment of the Department of Labor. It argued that the BAT should continue to limit its role to promoting sound apprenticeship programs and providing technical assistance to the unions and employers who operated them. The resolution pointed out that the BCTD had voluntarily adopted a nondiscrimination program on June 21, 1963, ordering local unions to accept and refer apprenticeship applicants without regard to race and other irrelevant factors. BCTD president C. J. Haggerty forwarded the resolution to Wirtz in December. Wirtz then met with Haggerty to discuss "further consideration of the points covered by this Resolution."

In October 1963 B. A. Gritta, president of the AFL-CIO's Metal Trades Department (MTD), added his voice to the opposition to the proposed regulations. While affirming the commitment of the twenty-two unions of the MTD to fair treatment in apprenticeships, he also conveyed their view that apprenticeship should be a voluntary "labor-management program grounded in the employment relationship and mutually worked out and administered by management and labor." Gritta argued that, instead of issuing mandatory regulations providing the sanction of deregistration, the Department of Labor should work on a voluntary basis with unions and management to promote nondiscrimination. He noted that the department had never before issued a rule providing for revocation of registration on the basis of any other aspect of apprenticeship. He argued that singling out nondiscrimination as the sole basis "runs contrary to past practices and policies of the Department [of Labor and] . . . can only do injury to the continued growth and promotion of apprenticeship." Responding for Wirtz, Under Secretary John Henning indicated that nondiscriminatory programs had nothing to fear from the regulations and expressed confidence that organized labor would work with the department to ensure equal employment opportunity. However, turning Gritta's position against singling out the nondiscrimination area on its head, Henning indicated that Wirtz agreed and was in favor of a broader policy that would allow deregistration for a variety of reasons.[26]

Michael Fox, president of the AFL-CIO's Railway Employees' Department, was another labor representative who opposed the regulation. He pointed out that the ACA, of which he was a member, had unanimously rejected the regulation. He expressed his disappointment at the manner in which the whole issue was being handled. Fox argued that the apprenticeship system was premised on the assumption that the federal government serves as a cooperative facilitator. It appeared to him that the regulations would turn the BAT into a policeman.[27]

Issuing the First Affirmative Action Regulation

After receiving and considering seventeen comments, most of them negative, the Department of Labor published the final regulation in the *Federal Register* on December 18, 1963.[28] It took effect January 17, 1964. In the face of a consensus of opposition from management and labor, the department made a few significant concessions in the final rule. First, it backed away from expressly requiring apprenticeship programs to take compensatory action for any past discrimination they may have committed when they established the lists of those deemed eligible for apprenticeship positions. The proposed regulation had required "offsetting" the effects of previous discrimination, that is, a lack of blacks on the hiring lists. The final rule simply required the "removing" of any discriminatory results without setting any requirements or specifying how it should be accomplished. However, the programs still had a duty to rectify the discrimination.

The final regulation also backed away from actually, or implicitly, setting racial quotas in apprenticeship programs. Wirtz had decreed in June that candidate lists were to be disregarded to the extent needed to provide opportunities to minorities for "a significant number of positions." To many, this statement implied the application of a quota of black apprentices. The final rule specifically and categorically eliminated that possibility. First, it deleted the phrase "significant number" and replaced it with a vague assertion that programs should provide "current opportunities for selection of qualified members" of minority groups. To hammer the point home, the rule added a paragraph titled "Quota system barred":

> Nothing contained in this part shall be construed to require any program sponsor or employer to select or employ apprentices in the proportion which their race, color, religion, or national origin bears to the total population.

The department, however, held firm on two pillars of the regulation. It retained intact the enforcement "stick": deregistration of programs which the BAT determined were "not in conformity" with the standard. It also maintained Wirtz's basic, two-option approach to compliance by existing programs: (1) evidence of opening opportunities to blacks with, basically, no questions asked; or failing that, (2) demonstration of an objective, fair selection system. As was provided in Section I of the proposed rule, new programs could only exercise the second option.

Immediately after the January 18, 1964, effective date of the rule, the BAT began applying it to all new apprenticeship programs that sought registration. In the first five months of enforcement, the BAT reviewed 383 new apprenticeship programs and determined that all were in compliance. In succeeding years, enforcement of the rule became an uncontroversial, routine function.[29]

The apprenticeship rule was not represented or described as affirmative action at the time of issuance. In the process of developing the rule, the department had edged toward, and then backed firmly away from mandatory quotas or goals. However, it made it clear that apprenticeship programs needed to go out of their way to somehow include more African Americans and other minorities. This was the essence of affirmative action as it was understood at the time. In many ways, this historic rule set the tone and parameters for future debate on affirmative action, and it broke ground for the raft of equal employment opportunity regulations and programs that emerged in the years after passage of the Civil Rights Act of 1964.

Epilogue

There are many facts and ideas that a reader might take away from this book. Each reader's list may be slightly different. However, there are three central points that will hopefully appear on everyone's list: first, there were significant, measurable advances for African American workers; second, the concept of affirmative action was born and underwent significant development before the Civil Rights Act; and third, most major actions by the executive branch were taken only in response to pressure, direct or indirect, from the African American community. It bears repeating some key facts from the preceding nine chapters that buttress these points.

First, while data on black employment is fragmentary, there are enough examples of progress to indicate that the general tendency was toward advancement. Federal employment, including hiring, promotions, and working conditions, was the brightest area. The Jim Crow practices introduced during the Wilson administration gradually loosened their hold, beginning with the desegregation of the Commerce Department in the 1920s, and were virtually eliminated by the 1950s. During World War II, the number of black civil servants more than tripled, and their percentage rose to approximate the black percentage in the general population. The push to hire African Americans accelerated greatly during the early 1960s. Between 1961 and 1963, 19 percent of new federal hires were black.

EPILOGUE

Also, the representation of African Americans in supervisory and professional job series, while always lagging that of whites, grew from virtually nil to a respectable level by 1964. In the period 1956-1960 alone, black employment in the middle and upper civil service grades grew from 3.7 percent of all employees to 5.9 percent.

Beginning with the New Deal, government-funded projects and government contractors began to incorporate principles of fair employment. It is true that New Deal racial fairness policies set in Washington were often thwarted in the segregated South, and legislation such as the Social Security Act and Fair Labor Standards Act were crafted to exclude large numbers of black citizens.[1] Nevertheless, most New Deal work-relief programs had some success in providing equal treatment for unemployed African Americans. The Public Works Administration (PWA), for example, specifically banned discrimination on the basis of race or religion. Fourteen percent of all Work Projects Administration beneficiaries were African Americans. Under fair employment executive orders, the black proportion of employment by defense contractors more than doubled during World War II, and black employment in white-collar jobs in the defense industry gained significantly in the 1960s. Some 10.65 percent of new hires in 1962 and 1963 in this area were African Americans.

Second, affirmative action, while not usually touted under that name, began to manifest itself during the New Deal. Harold Ickes set racial hiring goals for the PWA, requiring that blacks be hired in proportion to the population. Failure to meet what amounted to a quota was deemed prima facie proof of discrimination. After World War II, the Bureau of Engraving and Printing came under pressure from the civil rights community to open its skilled jobs to blacks. When the bureau did not act, Truman ordered it to begin placing well-qualified blacks in its apprenticeship programs. In 1961 E.O.

10925 included the phrase "affirmative action" and required federal government contractors to ensure fair treatment of their workers. The Department of Labor's historic apprenticeship regulation of 1963, while specifically banning quotas, required affirmative action in appointments to apprenticeship programs.

Lastly, most federal action, and therefore most progress, resulted from direct petitions by African American groups, civil rights activism, dramatic violence against blacks, or all of the above. The NAACP, William Monroe Trotter, and others objected strongly to Woodrow Wilson's imposition of Jim Crow racial strictures in Washington. As a result, the tide of segregation within the federal government was stemmed, although it did not fully recede for many years. The Division of Negro Economics in World War I was created only after civil rights groups demanded establishment of a government agency devoted to black problems. African American watchdog groups monitored the New Deal's National Recovery Act and denounced it for discriminating against black workers. A. Philip Randolph's mere threat to mount a march of ten thousand blacks on Washington convinced FDR to issue E.O. 8802. Postwar violence against blacks in the 1940s, including several shocking murders, prompted protests by civil rights leaders and led President Truman to establish the Committee on Civil Rights. Black leaders clamored for another Fair Employment Practices Committee when the defense industry started gearing up to meet the Korean War emergency. In response, Presidents Truman and Eisenhower established committees to promote equal treatment in that area.

Both black pressure and the government's responses escalated during the Kennedy administration. In the late 1950s, the NAACP and other civil rights groups had called on the Department of Labor to open up more apprenticeship opportunities for black youths. Initially it had resisted, but in the early 1960s, it took a number of

EPILOGUE

steps on apprenticeship, culminating in Secretary Wirtz's affirmative action order of 1963. The explosion of the civil rights movement in 1960 prompted the Kennedy administration to establish the President's Committee on Equal Employment Opportunity (PCEEO). In 1961, as a result of discrimination complaints filed by the NAACP, the PCEEO initiated Plans for Progress. When this program did not live up to expectations, black civil rights leaders denounced it. Their denunciation led to the *Kheel Report* and a revamping to orient the program toward compulsory, rather than voluntary, compliance. In response to extreme violence against civil rights marchers in Birmingham and to the murder of Medgar Evers, the government accelerated its antidiscrimination efforts. It also began to seek enactment of a comprehensive civil rights law. The March on Washington for Jobs and Freedom, at which Martin Luther King Jr. gave his immortal "I have a dream" speech, provided a further push toward passage. President Kennedy's assassination in 1963 and a strong effort by LBJ contributed to enactment in 1964.

In his 1963 "Letter from Birmingham Jail," Martin Luther King Jr. wrote, "freedom is never voluntarily given by the oppressor; it must be demanded by the oppressed." Perhaps some day the federal government will routinely do the right thing before African Americans, women, gays, and other oppressed groups have had to march, pressure, protest, and beg for their rights. Only when America has reached that point will we be able to claim, with any validity, that we have finally become an equalitarian society.

Notes

CHAPTER 1.

1. The [Dillingham] Immigration Commission, pp. 37-38, 322; Kennedy, p. 43.

2. Gottlieb, p. 5.

3. Hill, "Black Labor and Affirmative Action," p. 217; Trotter, p. 60.

4. Wilson's victory was mainly attributable to a split in the Republican vote. The split resulted when the incumbent Republican president, William Howard Taft, sought reelection and the former Republican president, Theodore Roosevelt, ran as an independent on the Bull-Moose ticket.

5. Ballew, pp. 16-24; Scheiber and Scheiber, p. 111; Clements, pp. 45-46.

6. Ballew, pp. 11-15, 30; Clements, pp. 45, 160.

7. Among these positions were the Assistant Attorney General, the Register of the Treasury, and the Recorder of Deeds for Washington, DC. In addition, numerous black postmasters were also replaced with whites.

NOTES

8. Ballew, pp. 24-31, 52-53, 86; Scheiber and Scheiber, pp. 111-114; Franklin and Moss, p. 384; Patler, pp. 11, 55.

9. Patler, pp. 11, 15; King, pp. 40-46.

10. Ballew, pp. 24-31, 86; Scheiber and Scheiber, pp. 111-114.

11. King, pp. 48-49.

12. Patler, pp. 17-20, 56; Ballew, p. 26; Scheiber and Scheiber, pp. 112-113; Clements, p. 45.

13. Clements, pp. 46, 60; Scheiber and Scheiber, p. 113; Finch, p. 254.

14. Finch, p. 35.

15. Patler, pp. 62-67.

16. Ballew, pp. 27-28, 44-46, 61-63; Patler, pp. 133-142, 196-199.

17. Ballew, pp. 63-67; Patler, pp. 175-183; Booker.

18. Robert Zieger, *America's Great War*, p. 129.

19. Ellis, p. 228.

20. Scheiber and Scheiber, pp. 114-117.

21. Finch, pp. 40-41.

22. Scott, *Scott's Official History*, pp. 173-283.

23. Scheiber and Scheiber, pp. 118-124.

24. Ellis, p. 54; Scott, *Scott's Official History*, pp. 40-45, 51-65; Zieger, *America's Great War*, p. 131; Scheiber and Scheiber, pp. 124-126.

25. Scheiber and Scheiber, pp. 131-132; Robert Zieger, "African Americans and the Great War Decade"; Zieger, *America's Great War*, pp. 132-135.

26. William B. Wilson served as the first secretary of the Department of Labor from 1913 to 1921. With WWI, he put the Department of Labor on the map. Many of the current departmental activities trace back to that period, including employment services, employment of women, fair employment for minorities, and labor management relations. The department helped in winning the war by mobilizing an effective workforce for defense production.

27. Zieger, *America's Great War*, pp. 54-65; Wilhelm, p. 180; Guzda, "Social Experiment," pp. 9-10; Chicago NAACP to Sec. Wilson, Sept. 12, 1913, [folder number] 16/150, RG 174; New York City Republican Club to Sec. Wilson, Dec. 30, 1913, 16/150, RG 174.

28. This USES is not to be confused with the body of the same name created by the Wagner-Peyser Act of 1933.

29. DOL Circular No. 5, Jan. 22, 1915, 16/119, RG 174; Breen, *Labor Market Politics*, pp. 10-11.

30. *Annual Report of the Chief of the Division of Information* [1915], pp. 7-14.

31. Ibid.; Breen, *Labor Market Politics*, p. 11.

32. Lombardi, p. 263; Emmett J. Scott, *Negro Migration*, p. 53; *Annual Reports* [1917], DOL, p. 79; Johnson, p. 22.

33. A spectacular boom in cotton prices had encouraged farmers to greatly increase the acreage devoted to this crop. However, cotton growing and harvesting was very labor intensive, which meant

that the demand for labor was expanding just as the supply was decreasing due to the migration.

34. Hahamovitch, p. 83; *Annual Reports* [1917], DOL, pp. 79-80; Lombardi, p. 263; Charles Johnson, p. 22; Scott, *Negro Migration*, p. 78.

35. There was ample precedent for such a report on black conditions and life. When its predecessor agency, the US Bureau of Labor, was created by act of Congress in 1884, Carroll D. Wright, the first commissioner of the bureau, sought permission from the president to conduct a study of the economic and social conditions of black Americans. Permission was not granted at that time, but Wright revived the idea a few years later and the bureau commissioned and published a series of nine studies of the living conditions of blacks in various areas, mostly in the South. The principal author was W. E. B. DuBois, later a founder of the NAACP. See Guzda, "Social Experiment," p. 9; Grossman, "Black Studies," pp. 17-26.

36. Guzda, "Social Experiment," p. 11.

37. *Negro Migration in 1916-17*, p. 7; *Annual Reports* [1917], DOL, p. 80; Guzda, "Social Experiment," p. 13.

38. *Negro Migration in 1916-17*, pp. 9-15.

39. Ibid.

40. Zieger, "African Americans and the Great War Decade."

41. Louis Post Statement, April 4, 1919; J. S. Cullinen to Sec. Wilson, June 26, 1917; Cong. John T. Watkins to Sec. Wilson, July 14, 1917; Sec. Wilson to Cong. Watkins, July 17, 1917, all found in 8/102, RG 174.

42. Breen, *Labor Market Politics*, p. 127.

43. Zieger, "African Americans and the Great War Decade."

44. Guzda, "Social Experiment," pp. 16-17; Breen, *Labor Market Politics*, pp. 127-128.

45. Petition from Giles Jackson, undated [c. June 1917]; Giles Jackson to Hugh Kerwin, Jan. 14, 1918; Samuel Gompers to Sec. Wilson, Jan. 23, 1918, all three found in 8/102A, RG 174; John A. Ross to Sec. Wilson, July 18, 1917, 16/38, RG 174.

46. Scott, *Negro Migration*, pp. 143-150; N. Weiss, pp. 133-134.

47. R. Moton et al. to Sec. Wilson, Feb. 12, 1918; Louis Post to Sec. Wilson, Feb. 15, 1918, both found in 8/102A, RG 174.

48. Louis Post to Sec. Wilson, Feb. 15, 1918, 8/102A, RG 174; PL 426-62, March 4, 1913.

49. Advisory Council to Sec. Wilson, Feb. 27, 1918; DOL Press Release, April 1918, 8/102A; Louis Post Statement, April 4, 1919, all three found in 8/102, RG 174.

50. *The Negro at Work*, p. 12; DOL Press Release, April 1918, 8/102A, RG 174.

51. Guzda, "Social Experiment," pp. 17-18; N. Weiss, pp. 30-33, 133-134; DOL Press Release, April 1918, 8/102A, RG 174.

52. Guzda, "Labor Department's First Program," p. 40.

53. Breen, *Labor Market Politics*, p. 128; *Annual Report of the Director General* [1918], p. 28.

54. *Annual Report of the Director General* [1918], p. 28.

NOTES

55. Haynes to Wilson, Jan. 10, 1919, 20/40A, RG 174; *The Negro at Work*, p. 12.

56. Memo to Dir. General [USES], April 10, 1918, 8/102, RG 174.

57. Haynes to Sec. Wilson, May 7, 1918, 8/102, RG 174.

58. Ibid.

59. In this memo, Director Haynes stated his belief that such collegial joint undertakings "is fundamental."

60. Haynes to Sec. Wilson, May 7, 1918, 8/102, RG 174.

61. Ibid.; Post to Sec. Wilson, May 10, 1918, 8/102, RG 174; Louis Post Statement, April 4, 1919, 8/102, RG 174; *The Negro at Work*, pp. 12-13.

62. Report on DNE, Jan. 10, 1919, 20/40A, RG 174; "Matters of Record," undated (c. Jan. 1919), DNE, RG 174; *The Negro at Work*, pp. 20-21.

63. Report on DNE, Jan. 10, 1919, 20/40A, RG 174; *The Negro at Work*, p. 22.

64. Ltr. to Sec. Wilson, April 12, 1919, 8/102A, RG 174; "Matters of Record."

65. *The Negro at Work*, pp. 19-20; Memo from Haynes to Post, May 28, 1918, 8/102A, RG 174; Report on DNE, Jan. 10, 1919, 20/40A, RG 174.

66. *The Negro at Work*, pp. 13-14; Report on DNE, Jan. 10, 1919, 20/40A, RG 174; "Matters of Record."

67. "Matters of Record"; *The Negro at Work*, pp. 13-14, 97-98.

68. *The Negro at Work*, p. 107.

69. The last point was a key concern because whites feared that the arrival of black workers meant employers would use them as strikebreakers.

70. *The Negro at Work*, pp. 106-107.

71. Ibid., pp. 68-69.

72. Ibid., pp. 14-15, 19, 105-108.

73. Ibid., pp. 22, 65-71, 100, 106-107; George L. Boyle to Sec. Wilson, April 12, 1919, 8/102A, RG 174.

74. "Matters of Record."

75. *The Negro at Work*, pp. 111-114.

76. "Summary of Report on Forrester B. Washington," George Haynes, July 30, 1918, 8/102A, RG 174.

77. *The Negro at Work*, pp. 77-81.

78. The first such black business enterprise in the state was set up by a Butcher Workmen's local union in Chicago.

79. *The Negro at Work*, pp. 73-76, 90-91, 95-96, 116-118.

80. *The Negro at Work*, pp. 17-18, 137-138.

81. Post memo, Aug. 13, 1918, 8/102A, RG 174.

82. *The Negro at Work*, pp. 22-25.

83. Draft of speech, Haynes, undated (c. early 1919), DNE, RG 174.

84. The Division of Negro Economics found that in Chicago a shocking 99 percent of all black veterans were unemployed.

85. "Function and Work of the Division of Negro Economics," personal memo, George Haynes, March 15, 1919, DNE, RG 174; Ellis, pp. 224-225.

86. *The Negro at Work*, pp. 15-17, 92.

87. "Antagonisms Meet [sic] With," undated typescript (c. April 1919), 8/102A, RG 174; Guzda, "Social Experiment," pp. 29-30.

88. Haynes to Sec. Wilson, July 8, 1919, 8/102C, RG 174.

89. *The Negro at Work*, pp. 26-31.

90. *The Negro at Work*, pp. 111-114; Charles Haase to Sec. Wilson, March 5, 1919, 8/102A, RG 174.

91. Zieger, *America's Great War*, pp. 206-207; Finch, pp. 54-55.

92. *Annual Reports* [1920], DOL (Washington, DC: GPO, 1920), p. 41; Guzda, "Labor Department's First Program," p. 43; Guzda, "Social Experiment," pp. 33-36.

93. *The Negro at Work*, pp. 135-136.

94. Because there was always a significant amount of return migration every year, the gross annual migration out of the South was much larger than 34,000.

95. Haynes, p. 65; Finch, p. 75; Kusmer.

96. Guzda, "Social Experiment," p. 36; Ellis, p. 232.

97. William Monroe Trotter, the NAACP, and others pressed Presidents Harding and Coolidge to eliminate Jim Crow practices

in the government. Harding had promised during his election campaign in 1920 to banish it through an executive order. In 1926 Coolidge made a similar promise. Neither president, however, followed up, despite continual pressure from the black and white presses.

98. King, p. 49; Patler, pp. 206-207; Ritchie.

CHAPTER 2.

1. Communication with Ray Marshall, Feb. 2008.
2. Cole, Jr., p. 11; Franklin and Moss, pp. 94, 383-384.
3. Sitkoff, *A New Deal for Blacks*, pp. 39-42, 84-88; Franklin and Moss, p. 387.
4. Watkins, pp. 288-289.
5. Clarke, pp. 20-22.
6. Thereby she made history as the first female cabinet member in US history.
7. Guzda, "Frances Perkins' Interest," p. 336.
8. Macmahon, Millett, and Ogden, pp. 189-190; Clarke, pp. 140-142.
9. Zangrando and Zangrando, pp. 91-92.
10. "Industrial and Labor Conditions," *Monthly Labor Review*, July 1933, pp. 42-44.
11. Sitkoff, *A New Deal for Blacks*, pp. 42-45.
12. Blumberg, p. 29.

NOTES

13. Blumberg, pp. 29-31; Franklin and Moss, p. 398; Watkins, p. 644; Macmahon, Millett, and Ogden, pp. 17-18, 190; Sitkoff, *A New Deal for Blacks*, pp. 36-38; Hahamovitch, pp. 138-139.

14. Freidel, pp. 312-319.

15. "Negro Workers under the NRA," Joint Committee on National Recovery, 1933-1935, undated (1934?), USES/Oxley, RG 183; Sitkoff, *A New Deal for Blacks*, pp. 54-55, 104; Freidel, pp. 320-321; Franklin and Moss, p. 395.

16. Macmahon, Millett, and Ogden, p. 17; Ickes, pp. 1-5; Clarke, p. 145.

17. Ickes, pp. 30-33, 199.

18. Ibid., pp. 33-34.

19. Franklin and Moss, p. 398; Sitkoff, *A New Deal for Blacks*, pp. 66-68; Clarke, p. 96; Moreno, pp. 55-65.

20. Ickes, pp. 77-78, 207; Clarke, p. 45.

21. According to the Fair Labor Standards Act of 1938, scrip, tokens, credit cards, "dope checks," coupons, and similar devices are not proper mediums of payment.

22. Clarke, p. 98; Watkins, p. 647.

23. Walker, p. 23.

24. Macmahon, Millett, and Ogden, p. 18; Watkins, p. 391; Walker, p. 50.

25. Blumberg, pp. 33-34; Walker, pp. 82-88.

26. Walker, pp. 66-81, 104-130.

27. Freidel, p. 323; Walker, pp. 79, 147, 155-156, 161.

28. Cole Jr., pp. 9-10; Watkins, pp. 338-339.

29. Watkins, pp. 339-340; Cole Jr., p. 10.

30. Sterner, pp. 255-259, 269; Cole Jr., p. 14; Sitkoff, *A New Deal for Blacks*, p. 74.

31. Sitkoff, *A New Deal for Blacks*, p. 51; Cole Jr., pp. 14, 16.

32. Sterner, p. 255; Watkins, p. 641; Telegram copy/Confidential, from Frances Perkins, May 20, 1933, CCC, RG 174.

33. Perkins to Persons, July 29, 1935, Employment-Labor Policies, RG 174.

34. Cole Jr., pp. 18-26, 55-56; Guzda, "Frances Perkins' Interest," p. 34; Watkins, pp. 641-642.

35. Watkins, p. 642; Cole Jr., pp. 16-17.

36. Cole Jr., pp. 46-48; Watkins, pp. 642-643.

37. Franklin and Moss, p. 397; Cole Jr., pp. 50-52, 61-62.

38. Clarke, pp. 40, 43-45; Finch, pp. 84-86.

39. Watkins, pp. 644, 648; Sitkoff, *A New Deal for Blacks*, p. 66; Clarke, p. 45.

40. Watkins, p. 645.

41. Sitkoff, *A New Deal for Blacks*, pp. 77-78; Watkins, pp. 644-646; Clarke, pp. 43-45.

42. Sitkoff, *A New Deal for Blacks*, pp. 76-78; Franklin and Moss, pp. 392-394.

43. Moreno, p. 56; Sitkoff, *A New Deal for Blacks*, p. 78; Watkins, p. 646.

44. Perkins to Edward McGrady, Feb. 11, 1935, Admin/McGrady, RG 174; Isador Lubin to Harold Ickes, March 27, 1935, Interior Dept., RG 174.

45. Oxley to Isador Lubin, Weekly Progress Reports, June 1935 to June 1937, USES/Oxley Misc. Records, RG 183.

46. Guzda, "Frances Perkins' Interest," pp. 32-33; Oxley to Isador Lubin, Weekly Progress Reports, June 1935 to June 1937, USES/Oxley Misc. Records, RG 183; *Annual Reports* [1939], DOL, p. 28; Oxley to Sec. Perkins, May 22, 1939, USES, RG 174; Oxley to Governor of Alabama, Sept. 4, 1934, Oxley file, RG 183; Clipping (unidentified Winston-Salem, NC, newspaper), May 7, 1939, DOL Historical Office.

47. Sitkoff, *A New Deal for Blacks*, pp. 88-89; Franklin and Moss, p. 388.

48. Hahamovitch, p. 155.

49. Macmahon, Millett, and Ogden, p. 1; Sitkoff, *A New Deal for Blacks*, pp. 55-59; Freidel, pp. 329-330; Olson, p. 444.

50. McCarthy, p. 219.

51. Olson, pp. 427-429; Sitkoff, *A New Deal for Blacks*, pp. 59-60; Wandersee, pp. 63-64; Franklin and Moss, p. 389; Zangrando and Zangrando, pp. 92-93; Hareven, pp. 54, 210.

52. Olson, p. 147.

53. Watkins, pp. 392-395; Macmahon, Millett, and Ogden, p. 75; Blumberg, pp. 45-46.

54. Olson, pp. 548-549; Freidel, pp. 332-333; Macmahon, Millett, and Ogden, pp. 1-6; Blumberg, pp. 96, 291-292.

55. Macmahon, Millett, and Ogden, pp. 3-6, 253-258; Olson, p. 170; Blumberg, p. 216.

56. The WPA was one of more than 20 New Deal laws that banned discrimination on account of race or religion.

57. Macmahon, Millett, and Ogden, p. 101; Sitkoff, *A New Deal for Blacks*, p. 69.

58. Howard, p. 286. A similar situation arose during the Kennedy administration. See chapter 9.

59. Macmahon, Millett, and Ogden, pp. 148-155.

60. Sitkoff, *A New Deal for Blacks*, p. 71; Blumberg, pp. 153-155, 166-168.

61. Blumberg, pp. 186-198, 205, 212-213; Sitkoff, *A New Deal for Blacks*, pp. 207-208, 212; Howard, pp. 294-295.

62. Macmahon, Millett, and Ogden, p. 193; Watkins, pp. 643-644; Sterner, p. 253; Howard, pp. 286-287, 294.

63. There is anecdotal evidence that WPA jobs may have contributed to migration northward as workers in the South used WPA earnings to leave the area and take their families with them. In March 2000 the author received a telephone query on an unrelated topic from a journalist named Holsendolph (not the well-known Ernest Holsendolph but possibly his son). In the course of the conversation, Mr. Holsendolph described how his father migrated in just such a manner.

NOTES

64. Franklin and Moss, p. 398; Howard, pp. 288-290; Sitkoff, *A New Deal for Blacks*, p. 70.

65. Blumberg, pp. 298-299; Howard, pp. 290-291; Sterner, pp. 239-243.

66. Sterner, pp. 243-246.

67. Ibid., pp. 246-251.

68. Howard, pp. 291-292.

69. Macmahon, Millett, and Ogden, pp. 165-166.

70. Some funding was restored in 1938 after the economy had faltered again, after seeming to climb out of the Depression.

71. Blumberg, pp. 87-88, 221-278; Olson, pp. 448-450.

72. Macmahon, Millett, and Ogden, pp. 85-86; Olson, pp. 367; Wandersee, pp. 66-68.

73. Macmahon, Millett, and Ogden, pp. 85-86.

74. Branch, Pillar of Fire, p. 188; Franklin and Moss, p. 397.

75. Sitkoff, *A New Deal for Blacks*, p. 73; Wandersee, pp. 68-69; Hareven, p. 208.

76. In tribute to Bethune's legacy, in 1974, on the 99th anniversary of her birth, a statue of her holding a cane that FDR had given her was erected in Lincoln Park in Washington, DC. It was the first public statue of an African American woman in the nation's capital. Source: http://www.kittytours.org/thatman2/index.html, accessed Feb. 22, 2005.

77. Olson, pp. 47-48; Sitkoff, *A New Deal for Blacks*, pp. 80-81; Watkins, p. 639.

78. Dorothy Height addressing Black Leadership Conference, Washington, DC, C-SPAN, March 28, 2005.

79. Watkins, p. 640; Sitkoff, *A New Deal for Blacks*, p. 73; Sterner, pp. 261-262, 270; "The Tenth Youth"; Kryder, p. 28.

80. Sterner, pp. 262-270; Sitkoff, *A New Deal for Blacks*, p. 73.

81. Sitkoff, *A New Deal for Blacks*, p. 79; Franklin and Moss, p. 391; Olson, p. 51.

82. Watkins, pp. 646-647; Sitkoff, *A New Deal for Blacks*, p. 79; Kryder, pp. 27-28.

83. Olson, p. 51; Franklin and Moss, p. 394; Sitkoff, *A New Deal for Blacks*, p. 79.

84. Olson, p. 48; "Two Years with the Joint Committee on National Recovery, 1933-1935," Nov. 1935, USES/Oxley, RG 183; "Second National Conference on the Problems of the Negro and Negro Youth" [Proceedings], Jan. 1939, USES/Oxley, RG 183; Sitkoff, A New Deal for Blacks, pp. 81-83; "The Negro in Industry: National Conference on Problems of the Negro and Negro Youth," *Monthly Labor Review*, Feb. 1937, pp. 345-348.

85. Hahamovitch, p. 151; Sitkoff, *A New Deal for Blacks*, pp. 169-189; Franklin and Moss, pp. 401-404; Olson, pp. 404-405; Kurian, pp. 414-415; Zieger, "Black and White," p. 5.

86. Witte, pp. 143-145.

NOTES

87. "Second National Conference on the Problems of the Negro and Negro Youth" [Proceedings], Jan. 1939, USES/Oxley, RG 183, pp. 36-37.

88. Grossman, "Fair Labor Standards," pp. 22-30.

89. Moreno, pp. 41-52; Sitkoff, *A New Deal for Blacks*, pp. 216-243.

90. Berman, pp. 5-6.

CHAPTER 3.

1. Kersten, p. 11; Anderson, 242-243; Dalfiume, pp. 44-81, 106; Sitkoff, *A New Deal for Blacks*, 300; Franklin and Moss, pp. 434-436; Fairchild and Grossman, p. 156.

2. Dalfiume, pp. 106-114; Reed, p. 11; Anderson, p. 243; Sitkoff, *A New Deal for Blacks*, p. 300; Zangrando and Zangrando, p. 96; Ruchames, pp. 13-14; Fairchild and Grossman, p. 156.

3. Hastie had been dean of the Howard University Law School and was the first African American to be appointed a federal judge. See Fairchild and Grossman, pp. 156-157.

4. Kryder, pp. 25, 39; Sitkoff, *A New Deal for Blacks*, pp. 308-309.

5. Kersten, pp. 12-13; Kryder, pp. 38-39; Fairchild and Grossman, p. 94.

6. Franklin and Moss, p. 436; Reed, p. 13; Sitkoff, *A New Deal for Blacks*, pp. 308-309; Ruchames, pp. 11, 15-16; Kryder, pp. 39-41, 57; Fairchild and Grossman, p. 94.

7. Ruchames, p. 16; Sitkoff, *A New Deal for Blacks*, pp. 310-311.

8. Anderson, pp. 244-251; Franklin and Moss, p. 436; Reed, p. 13; Dalfiume, pp. 115-118.

9. Anderson, pp. 251-259; Sitkoff, *A New Deal for Blacks*, pp. 320-321; Ruchames, pp. 17-21; Dalfiume, pp. 13-15; Kryder, pp. 58-66; Fairchild and Grossman, p. 158.

10. Sitkoff, *A New Deal for Blacks*, p. 322; Reed, p. 1.

11. Moreno, pp. 66-73.

12. Reed, pp. 21-22.

13. Ibid., pp. 22, 83.

14. Kersten, p. 19; Reed, p. 28.

15. Kersten, pp. 19-36; Reed, p. 44; Ross, p. 21.

16. Ruchames, pp. 22-59; Kersten, p. 32; Reed, p. 51.

17. Reed, pp. 69-88; Kryder, p. 95; Kersten, p. 40.

18. Reed, pp. 101-102; Kersten, pp. 40-41.

19. Ruchames, pp. 22-59; Reed, pp. 92-112; M. Ross, pp. 21-22.

20. Reed, pp. 109-112; M. Ross, p. 22.

21. *FEPC: How it Operates*, pp. 3-4; Morgan, pp. 38-40; R. Weiss, pp. 37-38; Ruchames, pp. 22-59.

22. Ruchames, p. 66; Kersten, pp. 43-44.

23. Kryder, p. 97.

24. Ruchames, p. 151.

25. Ibid., pp. 137-145; *FEPC: How it Operates*, pp. 5-10; Kersten, p. 111.

26. The cooperative, educational approach of the Second FEPC anticipated the predominant direction of postwar federal efforts to promote equal opportunity for African Americans (see chapters 4-8). The racially proportionalistic emphasis of New Deal agencies such as the PWA, NYA, CCC, and WPA largely faded away with the wartime demise of these programs. The FEPC's approach was tactical, not philosophical. It was a practical response to the limited powers granted it by E.O.s 8802 and 9346. However, its policies received an intellectual underpinning in 1944 with the publication of Gunnar Myrdal's monumental and influential study of prejudice and race relations in the United States—*An American Dilemma*. Myrdal, a distinguished Swedish sociologist, defined discrimination, not primarily as an economic or social problem, but as a personal, moral problem. In his Introduction, Myrdal wrote: *"The American Negro problem is a problem in the heart of the American. It is there that the interracial tension has its focus. It is there that the decisive struggle goes on."* (Myrdal, p. xliii, original emphasis.) Into the 1960s, Myrdal's ideas and rhetoric reinforced a noncoercive approach to equal opportunity in the workplace and the society that was widely accepted by public officials. (See Sugrue, pp. 145-173.) In 2014 former Secretary of Labor Ray Marshall, at the US Department of Labor website (http://www.dol.gov/100/books-shaped-work/marshall.htm), described An American Dilemma as being of seminal importance for American labor policies and as a positive influence on the leadership of the civil rights movement. This was high praise coming from a public official who argued for vigorous enforcement of labor regulations generally and who saw many shortcomings in voluntarism as advocated by Myrdal (see Marshall's Foreword to this book, p. vii).

27. Kersten, p. 45; Reed, p. 156.

NOTES

28. Ruchames, pp. 145-149; Reed, p. 6.

29. Boris and Honey, p. 30; Kryder, pp. 39, 111-112.

30. King, p. 182; Kryder, p. 112; Ruchames, pp. 148-149; Reed, p. 6; Fairchild and Grossman, p. 159.

31. Reed, pp. 175-204; King, pp. 97-101.

32. Ruchames, pp. 150-151, 159-163.

33. M. Ross, pp. 38-39.

34. Ruchames, pp. 163-164; Moreno, pp. 66-73; Kryder, pp. 74-85, 90; Kersten, pp. 126-130; Reed, pp. 156-166.

35. Ruchames, pp. 159-163; R. Weiss, p. 38; Moreno, p. 72.

36. Ruchames, pp. 159-163; Reed, p. 10; Kersten, p. 135.

37. Kersten, pp. 136-137.

38. Kryder, pp. 113-130; Finch, pp. 111-113.

39. Palmer later chaired a successor to the FEPC in the Truman administration (see chapter 4); Kersten, p. 137.

40. Fairchild and Grossman, p. 160.

41. Ibid., p. 168.

42. Franklin and Moss, p. 437.

CHAPTER 4.

1. Berman, p. 34; R. Weiss, p. 39; Minchin, pp. 28-29; Reed, pp. 167-171; Kersten, pp. 131-133.

NOTES

2. Kersten, pp. 133-134; E.O. 9664, Dec. 20, 1945, RG 174.

3. R. Weiss, p. 39; McCoy and Ruetten, pp. 19-54; Morgan, p. 31.

4. *Growth of Labor Law in the United States*, pp. 257-260; R. Weiss, pp. 97, 40; Sugrue, p. 151.

5. McCoy and Ruetten, pp. 31-33; Lekachman, pp. 66, 165-175; Kurian, pp. 652-653.

6. Finch, p. 116; Berman, pp. 44-47.

7. McCoy and Ruetten, pp. 47-53, 86-91; Berman, pp. 51-57, 66-73; Dalfiume, pp. 144-145.

8. Berman, pp. 104-116; Dudziak, p. 82.

9. McCoy and Ruetten, pp. 97-130.

10. Ibid., pp. 156-157.

11. Truman had wanted to keep Perkins on as secretary and initially refused to accept her resignation. However, he encountered resistance to her remaining from the male members of his cabinet, despite the fact that she had served with distinction under FDR. Truman, evidently more tolerant of blacks than of women in the workplace, thereupon accepted the once-spurned resignation. As a consolation prize, he appointed her as a member of the US Civil Service Commission. Telephone conversation with Kirstin Downey (see bibliography). Feb. 21, 2008.

12. Anon. to Secretary of Labor, July 16, 1945, LS18, RG 174.

13. Robert Goodwin to Victor Reuther, Jan. 25, 1946 (and earlier attached items), Minority Group Policy, Gibson Box 6, RG 174.

14. Speech, Sec. Schwellenbach, Nov. 14, 1946, Historical Office, DOL.

15. The Tuskeegee Institute, *The Negro Yearbook*, 1947, p. 229; A.A. Liveright to Albert Abramson, letter, DOL, March 26, 1946, ACRR, Gibson Box 5, RG 174; Agenda, Emergency National Conference, April 5, 1946, AACRR, Gibson Box 5, RG 174.

16. The Bureau of Apprenticeship and Training was originally called the Apprenticeship Division, which was renamed a few years later. The BAT's function was to register and certify apprenticeship programs, which were privately run—usually jointly by employers and unions. It did not itself organize or operate apprenticeship programs.

17. ACRR Memo, April 12, 1946, A.A. Liveright to Robert Goodwin, April 30, 1947, AACRR, Gibson Box 5, RG 174.

18. Dalfiume, p. 149.

19. A. A. Liveright to William Patterson, April 29, 1946; William Patterson to A. A. Liveright, May 31, 1946, both found in ACRR, Gibson Box 5, RG 174.

20. A. A. Liveright to Maj. Gen. Graves Erskine, April 30, 1946, ACRR, Gibson Box 5, RG 174.

21. Memo from Sydney Taylor Brown, June 4, 1946; Agenda, National Action Conference on Minority Veterans' Problems, July 12, 1946, both found in ACRR, Gibson Box 5, RG 174.

22. Memo, Edward Cushman to John Gibson, Aug. 14, 1946, Minority Group Policy, Gibson Box 5, RG 174.

NOTES

23. *Current Biography*, 1947, pp. 335-337; *New York Post*, Sept. 24, 1946, p. 41. As a representative of the black social aid group Alpha Kappa Alpha, Thomasina Johnson was, according to the *New York Post*, "the first full-time Negro lobbyist in the nation's capital."

24. Sec. Schwellenbach to Robert Goodwin, Feb. 24, 1947, USES-General, Box 192, RG 174.

25. Thomasina Johnson to David Morse, Dec. 19, 1947, Minority Groups, Morse files, Box 6, RG 174.

26. Roy Patterson to Sec. Schwellenbach, Dec. 16, 1947, Discrimination, Box 31, RG 174.

27. David Morse to Sec. Schwellenbach, Jan. 6, 1948 (and attached correspondence), Discrimination, Box 31, RG 174.

28. Sec. Schwellenbach died in office on June 10, 1948.

29. DOL Press Release, Aug. 12, 1948; John Gibson to William Oliver, Aug. 31, 1948 (and attached material); John Gibson to Ruth Steele, Aug. 19, 1948 (and attached material), all found in FEPC Dir. Mat., Gibson Box 3, RG 174.

30. Speeches, Sec. Tobin, Nov. 15, 1949 and Sept. 11, 1950, Historical Office, DOL.

31. McCoy and Ruetten, pp. 190-192; Roy Wilkins to Sec. Tobin, Feb. 9, 1949, Gen. Corres. - Nat. A, Box 58, RG 174.

32. McCoy and Ruetten, pp. 113-114, 124, 134-135.

33. Sec. Tobin to Sen. Paul Douglas, Jan. 12, 1950, 1950—Cong.—D, Box 51, RG 174.

34. Clarence Mitchell to Sec. Tobin, Nov. 29, 1949; Thomasina Norford to John Gibson, Feb. 10, 1950, both found in FEPC Dir. Mat., Gibson Box 3, RG 174.

35. Winslow to Sec. Tobin, May 24, 1949; Winslow to John Gibson, Feb. 28, 1950, both found in FEPC Dir. Mat., Gibson Box 3, RG 174; Winslow to Sec. Tobin, Nov. 21, 1949, Admin.—Winslow, Box 1, RG 174; Winslow to Sec. Tobin, March 17, 1950, Admin.—Winslow, Box 32, RG 174.

36. John Gibson to Sec. Tobin, April 3, 1950, FEPC Dir. Mat., Gibson Box 3, RG 174; G.O. No. 40 [revised], Amendment No. 1, July 6, 1950, DOL Historical Office.

37. McCoy and Ruetten, pp. 251-266.

38. Rung.

39. King, p. 104.

40. McCoy and Ruetten, pp. 266-268; Clarence Mitchell to Sec. Tobin, Aug. 9, 1950; Sec. Tobin to Clarence Mitchell, Aug. 24, 1950, both found in Gen. Corres.—Nat. A., Box 58, RG 174.

41. Sec. Tobin to Walter White, Nov. 27, 1950, Gen. Corres. —Nat. A., Box 58, RG 174.

42. Sec. Tobin to David Niles, Dec. 27, 1950, FEPC Dir. Mat., Gibson Box 3, RG 174.

43. McCoy and Ruetten, pp. 268-275; Berman, pp. 185-186; Morgan, pp. 42-43.

44. McCoy and Ruetten, pp. 275-281; Berman, pp. 192-193.

NOTES

45. Transcript, Conference re: Nondiscrimination in Employment, July 15, 1952, PCGCC, Straub Box 2, RG 174.

46. PCGCC, Tentative Agenda for Meeting (and attachments), Oct. 7, 1952, Non-Discrim. Clause, Straub Box 5, RG 174.

47. Moreno, p. 179.

CHAPTER 5.

1. Burk, pp. 15-20; Berman, p. 231.

2. Burk, p. 39; Guzda, *Dictionary*, s.v. "Mitchell, James Paul," p. 543.

3. Branch, *Parting the Waters*, pp. 128-129, 216-218, 245, 255.

4. The American Federation of Labor (AFL) and the Congress of Industrial Organizations (CIO) merged in 1955 to form the AFL-CIO.

5. Patterson, pp. 19, 380-406; Branch, *Parting the Waters*, p. 269; Franklin and Moss, pp. 463, 466-473.

6. Burk, pp. 23-24, 262; Zieger, "'Uncle Sam Wants You," p. 97; Speech, Sec. Mitchell, Oct. 9, 1954, Historical Office, DOL.

7. Burk, pp. 69-70, 77-87; McCoy and Ruetten, p. 209; Speech, Sec. Mitchell, Aug. 30, 1956, Historical Office, DOL; DOL: Office of the Assistant Secretary for Administration and Management, s.v. "History at the Department of Labor," http://www.dol.gov/asp/programs/history/main.htm, also "Timeline," http://www.dol.gov/oasam/programs/history/dpt.htm (both accessed June 1, 2004).

8. Burk, pp. 45-60; Dulles, pp. 1-2; Branch, *Parting the Waters*, pp. 233-237; Franklin and Moss, p. 498.

9. Speech, Sec. Mitchell, Aug. 30, 1956, Historical Office, DOL; Burk, p. 44; Franklin and Moss, pp. 463-465.

10. Speech, Sec. Mitchell, Nov. 18, 1954, Historical Office, DOL.

11. Burk, p. 93; Morgan, pp. 43-44.

12. R. Weiss, pp. 42-43; Morgan, pp. 43-44; Burk, p. 93.

13. Burk, p. 95; Morgan, p. 44; Moreno, p. 180; Speech, Sec. Mitchell, Dec. 28, 1954, Historical Office, DOL.

14. Speech, Sec. Mitchell, Nov. 13, 1953, Historical Office, DOL.

15. Morgan, p. 44; Burk, p. 98.

16. Speeches, Sec. Mitchell, Nov. 13, 1953 and Oct. 25, 1955, Historical Office, DOL; Burk, pp. 95-96.

17. Burk, pp. 93, 98-100; Morgan, p. 44; Speech, Sec. Mitchell, Jan. 21, 1956, Historical Office, DOL; Moreno, p. 182.

18. Morgan, p. 44; Burk, p. 98; Speeches, Sec. Mitchell, Nov. 13, 1953, June 28, 1955, and Jan. 21, 1956, Historical Office, DOL.

19. Burk, p. 98; William P. Rogers later served as attorney general in the Eisenhower administration and secretary of state in the Richard Nixon administration.

20. Speeches, Sec. Mitchell, Dec. 28, 1954 and Jan. 21, 1956, Historical Office, DOL.

21. Burk, pp. 95-99; Morgan, p. 44; Speech, Sec. Mitchell, Dec. 28, 1954, Historical Office, DOL.

22. Burk, p. 98; Speeches, Sec. Mitchell, June 28, 1955 and Oct. 25, 1955, Historical Office, DOL.

NOTES

23. Speech, Sec. Mitchell, Jan. 21, 1956, Historical Office, DOL.

24. Speech, Sec. Mitchell, Oct. 25, 1955, Historical Office, DOL.

25. Burk, pp. 96-97.

26. R. Weiss, p. 43; Burk, pp. 93, 100, 101.

27. Moreno, pp. 184-188.

28. Speech, Sec. Mitchell, Sept. 20, 1955, Historical Office, DOL; R. Weiss, p. 43; Burk, pp. 102-108.

29. Burk, pp. 99-100, 104-105.

30. R. Weiss, p. 44.

31. Morgan, p. 45.

32. Burk, pp. 71-76, 87-88.

33. Speech, Sec. Mitchell, June 28, 1955, Historical Office, DOL; *Marquis Who's Who*, s.v. "Church, Roberta."

34. Robert Goodwin to Sec. Mitchell, March 11, 1954, Administrative DOL Programs, Box 42, RG 174.

35. Sec. Mitchell to Staff, July 13, 1957, att. to Church to Mitchell, Dec. 2, 1957, Admin.—Miss Church, Box 180, RG 174; Robert Goodwin to Sec. Mitchell, March 11, 1954, Administrative DOL Programs, Box 42, RG 174.

36. Church to Sec. Mitchell, Oct. 27, 1957, Admin.—Miss Church, Box 180, RG 174.

37. Record of Minority Groups Conference of July 1956, Nov. 1956, Box 148, RG 174.

38. BES Program Letter, Dec. 17, 1953, att. to Robert Goodwin to Mitchell, March 11, 1954, Administrative DOL Programs, Box 42, RG 174.

39. Robert Goodwin to Rocco Siciliano, March 26, 1956, State Correspondence—Arkansas, RG 174.

40. Bland to Goodwin, April 26, 1956, State Correspondence—Arkansas, RG 174.

41. Mitchell to Bland, May 16, 1956, State Correspondence—Arkansas, RG 174.

42. Newell Brown to Sec. Mitchell, Feb. 16, 1959, ES-2-1, RG 174.

43. Record of Minority Groups Conference of July 1956, Nov. 1956, Box 148, RG 174; *Annual Reports* [1956], DOL, pp. 8-9.

44. Robert Goodwin to Sec. Mitchell, March 11, 1954, Administrative DOL Programs, Box 42, RG 174; *Annual Reports* [1953], DOL, p. 23; Report, Sec. Goldberg to Vice President Johnson, May 25, 1961, PCEEO, Box 42, RG 174.

45. Newell Brown to O'Connell, March 16, 1960, AT-2-1, Box 334, RG 174.

46. Minchin, p. 9.

CHAPTER 6.

1. "February One," Independent Lens program, PBS, Feb. 1, 2005.

2. Brauer, pp. 30-40; Franklin and Moss, pp. 498-499.

3. President Kennedy followed this up during his tenure by frequently entertaining prominent blacks at the White House, something previous presidents did only rarely.

4. Inaugural Address of President Kennedy, Jan. 20, 1961, *Public Papers of the President*.

5. Robert Weaver was later appointed secretary of the new Department of Housing and Urban Development in 1965 and thereby became the first African American to serve in the cabinet.

6. Marshall was later appointed to the US Supreme Court.

7. Brauer, p. 84; Franklin and Moss, p. 500; Wirtz, transcript of interview conducted by the author, Dec. 11, 1998, pp. 2-4.

8. Moreno, p. 189; Reed, pp. 111-112; Graham, pp. 28, 33-34; Wirtz, untranscribed interview conducted by the author, June 15, 2004; Wirtz interview, Dec. 11, 1998, p. 29.

9. Press Release, April 5, 1961, Historical Office, DOL.

10. JFK Memo to Executive Departments, April 18, 1961, PCEEO, Box 42, RG 174.

11. Graham, pp. 43-46.

12. Meany, Reuther, and Lazarus had also served on President Eisenhower's PCGC.

13. Press Release, April 5, 1961, Historical Office, DOL; Sec. Goldberg to Agency Heads, April 3, 1961, PCEEO, Box 42, RG 174; Speech, Arthur Chapin, April 8, 1961, PE-4-2, Box 82, RG 174.

14. Press Release, April 5, 1961, Historical Office, DOL; Lundquist to Shulman, March 8, 1961, PCEEO, Box 42, RG 174.

15. Sec. Goldberg to DOL Employees, March 7, 1961, White House, Box 23, RG 174.

16. Ibid.

17. Ibid.

18. Sec. Goldberg to Vice Pres. Johnson, March 9, 1961, White House, Box 23, RG 174; Wirtz interview, Dec. 11, 1998, pp. 14-17; Press Release, Feb. 17, 1961, Historical Office, DOL; Vice Pres. Johnson to Sec. Goldberg, March 11, 1961, White House, Box 23, RG 174.

19. Press Release, April 5, 1961, Historical Office, DOL; Speech, Arthur Chapin, April 8, 1961, PE-4-2, Box 82, RG 174.

20. First Meeting of PCEEO [minutes], April 11, 1961, PCEEO, Box 42, RG 174.

21. Underlining this point, Executive Vice Chair Jerry Holleman reminded the members that they were expected to attend meetings in person whenever possible rather than relying on proxies.

22. First Meeting of PCEEO [minutes], April 11, 1961, PCEEO, Box 42, RG 174.

23. Ibid.

24. PCEEO, Newsletter, July 1961; *Rules and Regulations*.

25. Graham, p. 46.

26. Brauer, p. 80.

27. *The First Nine Months*, pp. 49-52.

28. PCEEO, Newsletter, June 1961, July 1962; Jerry Holleman to Agency Heads, April 28, 1961, PCEEO, Box 42 RG 174; *The First*

NOTES

Nine Months, pp. 2-3, 49-52; Statement by Arthur Goldberg, PCEEO Press Release, May 2, 1961, PCEEO, Box 42, RG 174; *Rules and Regulations*.

29. Graham, pp. 33, 48; Wirtz interview, June 15, 2004.

30. *The First Nine Months*, pp. 49-52.

31. Sen. Lister Hill to PCEEO, July 12, 1961, PCEEO, Box 43, RG 174.

32. PCEEO, Newsletter, Jan. 1962.

33. Report of the PCEEO, *The First Nine Months*, Jan. 15, 1962, pp. 49-52.

34. Sen. Lister Hill to PCEEO, July 12, 1961, PCEEO/Box 43, RG 174.

35. PCEEO, Newsletter, Jan. 1962.

CHAPTER 7.

1. PCEEO, Newsletter, various issues, 1961-1962.

2. *The First Nine Months*, pp. 6-7; PCEEO, Newsletter, June 1961.

3. Report to the President by the PCEEO, Washington, DC, Nov. 26, 1963, pp. 1-3.

4. PCEEO, Newsletter, June 1961; Statement by Sec. Goldberg, PCEEO Press Release, May 2, 1961, PCEEO, Box 42, RG 174.

5. *The First Nine Months*, pp. 2-3.

6. PCEEO, Newsletter, July 1962; *The American Dream—Equal Opportunity*, p. 12.

7. *The American Dream—Equal Opportunity*, p. 12; *The First Nine Months*, pp. 3, 45.

8. *The First Nine Months*, pp. 42-45.

9. Ibid.

10. PCEEO, Newsletter, June and July 1961.

11. PCEEO, Newsletter, April and July 1962.

12. *The First Nine Months*, pp. 2-3, 36; PCEEO, Newsletter, July 1961.

13. PCEEO, Newsletter, Sept. 1961.

14. Graham, pp. 47-49.

15. Support in this case later grew into a broader commitment to the PCEEO by the Pentagon that included provision of both policy and staff support in other defense contract enforcement actions.

16. PCEEO, Newsletter, June 1961; Graham, pp. 47-49.

17. *The First Nine Months*, p. 36.

18. *The First Nine Months*, p. 2; Moreno, pp. 191-192.

19. The subcommittee's other members included progressive businessmen Edgar Kaiser and Fred Lazarus, Jr.; UAW president Walter Reuther; and DHEW Secretary Abraham Ribicoff.

20. Graham, pp. 50-52; Report to the President by the PCEEO, Washington, DC, Nov. 26, 1963, p. 108.

21. PCEEO, Newsletter, July and Sept. 1961, Jan. 1962.

NOTES

22. Report to the President by the PCEEO, Washington, DC, Nov. 26, 1963, p. 109.

23. Ibid., p. 2.

24. PCEEO, Newsletter, July 1962.

25. Minchin, pp. 9-10; George Meany to Vice Pres. Johnson, March, 7, 1961, PCEEO, Box 42, RG 174.

26. Francis Shane to Sec. Goldberg, Aug. 11, 1961, PCEEO, Box 43, RG 174.

27. *The First Nine Months*, pp. 36-37, 61-62; *The American Dream—Equal Opportunity*, p. 13; PCEEO Meeting [minutes], Feb. 15, 1962, PCEEO, Box 155, RG 174, p. 64.

28. *The First Nine Months*, p. 61.

29. *The First Nine Months*, pp. 63-64; *The American Dream—Equal Opportunity*, p. 13.

30. *The American Dream—Equal Opportunity*; *The First Nine Months*, pp. 63-64; PCEEO, Newsletter, July 1962.

31. *The First Nine Months*, pp. 63-64; Report to the President by the PCEEO, Washington, DC, Nov. 26, 1963, p. 130.

32. *The First Nine Months*, p. 5.

33. Jerry Holleman to Agency Heads, Oct. 23, 1961, PCEEO, Box 43, RG 174.

34. Jerry Holleman to Agency Heads, April 28, 1961, PCEEO, Box 42 RG 174; *The First Nine Months*, p. 13; PCEEO, Newsletter, July 1962; *The American Dream—Equal Opportunity*, p. 12.

35. John Feild to Sec. Goldberg, June 22, 1962, PCEEO, Box 156, RG 174.

36. Jerry Holleman to Agency Heads, April 28, 1961, PCEEO, Box 42 RG 174; *The First Nine Months*, p. 1; *The American Dream—Equal Opportunity*, p. 11; PCEEO, Newsletter, June 1961; Brauer, pp. 83-85.

37. *The First Nine Months*, p. 1; Report to the President by the PCEEO, Washington, DC, Nov. 26, 1963, p. 3; *The American Dream—Equal Opportunity*, p. 11; Franklin and Moss, p. 500.

38. John McCully to Jerry Holleman (with attachments), April 2, 1962, PCEEO, Box 156, RG 174.

39. Sumner Stone to Vice Pres. Johnson, March 9, 1962 [Under March 28, 1962], PCEEO, Box 155, RG 174.

40. Herbert Hill to Sec. Goldberg, April 11, 1962, PCEEO, Box 156, RG 174; Moreno, pp. 191-192.

41. Graham, pp. 51-57.

42. *New York Times*, June 20, 1962.

43. Graham, pp. 57-58; Press Release, May 11, 1962, Historical Office, DOL.

44. Jerry Holleman to Federal Agency Heads, May 11, 1961, PCEEO, Box 156, RG 174.

CHAPTER 8.

1. *Kheel Report*, July 1962, PCEEO, Box 156, RG 174.

NOTES

2. "Plans for Progress, One-Year Goals and One-Year Results," Memorandum to the President and the Vice President, Aug. 20, 1962, PCEEO, Box 156, RG 174.

3. Brauer, pp. 149-150.

4. "Plans for Progress, One-Year Goals and One-Year Results."

5. Stanley Simmons to Sec. Goldberg, Aug. 31, 1962, PCEEO, Box 156, RG 174.

6. Brauer, pp. 149-151.

7. PCEEO Press Release, Jan. 17, 1963, PCEEO, Box 64, RG 174; "Special Report, Plans for Progress: Atlanta Survey," Southern Regional Council (Atlanta, GA, Jan. 1963).

8. *Newsweek*, Feb. 25, 1963, p. 27.

9. John Feild to Hobart Taylor, Feb. 28, 1963 (several related memos attached), PCEEO, Box 65, RG 174.

10. Brauer, pp. 214-215.

11. Meeting of the Vice President's Study Group [minutes], March 7, 1963, PCEEO, Box 64, RG 174.

12. PCEEO Meeting [minutes], July 18, 1963, PCEEO, Box 64, RG 174; Brauer, p. 216.

13. Hobart Taylor to Wirtz, July 18, 1963, PCEEO, Box 66, RG 174; Report to the President by the PCEEO, Washington, DC, Nov. 26, 1963, p. 110.

14. Nevertheless, in December 1963, DOL officials reviewing the draft PCEEO annual report sought to downplay claims of progress.

Special Assistant Tom Powers recommended to Sec. Wirtz that "our objectives should be to claim as much progress as we can without subjecting ourselves to attack" (Powers to Sec. Wirtz, Dec. 17, 1963, PCEEO, Box 64, RG 1740). In a measure of the extent to which critics had been appeased, this claim passed without comment. (Remarks of Pres. Johnson, Plans for Progress Meeting, Jan. 16, 1964, PCEEO, Box 153, RG 174.)

15. *Proceedings*, PCEEO, May 12, 1964, DOL Library, pp. 35-39; Wirtz interview, June 15, 2004.

16. Brauer, p. 150.

17. Boris Shiskin to Sec. Goldberg, June 30, 1961, PI-6-3-6, Box 89, RG 174; Sec. Goldberg to Francis Shane, United Steelworkers of America (further correspondence attached), Aug. 17, 1961, PCEEO, Box 43, RG 174; Walter Reuther to Sec. Goldberg, Nov. 28, 1961, PCEEO, Box 43, RG 174; Francis Shane to Sec. Goldberg, Nov. 29, 1961, PCEEO, Box 43, RG 174.

18. PCEEO meeting [minutes], Feb. 15, 1962, pp. 64-65, PCEEO, Box 155, RG 174.

19. Wirtz interview, June 15, 2004; PCEEO meeting [minutes], Feb. 15, 1962, PCEEO, Box 155, RG 174, pp. 64-65; *The American Dream—Equal Opportunity*, p. 13; *The First Nine Months*, p. 62; PCEEO, Newsletter, Sept. 1961; Report to the President by the PCEEO, Washington, DC, Nov. 26, 1963, pp. 2, 118-127.

20. AFL-CIO Release, June 28, 1963, PCEEO, Box 66, RG 174; Report to the President by the PCEEO, Washington, DC, Nov. 26, 1963, p. 119; Sec. Wirtz to George Meany, March 14, 1963, PCEEO, Box 65, RG 174.

NOTES

21. Report to the President by the PCEEO, Washington, DC, Nov. 26, 1963, pp. 119-120.

22. Sec. Wirtz telegram to UPFP unions, June 10, 1963; Sec. Wirtz letters to UPFP unions, Aug. 7, 1963, both found in PCEEO, Box 66, RG 174; Tom Powers to Sec. Wirtz, Aug. 28, 1963, PCEEO, Box 66, RG 174; Report to the President by the PCEEO, Washington, DC, Nov. 26, 1963, pp. 118-119.

23. James R. Hoffa to Vice Pres. Johnson, July 3, 1963, PCEEO, Box 66, RG 174.

24. Minchin, pp. 111-112.

25. Sec. Wirtz to Robert Kennedy, June 12, 1963, White House—President, Box 38, RG 174.

26. PCEEO Press Release, March 17, 1964, PCEEO, Box 153, RG 174.

27. Remarks of President Johnson, March 16, 1964, Public Papers of the President, PCEEO, Box 153, RG 174.

28. Graham, p. 59.

29. *Proceedings*, PCEEO, May 12, 1964, Washington, DC, pp. 13-14.

30. Report to the President by the PCEEO, Washington, DC, Nov. 26, 1963, pp. 10-13.

31. Ibid., pp. 21-22.

32. Ibid., pp. 34-39; Moreno, p. 193.

33. Report to President by PCEEO, Nov. 26, 1963, p. 29.

34. PCEEO Meeting, July 18, 1963, PCEEO, Box 64, p. 3.

35. PCEEO Meeting, May 29, 1963, PCEEO, Box 65, p. 2; Wirtz interview, Dec. 11, 1998, pp. 11-12; Brauer, p. 283; Branch, *Pillar of Fire*, pp. 90-91.

36. John Donovan to Sec. Wirtz, Oct. 10, 1963, PCEEO, Box 64, RG 174; *Proceedings*, PCEEO, May 12, 1964, pp. 16-18.

37. Graham, pp. 64-67.

38. PCEEO Meeting, July 18, 1963, PCEEO, Box 64, RG 174.

39. E.O. 1114, June 22, 1963, Presidential Documents, Part II, Sect. 202.

40. *Proceedings*, PCEEO, May 12, 1964; Wirtz interview, June 15, 2004.

CHAPTER 9.

1. Charles Donohue to Sec. Wirtz, Oct. 4, 1962, AT 2-1, Box 9, RG 174.

2. Robert Goodwin to Sec. Wirtz, Dec. 4, 1962, Conf. Misc., Box 11, RG 174; Speech, Sec. Wirtz, Jan. 23, 1964, Historical Office, DOL.

3. PCEEO meeting, Feb. 15, 1962, PCEEO, Box 156, RG 174; National Urban League Conference, May 16, 1962, Secretary's Cfces., Box 152, RG 174; Sub-Cabinet Group on Civil Rights, Report, March 12, 1962, Sub-Cabinet Committee, Box 159, RG 174.

4. Charles Donohue to Sec. Wirtz, Oct. 4, 1962, AT 2-1, Box 9, RG 174; PCEEO Meeting, Feb. 15, 1962, PCEEO, Box 156, RG 174; Sub-Cabinet Group on Civil Rights, Report, March 12, 1962,

Sub-Cabinet Committee, Box 159, RG 174; National Urban League Conference, May 16, 1962, Secretary's Cfces., Box 152, RG 174.

5. Press Release, July 17, 1961, Historical Office, DOL; Sec. Goldberg to Gov. John Swainson (MI), Aug. 24, 1961, AT 2-1, Box 29, RG 174; Civil Rights Sub-Cabinet Group, Feb. 1962 Report, Committees-Sub-Cabinet Group, Box 159, RG 174.

6. Ansel Cleary to George Meany, Nov. 3, 1961, AT-2-1, Box 29, RG 174.

7. Meeting on Recruitment of BAT Representatives [minutes], Nov. 9, 1963, AT 2-1, Box 29, RG 174.

8. Press Release, June 25, 1962, Historical Office, DOL.

9. Sec. Wirtz to Robert Kennedy, June 5, 1963, PCEEO, Box 66, RG 174; Press Releases, Feb. 27, May 23, June 10 and 17, 1963, Historical Office, DOL.

10. Manpower Administration Order No. 12, Nov. 12, 1963, AT-1, Box 49, RG 174.

11. John Henning to Sec. Wirtz, May 22, 1963, Advisory Committee, Box 69, RG 174.

12. Statement of the President, June 4, 1963, PCEEO, Box 66, RG 174.

13. Sec. Wirtz to Robert Kennedy, June 5, 1963, PCEEO, Box 66, RG 174; Sec. Wirtz to state apprenticeship offices (30 letters), June 5, 1963, PCEEO, Box 66, RG 174; Sugrue, p. 164.

14. See Moreno, pp. 193-197.

15. Sec. Wirtz to state apprenticeship offices (30 letters), June 5, 1963, PCEEO, Box 66, RG 174.

16. Sec. Wirtz to Edward Goshen, June 11, 1963, AT-1, Box 49, RG 174.

17. Sec. Wirtz to Edward Goshen, July 2, 1963, AT-1, Box 49, RG 174.

18. Sec. Wirtz to Edward Goshen, June 11, 1963, AT-1, Box 49, RG 174.

19. BAT Circular 64-7, July 17, 1963, AT-2-1, Box 49, RG 174.

20. David Christian to John Donovan, July 17, 1963, AT-1, Box 49, RG 174.

21. "Nondiscrimination in Apprenticeship and Training," Notice of Proposed Rule Making, *Federal Register*, Oct. 23, 1963, pp. 11313-11316.

22. R. P. Sornsin to Sec. Wirtz, Nov. 8, 1963, AT-2-1, Box 49, RG 174.

23. Herrick S. Roth, Nov. 6, 1963, AT-2-1, Box 49, RG 174.

24. M. L. Katke to John Henning, Nov. 4, 1963, AT-2-1, Box 49, RG 174.

25. Sec. Wirtz to C. J. Haggerty, Dec. 9, 1963, AT-2-1, Box 49, RG 174.

26. John Henning to B. A. Gritta, Dec. 6, 1963, AT-2-1, Box 49, RG 174.

27. Michael Fox to Sec. Wirtz, Nov. 4, 1963, AT-2-1, Box 49, RG 174.

28. "Nondiscrimination in Apprenticeship and Training," 29 CFR Part 30, *Federal Register*, Dec. 18, 1963, pp. 13775-13778. In June

1964 the PCEEO, which had developed the original basis for the standard, adopted the rule. (See also Sec. Wirtz to PCEEO Subcommittee, April 3, 1964, PCEEO, Box 153, RG 174; and PCEEO Press Releases, May 1, June 5, 1964, PCEEO, Box 144, RG 174.)

29. *Annual Reports*, DOL: 1964, p. 40; 1965, pp. 44-45; and 1966, p. 41.

EPILOGUE.

1. See Ira Katznelson, *When Affirmative Action Was White*, for a full discussion of this point.

Bibliography

I. Books (non-government) and Articles:

Abrams, Richard M. *The Issues of the Populist and Progressive Eras, 1892-1912*. Columbia, SC: University of South Carolina Press, 1969.

Altmeyer, Arthur J. *The Formative Years of Social Security*. Madison, WI: University of Wisconsin Press, 1966.

Anderson, Jervis. A. *Philip Randolph: A Biographical Portrait*. New York: Harcourt Brace Jovanovich, 1972.

Ballew, Charles LeBron. "Woodrow Wilson and the Negro." MA thesis, University of Maryland, 1965.

Barde, Robert. "An Alleged Wife: The Mysterious Detention and Trials of a Chinese Immigrant Early in the 20th Century." Unpublished manuscript, October 4, 1999.

Berman, William C. *The Politics of Civil Rights in the Truman Administration*. Columbus, OH: Ohio State University Press, 1970.

Blumberg, Barbara. *The New Deal and the Unemployed: The View from New York City*. Lewisburg, PA: Bucknell University Press, 1979.

Booker, Christopher B. "Woodrow Wilson: The Last Confederate." Web-published excerpt from *African Americans and the Presidency*. New York: Scholastic, 2000. www.pressroom/~afrimale/wilson.htm (accessed November 7, 2001).

Boris, Eileen, and Michael Honey. "Gender, Race, and the Policies of the Labor Department." *Monthly Labor Review*, February 1988, pp. 26-36.

Branch, Taylor. *Parting the Waters: America in the King Years, 1954-1963*. New York: Simon and Schuster, 1988.

———. *Pillar of Fire: America in the King Years, 1963-1965*. New York: Simon and Schuster, 1998.

Brauer, Carl M. *John F. Kennedy and the Second Reconstruction*. New York: Columbia University Press, 1977.

Breen, William J. "Black Women and the Great War: Mobilization and Reform in the South." *Journal of Southern History*, August 1978, pp. 421-40.

———. *Labor Market Politics and the Great War: The Department of Labor, the State and the First U.S. Employment Service, 1907-1933*. Kent, OH: Kent State University Press, 1997.

Brown, Josephine Chapin. *Public Relief 1929-1939*. New York: Henry Holt and Company, 1940.

Burg, David F. *The Great Depression: An Eyewitness History*. New York: Facts On File, 1996.

Burk, Robert Fredrick. *The Eisenhower Administration and Black Civil Rights*. Knoxville, TN: University of Tennessee Press, 1984.

Burkey, Richard M. *Racial Discrimination and Public Policy in the United States*. Lexington, MA: Heath Lexington Books, 1971.

Burstein, Paul. *Discrimination, Jobs, and Politics: The Struggle for Equal Employment Opportunity in the United States since the*

New Deal. 2nd ed. Chicago: University of Chicago Press, 1998.

Cantor, Milton. *Black Labor in America.* Westport, CT: Negro Universities Press, 1969.

Cayton, Horace R., and George S. Mitchell. *Black Workers and the New Unions.* Chapel Hill: University of North Carolina Press, 1939.

Chase, Stuart. *Men and Machines.* New York: MacMillan, 1924.

Clarke, Jane Nienaber. *Roosevelt's Warrior: Harold L. Ickes and the New Deal.* Baltimore, MD: Johns Hopkins University Press, 1996.

Clements, Kendrick A. *The Presidency of Woodrow Wilson.* Lawrence, KS: University of Kansas Press, 1992.

Cole, Olen, Jr. *The African-American Experience in the Civilian Conservation Corps.* Gainesville, FL: University of Florida Press, 1999.

Dalfiume, Richard M. *Desegregation of the U.S. Armed Forces: Fighting on Two Fronts, 1939-1953.* Columbia, MO: University of Missouri Press, 1969.

Dallek, Robert. *Flawed Giant: Lyndon Johnson and His Times, 1961-1973.* New York: Oxford University Press, 1998.

Degler, Carl N., ed. *The New Deal.* Chicago: Quadrangle Books, 1970.

DeNoon, Christopher. *Posters of the WPA.* Los Angeles: The Wheatley Press, 1987.

Derber, Milton. *Labor in Illinois: The Affluent Years, 1945-80.* Urbana, IL: University of Illinois Press, 1989.

Detweiler, Frederick G. *The Negro Press in the United States.* Chicago: University of Chicago Press, 1922.

Downey, Kirstin. *The Woman Behind the New Deal: The Life of Frances Perkins, FDR's Secretary of Labor and His Moral Conscience.* New York: Doubleday, 2009.

Draper, Alan. *Conflict of Interests: Organized Labor and the Civil Rights Movement in the South, 1954-1968.* Ithaca, NY: ILR Press, 1994.

DuBois, W. E. Burghardt. *The Souls of Black Folk.* Greenwich, CT: Fawcett, 1961.

Dudziak, Mary L. *Cold War Civil Rights: Race and the Image of American Democracy.* Princeton, NJ: Princeton University Press, 2000.

Dulles, Foster Rhea. *The Civil Rights Commission: 1957-1965.* East Lansing, MI: Michigan State University Press, 1968.

Dutcher, Dean. *The Negro in Modern Industrial Society: An Analysis of Changes in the Occupations of Negro Workers 1910-1920.* Lancaster, PA: The Science Press, 1930.

Egerton, John. *Speak Now Against the Day: The Generation before the Civil Rights Movement in the South.* New York: Knopf, 1994.

Ellis, Mark. *Race, War, and Surveillance: African Americans and the United States Government during World War I.* Bloomington, IN: Indiana University Press, 2001.

Fairchild, Byron, and Jonathan Grossman. *The Army and Industrial Manpower in World War II.* Reprinted, Washington, D.C.: Center of Military History, Department of the Army, 2002.

Falzone, Vincent J. *Terence V. Powderly: Middle Class Reformer.* Washington, D.C.: University Press of America, 1978.

"February One." Independent Lens program, PBS, Feb. 1, 2005.

Finch, Minnie. *The NAACP: Its Fight For Justice.* Metuchen, NJ: The Scarecrow Press, 1981.

Foner, Philip S., and Ronald L. Lewis. *Black Workers: A Documentary History from Colonial Times to the Present.* Philadelphia: Temple University Press, 1989.

Franklin, John Hope, and Alfred A. Moss, Jr. *From Slavery to Freedom: A History of African Americans.* 7th ed. New York: Alfred A. Knopf, 1994.

Freidel, Frank Burt. *America in the Twentieth Century.* New York: Knopf, 1965.

Giffin, William W. *African Americans and the Color Line in Ohio, 1915-1930.* Columbus: Ohio State University Press, 2005.

Gill, Flora. *Economics and the Black Exodus: An Analysis of Negro Emigration from the Southern United States: 1910-70.* New York: Garland Publishing, 1979.

Goodwin, Doris Kearns. *Lyndon Johnson and the American Dream.* New York: Harper and Row, 1976.

Gottlieb, Peter. "Migration and Jobs: The New Black Workers in Pittsburgh, 1916-1930," *The Western Pennsylvania Historical Magazine*, January 1978, pp. 1-15. Reproduced in Kusmer, *The Great Migration and After*, 297-311. [see separate citation for Kusmer]

Graham, Hugh Davis. *The Civil Rights Era: Origins and Development of National Policy 1960-1972.* New York: Oxford University Press, 1990.

Grant, Robert B. *The Black Man Comes to the City.* Chicago: Nelson-Hall Company, 1972.

Greene, Lorenzo J., and Carter G. Woodson. *The Negro Wage Earner.* Washington, D.C.: Association for the Study of Negro Life and History, 1930.

Grossman, Jonathan. *The Department of Labor.* New York: Praeger Publishers, 1973.

———. "Black Studies in the Department of Labor, 1897-1907." *Monthly Labor Review*, June 1974, pp. 17-27.

———. "Fair Labor Standards Act of 1938: Maximum Struggle for a Minimum Wage." *Monthly Labor Review*, June 1978, pp. 22-30.

Guzda, Henry P. "Frances Perkins' Interest in a New Deal for Blacks." *Monthly Labor Review*, April 1980, pp. 31-35.

———. "Labor Department's First Program to Assist Black Workers." *Monthly Labor Review*, June 1982, pp. 39-44.

———. "Mitchell, James Paul." In *Dictionary of American Biography Supplement Seven: 1961-1965*, pp. 542-44. New York: Scribner's Sons, 1981.

———. "Social Experiment of the Labor Department: the Division of Negro Economics." *The Public Historian* 4, no. 4 (1982): pp. 7-37.

Guzman, Jessie Parkhurst, ed. *Negro Year Book: A Review of Events Affecting Negro Life, 1941-1946*. Tuskegee, AL: Tuskegee Institute, 1947.

Hahamovitch, Cindy. *The Fruits of Their Labor: Atlantic Coast Farmworkers and the Making of Migrant Poverty, 1870-1945*. Chapel Hill, NC: University of North Carolina Press, 1997.

Hareven, Tamara. "ER and Reform." In *Without Precedent: The Life and Career of Eleanor Roosevelt*, edited by Joan Hoff-Wilson and Marjorie Lightman, pp. 201-12. Bloomington, IN: Indiana University Press, 1984.

Harrison, Robert. *State and Society in Twentieth-Century America*. New York: Longman, 1997.

Haynes, George E. "Negro Migration—Its Effect on Family and Community Life in the North." In *Proceedings of the*

National Conference of Social Work, pp. 62-75. June-July 1924. Chicago: University of Chicago Press, 1924.

Hiestand, Dale L. *Economic Growth and Employment Opportunities for Minorities*. New York: Columbia University Press, 1964.

Higgs, Robert. "Black Progress and the Persistence of Racial Economic Inequalities, 1865-1940." In *The Question of Discrimination: Racial Inequality in the U.S. Labor Market*, edited by Steven Shulman and William Darity, Jr., pp. 9-31. Middletown, CT: Wesleyan University Press, 1989.

Hill, Herbert. "Black Labor and Affirmative Action: An Historical Perspective." In *The Question of Discrimination*, pp. 190-267.

———. *Black Labor and the American Legal System: Race, Work and the Law*. Madison, WI: University of Wisconsin, 1985.

Howard, Donald S. *The WPA and Federal Relief Policy*. New York: Russell Sage Foundation, 1943.

Hunter, Tera W. *To 'Joy My Freedom: Southern Black Women's Lives and Labor after the Civil War*. Cambridge, MA: Harvard University Press, 1997.

Ickes, Harold L. *Back to Work: The Story of PWA*. New York: MacMillan, 1935.

Jaynes, Gerald David, and Robin M. Williams, Jr., eds. *A Common Destiny: Blacks and American Society*. Washington, D.C.: National Academy Press, 1989.

Johnson, Charles S. *The Negro in American Civilization: A Study of Negro Life and Race Relations in the Light of Social Research*. New York: Henry Holt, 1930.

Johnson, Lyndon Baines. *The Vantage Point: Perspectives of the Presidency*. New York: Holt, Rinehart, and Winston, 1971.

Katznelson, Ira. *When Affirmative Action Was White: An Untold History of Racial Inequality in Twentieth-Century America*. New York: W. W. Norton, 2005.

Kendricks, Ralph, and Claudette Levitt, eds. *Afro-American Voices, 1770's -1990's*. New York: Oxford Book Company, 1970.

Kennedy, Louise Venable. *The Negro Peasant Turns Cityward: Effects of Recent Migrations to Northern Centers*. New York: Columbia University Press, 1930.

Kersten, Andrew Edmund. *Race, Jobs, and the War: The FEPC in the Midwest, 1941-46*. Urbana, IL: University of Illinois Press, 2000.

King, Desmond S. *Separate and Unequal: Black Americans and the U.S. Federal Government*. Oxford: Clarendon Press, 1995.

Klug, Thomas. "Employers' Strategies in the Detroit Labor Market, 1900-1929." In *On the Line: Essays in the History of Auto Work*, edited by Melson Lichtenstein and Stephen Meyer, pp. 42-72. Urbana, IL: University of Illinois Press, 1988.

Kryder, Daniel. *Divided Arsenal: Race and the American State during World War II*. Cambridge, U.K.: Cambridge University Press, 2000.

Kurian, George, ed. *A Historical Guide to the U.S. Government*. New York: Oxford University Press, 1998.

Kusmer, Kenneth L. "Editor's Introduction." In *The Great Migration and After, 1917-1930*. New York: Garland Publishing, 1991.

Lawrence, Jacob. *The Great Migration: An American Story*. New York: HarperCollins, HarperTrophy Publishers, 1995.

Lekachman, Robert. *The Age of Keynes*. New York: Random House, 1966.

Levy, Peter B., ed. *Documentary History of the Modern Civil Rights Movement*. New York: Greenwood Press, 1992.

Lewis, Anthony. *Portrait of a Decade: The Second American Revolution [by] Anthony Lewis and the New York Times*. New York: Random House, 1964.

Lewis, David Levering. *W. E. B. DuBois: Biography of a Race, 1868-1919*. New York: Henry Holt, 1993.

Lewis, Edward E. *The Mobility of the Negro: A Study in the American Labor Supply*. New York: Columbia University Press, 1931.

Lombardi, John. *Labor's Voice in the Cabinet: A History of the Department of Labor from its Origin to 1921*. New York: Columbia University Press, 1942.

Macmahon, Arthur W., John D. Millett, and Gladys Ogden. *The Administration of Federal Work Relief*. Chicago: Public Administration Service, 1941.

Marquis Who's Who. "Church, Roberta." Dialog File 234. Reed Elsevier, Inc., 2004.

Marshall, F. Ray. *The Negro and Organized Labor*. New York: John Wiley and Sons, 1965.

———. *The Negro Worker*. New York: Random House, 1967.

Martin, George. *Madam Secretary: Frances Perkins*. Boston: Houghton Mifflin Company, 1976.

McCarthy, Abigail Q. "ER as First Lady." In *Without Precedent: The Life and Career of Eleanor Roosevelt*, edited by Joan Hoff-Wilson and Marjorie Lightman, pp. 214-25.

McCoy, Donald R., and Richard T. Ruetten. *Quest and Response: Minority Rights and the Truman Administration*. Lawrence, KS: The University Press of Kansas, 1973.

McJimsey, George. *Harry Hopkins: Ally of the Poor and Defender of Democracy*. Cambridge, MA: Harvard University Press, 1987.

Miller, Abie. *The Negro and the Great Society*. New York: Vantage Press, 1965.

Minchin, Timothy J. *The Color of Work: The Struggle for Civil Rights in the Southern Paper Industry, 1945-1980*. Chapel Hill, NC: University of North Carolina Press, 2001.

Moreno, Paul D. *From Direct Action to Affirmative Action: Fair Employment Law and Policy in America, 1933-1972*. Baton Rouge: Louisiana State University Press, 1997.

Morgan, Ruth P. *The President and Civil Rights: Policy-Making by Executive Order*. New York: St. Martin's Press, 1970.

Myrdal, Gunnar. *An American Dilemma: The Negro Problem and Modern Democracy*. New York: Harper and Brothers, 1944.

Nichols, David A. *A Matter of Justice: Eisenhower and the Beginning of the Civil Rights Revolution*. New York: Simon and Schuster, 2007.

Norgren, Paul H., and Samuel E. Hill. *Toward Fair Employment*. New York: Columbia University Press, 1964.

Northrup, Herbert R. *Organized Labor and the Negro*. New York: Harper and Brothers Publishers, 1944.

Northrup, Herbert R., and Richard L. Rowan, eds. *The Negro and Employment Opportunity: Problems and Practices*. Ann Arbor: University of Michigan, 1965.

Olson, James S., ed. *Historical Dictionary of the New Deal*. Westport, CT: Greenwood Press, 1985.

Patler, Nicholas. *Jim Crow and the Wilson Administration*. Boulder: University of Colorado Press, 2004.

Patterson, James T. *Grand Expectations: The United States, 1945-1974*. New York: Oxford University Press, 1996.

Pemberton, William E. *Bureaucratic Politics: Executive Reorganization during the Truman Administration.* Columbia, MO: University of Missouri Press, 1979.

Perkins, Dexter. *The New Age of Franklin Roosevelt, 1932-45.* Chicago: University of Chicago Press, 1957.

Perkins, Frances. *The Roosevelt I Knew.* New York: Viking Press, 1946.

Reed, Merl E. *Seedtime for the Modern Civil Rights Movement: The President's Committee on Fair Employment Practice, 1941-1946.* Baton Rouge, LA: Louisiana State University Press, 1991.

Reuter, Edward Byron. *The American Race Problem: A Study of the Negro.* New York: Thomas Y. Crowell, 1927.

Riddlesperger, Jr., James W., and Donald W. Jackson, eds. *Presidential Leadership and Civil Rights Policy.* Westport, CT: Greenwood Press, 1995.

Ritchie, Donald. "Electing FDR." Speech, Library of Congress, Washington, D.C., Feb. 14, 2008, televised on C-SPAN2, "Book TV."

Ross, Frank Alexander, and Louise Venable Kennedy. *A Bibliography of Negro Migration.* New York: Columbia University Press, 1934.

Ross, Malcolm. *All Manner of Men.* New York: Greenwood Press, 1948.

Ruchames, Louis. *Race, Jobs, & Politics: The Story of the FEPC.* New York: Columbia University Press, 1952. Reprinted, Westport, CT: Negro Universities Press, 1971. Citations are to the 1971 edition.

Rudwick, Elliott. *Race Riot at East St. Louis, July 2, 1917.* New York: Atheneum, 1972.

Rung, Margaret C. "The Fight for Fair Employment: The Politics of Race and Ethnicity in North America." Unpublished paper, annual meeting of the Organization of American Historians, Boston, MA, March 25, 2004.

Scheiber, Jane Lang, and Harry N. Scheiber. "The Wilson Administration and the Wartime Mobilization of Black Americans, 1917-1918." In *Black Labor in America*, edited by Milton Cantor, pp. 111-136. Westport, CT: Negro Universities Press, 1969.

Schlesinger, Arthur M. *The Coming of the New Deal*. Boston: Houghton Mifflin, 1958.

Scott, Emmett J. *Negro Migration during the War* [Carnegie Endowment Preliminary Economic Studies of the War]. New York: Oxford University Press, 1920.

———. *Scott's Official History of the American Negro in the World War*. Publisher unknown, 1919. Reprinted, New York: Arno, 1969.

Shor, Edgar L. "The Role of the Secretary of Labor." PhD diss., University of Chicago, 1954.

Shulman, Steven, and William Darity, Jr., eds. *The Question of Discrimination: Racial Inequality in the U.S. Labor Market*. Middletown, CT: Wesleyan University Press, 1989.

Sitkoff, Harvard. *A New Deal for Blacks: The Emergence of Civil Rights as a National Issue. Volume. I: The Depression Decade*. New York: Oxford University Press, 1978.

———. *The Struggle for Black Equality 1954-1980*. New York: Hill and Wang, 1981.

Skrentny, John David. *The Ironies of Affirmative Action: Politics, Culture, and Justice in America*. Chicago: University of Chicago Press, 1996.

Sterner, Richard. *The Negro's Share: A Study of Income, Consumption, Housing and Public Assistance.* New York: Harper and Brothers, 1943.

Sternsher, Bernard. *Hitting Home: The Great Depression in Town and Country.* Chicago: Quadrangle Books, 1970.

Sugrue, Thomas F. "Affirmative Action from Below: Civil Rights, the Building Trades, and the Politics of Racial Equality in the Urban North, 1945-1969." *Journal of American History*, June 2004, pp. 145-173.

Trotter, Joe W. "Class and Racial Inequality: The Southern West Virginia Black Coal Miners' Response, 1915-1932." In *Organized Labor in the Twentieth Century South*, edited by Robert H. Zieger, pp. 60-83. Knoxville, TN: University of Tennessee Press, 1991.

Walker, Forrest A. *The Civil Works Administration: An Experiment in Federal Work Relief, 1933-1934.* New York: Garland Publishing, 1979.

Wandersee, Winifred D. "ER and American Youth: Politics and Personality in a Bureaucratic Age." In *Without Precedent: The Life and Career of Eleanor Roosevelt*, edited by Joan Hoff-Wilson and Marjorie Lightman, pp. 63-87.

Watkins, Tom H. *Righteous Pilgrim: The Life and Times of Harold L. Ickes.* New York: Henry Holt and Company, 1990.

Weaver, Robert C. *Negro Labor: A National Problem.* New York: Harcourt, Brace and Company, 1946.

Weiss, Nancy J. *The National Urban League 1910-1940.* New York: Oxford University Press, 1974.

Weiss, Robert J. *"We Want Jobs": A History of Affirmative Action.* New York: Garland Publishing, 1997.

Wesley, Charles H. *Negro Labor in the United States, 1850-1925*. New York: Vanguard Press, 1927. Reissued, New York: Russell and Russell, 1967.

White, Walter F. "'Work or Fight' in the South," National Association for the Advancement of Colored People. Reprinted from *The New Republic*, March 1, 1919. Also available online through The University of Michigan, http://mirlyn.lib.umich.edu.

Wilhelm, Clarke L. "William B. Wilson: The First Secretary of Labor." PhD diss., Johns Hopkins University, 1967.

Witte, Edwin E. *The Development of the Social Security Act*. Madison, WI: University of Wisconsin Press, 1963.

Wolters, Raymond. *Negroes and the Great Depression: The Problem of Economic Recovery*. Westport, CT: Greenwood Publishing, 1970.

Woodward, C. Vann. *The Strange Career of Jim Crow*. Revised 2nd ed. New York: Oxford University Press, 1966.

Woofter, Thomas Jackson. *Negro Migration: Changes in Rural Organization and Population of the Cotton Belt*. New York: W. D. Gray, 1920.

Zangrando, Joanna Schneider, and Robert L. Zangrando. "ER and Black Civil Rights," In *Without Precedent: The Life and Career of Eleanor Roosevelt*. Edited by Joan Hoff-Wilson and Marjorie Lightman, pp. 88-107.

Zieger, Robert. "African Americans and the Great War Decade," unpublished manuscript, 2002.

———. *America's Great War: World War I and the American Experience*. Lanham, MD: Rowman and Littlefield, 2000.

———. "Black and White, Unite and Fight?: Race and Labor in U.S. History," unpublished paper, August 15, 2001.

———. *For Jobs and Freedom: Race and Labor in America since 1865.* Lexington, KY: University Press of Kentucky, 2007.

———. "'Uncle Sam Wants You ... to Go Shopping': A Consumer Society Responds to National Crisis, 1957-2001." *Canadian Review of American Studies* 34, no. 1 (2004): pp. 83-103.

Zieger, Robert H., ed. *Organized Labor in the Twentieth Century South.* Knoxville, TN: University of Tennessee Press, 1991.

II. State/Federal Government Documents

America Builds: The Record of the PWA. U.S. Public Works Administration. Washington, D.C.: Government Printing Office, 1939.

The American Dream—Equal Opportunity. Community Leaders' Conference Sponsored by the President's Committee on Equal Employment Opportunity [report]. May 19, 1962.

Annual Reports. U.S. Department of Labor. Washington, D.C.: Government Printing Office, 1913-present.

Annual Report of the Chief of the Division of Information. U.S. Bureau of Immigration, Division of Information. Washington, D.C.: Government Printing Office, 1906-1933.

Annual Report of the Director General. U.S. Employment Service. U.S. Department of Labor. Washington, D.C.: Government Printing Office, 1918-present.

The Anvil and the Plow: A History of the United States Department of Labor. U.S. Department of Labor. Washington, D.C.: Government Printing Office, 1963.

Correspondence Files of the Secretaries of Labor. Record Group 174, National Archives and Records Administration: College Park, MD.

Davis, John A. *How Management Can Integrate Negroes in War Industries.* New York State War Council, Committee on Discrimination in Employment, 1942.

[Dillingham] Immigration Commission [reports]. *Abstracts of Reports of the Immigration Commission, 1907-1910*, Vol. 1. Washington, D.C.: Government Printing Office, 1911.

Executive Orders. *Federal Register: Presidential Documents.* Washington, D.C.: Government Printing Office.

FEPC: How it Operates. U.S. Committee on Fair Employment Practice. 1944.

The First Nine Months. President's Committee on Equal Employment Opportunity [report]. Jan. 15, 1962.

Growth of Labor Law in the United States. U.S. Department of Labor. Washington, D.C.: Government Printing Office, 1967.

Historical Statistics of the United States: Colonial Times to 1970, Part 1. U.S. Department of Commerce. Bureau of the Census. Washington, D.C.: Government Printing Office, 1975.

Monthly Labor Review. U.S. Department of Labor. Bureau of Labor Statistics. 1915-present.

The Negro at Work during the World War and during Reconstruction [Second Study on Negro Labor]. U.S. Department of Labor. Division of Negro Economics. Washington, D.C.: Government Printing Office, 1921.

The Negroes in the United States: Their Economic and Social Situation. Unpublished report: U.S. Department of Labor. Bureau of Labor Statistics [Historical Office]. September 1965.

"The Negro in Industry: National Conference on Problems of the Negro and Negro Youth." *Monthly Labor Review*, February 1937, pp. 345-348.

Negro Migration in 1916-17. U.S. Department of Labor. Division of Negro Economics. Washington, D.C.: Government Printing Office, 1919.

Neustadt, Richard E. [U.S. Department of Labor, Historical Office]. "Notes on the White House Staff under President Truman." Typescript labeled "Confidential," provenance unknown: June 1953.

Newsletters. U.S. President's Committee on Equal Employment Opportunity. 1961-1964.

Press Releases. Historical Office, U.S. Department of Labor. 1961-present.

Proceedings. U.S. President's Committee on Equal Employment Opportunity. May 12, 1964.

"The Public Employment Service System, 1933-1953." U.S. Department of Labor. Bureau of Employment Security. *Employment Security Review*, June 1953.

Report: [Part] 3, Employment. United States Commission on Civil Rights. Washington, D.C.: Government Printing Office, 1961.

Report to the President. President's Committee on Equal Employment Opportunity. November 26, 1963.

Rules and Regulations, Effective July 22, 1961. President's Committee on Equal Employment Opportunity. Washington, D.C.: Government Printing Office, 1961.

"The Rural Negro on Relief, February 1935." U.S. Federal Emergency Relief Administration. *Research Bulletin*. Washington, D.C.: Federal Emergency Relief Agency. October 17, 1935. Reprinted New York: Arno Press, 1971.

Short, C.W., and R. Stanley-Brown. *Public Buildings: A Survey of Architecture of Projects Constructed by Federal and Other*

Governmental Bodies between the years 1933 and 1939 with the Assistance of the Public Works Administration. Washington, D.C.: Government Printing Office, 1939.

Smith, Marian [U.S. Department of Justice, Immigration and Naturalization Service]. *An Immigrant Nation: United States Regulation of Immigration, 1798-1991.* Washington, D.C.: Government Printing Office, 1991.

Special Studies: The Social and Economic Status of Negroes in the United States, 1970. U.S. Department of Commerce, Bureau of the Census. U.S. Department of Labor, Bureau of Labor Statistics. Washington, D.C.: Government Printing Office, 1971.

Speeches of the Secretaries of Labor, Historical Office, U.S. Department of Labor. 1930-1993.

"The Tenth Youth" [brochure]. The National Youth Administration. Washington, D.C.: Government Printing Office, 1940.

The U.S. Department of Labor Bicentennial History of the American Worker. Edited by Richard B. Morris. Washington. D.C.: Government Printing Office, 1976.

Wirtz, Willard. Interview by Judson MacLaury. December 11, 1998. Historical Office, U.S. Department of Labor, Washington, D.C.

———. Interview by Judson MacLaury. Untranscribed tape recording. June 15, 2004. Historical Office, U.S. Department of Labor, Washington, D.C.

www.ingramcontent.com/pod-product-compliance
Lightning Source LLC
Chambersburg PA
CBHW022104150426
43195CB00008B/265